Suspended For Life

To Keith James
SAVE OUR Children,
SAVE OUR future!
C. Tussey

Suspended For Life

The Road To Unemployment Crime And Death

C. Twiggy Billue

To order additional copies of this book, contact:
Xlibris LLC
1-888-795-4274
www.Xlibris.com
Orders@Xlibris.com
612233

Contents

Foreword

Cherylene Twiggy Billue is the embodiment of community activism. Her work, ethics, and passion help us all understand what an activist, who is rooted in the community, really looks like. She has lived in Syracuse since the 1980s and has raised children here. She still has nieces and nephews in the Syracuse City School District (SCSD). She is active in local NAN and has worked very closely with our chapter director, Barrie, on the issues of school suspensions and disproportionate impact on children of color and those with disabilities. She has come out on issues of gun violence. Twiggy sees the nuances of the situations around her and does the work necessary to rectify the situation on from multiple sides. She doesn't point fingers at just one side; she calls on her whole community to take action.

Much of her work has centered on youth in our community. In this work, she has helped parents, students, and administrators examine their rights and responsibilities as well as their biases and barriers to working together. This is all in an effort to help students get the quality education they deserve, parents to be involved meaningfully, and school buildings to be the community spaces they are supposed to be, and that starts with the leadership in those buildings. When there are children in need or a child or a parent who needs a voice, people call Twiggy. When a message comes from Twiggy, people take notice. She makes hard issues personal and calls on us all to make broad community problems personal. She shows people that she advocates on how to stand up for themselves and be their own advocate. She reminds people that it is not OK not to stand up. She encourages her community to combat the negative images and stereotypes and stand up for who they are.

She can do this because she is at the core of the community. Twiggy always has the history of what has happened, particularly as it relates to the South Side of Syracuse. She can tell you all about the background of any situation. She remembers because she was there. Communities need keepers of change and happenings.

When Twiggy opens her mouth, everyone turns their heads toward her. She voices out loud and in public what is being whispered. She does this in an intentional way; she is not just spouting off. She is convicted enough and sensitive enough to know that there will be benefits and consequences of how she chooses to speak the truth. It is most comfortable to get along and to stay professional and polite. Creating change and getting the real work done often require us to step out of our comfort zones. If someone in her community is disrespecting another activist, she will call that out, in front of everyone, and make it known that she demands respect for all people.

Twiggy asks for the seat to be created at the table and then calls on her community to fill that seat. This fearlessness and deep love for her community and the children and families she serves continues to be an inspiration to me as a parent of a child with a disability and as an activist. I hope this book will serve its purpose for the readers who will embark on this journey through her words. Learn from her experiences. Use the resources. When we know better, we do better. *Hotep!*

Talina Jones

Second Foreword

Twiggy Billue and I call each other sisters. We may look very different from the outside, but in our minds and in our passion for justice we are kin and kindred spirits. Over time, we have become steadfast allies whose different styles and experiences complement each other in our community action. Twiggy is one of the smartest people I know as well as the fiercest. Sometimes it seems that she runs intellectual circles around me, and I'm embarrassed to say that she can leave me spinning in the wake of her intellectual acuity. She perceives connections between people and their motives, and between events past and present, with an extreme clarity of vision. She dives into legal texts and policy documents with a vengeance, pulling out key language to throw directly at the obstacles in her way.

In this book, Twiggy relates stories about the forces of a whirlwind that she encountered as a parent and also about the way she used her tenacity and research skills to change the direction of these winds and direct them toward the local authorities who resisted her force for justice and social change. She can wield her skills with incredible power, so much so at times that some are intimidated by her delivery.

I have learned a great deal from Twiggy: about racism and class, about history and bureaucratic intrigues, about advocacy strategies, about working cross culturally, and about the reality of everyday lives. This book reflects the realities that Twiggy and her husband faced in their role as parents, raising, protecting, directing, teaching, and advocating for their children in an often hostile world. However, Twiggy's efforts didn't stop at her own children. Over the years, she has taken other people's daughters and sons under her wing, into her house, or under her protection. This has not been limited only to the children of relatives—sometimes it seems that she considers any at-risk student in the Syracuse district as her charge, especially when it seems that they were labeled or treated unfairly.

The stories that Twiggy tells about her children in this book, and the challenges she and her husband faced as parents, also tell the story of her own transformation. In order to advocate for her children, Twiggy had to gain new knowledge and skills, oftentimes very quickly. She empowered herself with knowledge and then took on the powers that be, and she didn't let up until she got what she was aiming for. As a result of her efforts, real change occurred. I just read an article that appeared in a March 2014 edition of the *Syracuse Post Standard* newspaper. It described the efforts taken by the County Department of Health to reduce levels of infant mortality in Syracuse City residents that in the 1980s mirrored rates in some third-world countries. The article talked about a multifaceted program that involved improved access to prenatal and infant healthcare, outreach, parental education, and case management. All I could think of as I read the article was that much of this had been initiated as a result of an advocacy campaign by Twiggy Billue. The rates of infant mortality in Onondaga County have gone down significantly, but what must be even more satisfying for Twiggy is the rates of infant mortality among African Americans are only slightly above the rates for Caucasian Americans.

Then Twiggy took on the City School District, when it seemed the teachers and administrators were hell-bent on labeling her sons as disruptive and denying them equal access to education. True to form, she researched the applicable laws, learned the ins and outs of the district's Code of Conduct, and won the services her sons were entitled to under the Individuals with Disabilities Education Act (IDEA). Her sons did not have ADHD or ADD. They were not being disruptive; they were frustrated because they each had undiagnosed learning disabilities. Now both her sons are fine young men, each with a Regents Diploma and a bright future.

When other parents and community members learned of her successes in the school district, they began to seek her out for advice and assistance. Twiggy turned her focus and energy to the problems of students in a troubled city school district. She took the most at-risk students under her wing, especially those who had experienced trauma in their families or community. She developed programs to guide and support these students. Then, as a leader in the local chapter of the National Action Network, Twiggy began to turn her attention to what seemed to be disproportionate suspension of African American and Latino American students as well as students with disabilities. In true form, Twiggy dived into the available data, finding clear confirmation of the disparities long before related documentation was released by the district.

Twiggy brought the problems of extreme student suspension to my attention, and we began to work as a team, speaking out publicly and as advocates for suspended students. We have seen amazing things in the district: partial and incomplete investigations, school staff and police stationed in schools using inappropriate or excessive force against students, principals imposing out-of-school suspension before asking the student for their version of events or considering whether a student's disability played a role in their behavior as required in the code of conduct, failure to ensure safety of students who had been victims or harassment or bullying, failure to notify parents about in-school suspension of their children, untimely notice of suspension hearings, schools failing to notify parents for months or years of academic problems of students with disabilities, students being denigrated by teachers or school staff, principals and administrators who were unfamiliar with due process procedures for students facing suspension, disciplinary paperwork with conflicting and missing information, and school policy documents written for compliance with the law rather than for communication with students, parents, or school staff.

This book tells stories about all these experiences, but it does more. It offers information. Twiggy had to teach herself—doing her own research, seeking the most effective advocacy strategies, learning how to put pressure on elected officials, learning relevant areas of law and regulation. In this book, Twiggy offers these stories and the lessons she learned to benefit other parents, community members, and all people of conscience who wish to see more justice in the world. These are not just cautionary tales; they are lessons in perception and advocacy, lessons that can be used for the benefit of many. The tales may be based in one Upstate New York City, in one urban school district, in one community, but Twiggy's experiences and the lessons she offers others are much more universal. What Twiggy faced and fought and learned and now offers to others may be applicable to any urban area in the United States with significant levels of poverty and segregation between communities of color and the dominant Caucasian communities who hold the key positions of influence and power.

As a closing note, I will let you know that Twiggy and I are of different races, but we both live on the southwest side of the city of Syracuse and we are both civil rights advocates. Twiggy knows that she can rely on me and I know that I can rely on her. But what I appreciate most about her is that while she constantly challenges me, she accepts me as I am. She never expects me to be anyone else and never makes me feel self-conscious about my nerdiness or my inevitable awkward moments of cluelessness.

Perhaps that is one of the secrets of her success and her ability to engage people across the spectrum of diversity. She doesn't judge people based on who they are or what they look like, but on how they act and how they treat others. She tries to walk a righteous path and she respects others who strive to do the same, not just in words but in deeds also.

Twiggy is also more likely to seek similarities and common interests rather than focus on things that separate people. She has taught me to do the same, and I'm frequently surprised with the connections I find rather than the separations. So whether you feel you have much in common with Twiggy or not, I suggest to you that there may be much to learn from what she has to say. This book is worth reading; her lessons are worth considering. She might just teach you something you can use to help you face life's challenges as an advocate for yourself, your children, your family, and your community.

Barrie Gewanter, Syracuse-based Human Rights Advocate

Preface

This book was written from a parent's perspective to help parents better understand how suspension is a life sentence for your children. It is intended to be a guide for any parent across the USA who has a child in school. My family's experiences with the health-care system and our children's experiences in education coupled with the suspension rate in Syracuse schools were the catalyst for the book. Life sentence is literally stated. It's a decision you are expected make that can guide the rest of your child's life and if made hastily can have very negative effects on your children's education, as well as health care. Health care, mental health, and medical privacy play a large role in schools, but they have become a crucial aspect of suspension and pushing out the students with disability in ostensibly ensuring them a life sentence of unemployment and potential crime.

Here are some things to remember about health care in schools as well as in a health-care setting. You have rights as a patient, a parent, or a student in health-care and education settings. Some of these rights include refusal of treatment, appealing decisions without the fear of reprisal, and due process.

We were not aware of our rights, and the health-care whirlwind we encountered could have resulted in a life sentence of regret, pain, and guilt. It was unlike anything we had ever experienced.

The education whirlwind we encountered from 1994 to 2007 was actually the prevention of a life sentence for our children. The suspension epidemic that parents were encountering in 2013 was the reason we decided to share our experiences. Suspension can equal a life sentence for some children. Have you ever felt like you were caught in a whirlwind or your world was spinning out of control?

My perception provided the understanding needed to connect the dots from past experiences, which allowed me to fully understand the present situation in Syracuse schools. From 1994 until the present (2013), war has been waged against African American students and their parents, especially students with different abilities. The only thing absent is that they do not know a war has been waged using suspensions as a weapon to push out or warehouse their children.

The plot to destroy African American children is a real conspiracy. It is a strategy aimed at all African American children, but it more covertly targets the African American male students and the disabled. The force of the wind pushing our children out of the educational system is at epidemic proportions.

Have you ever felt as if your children were issued a life sentence in school? Have you ever wanted to scream out for help though your screams for help were viewed as unwarranted? Would you be surprised if you had these feelings about your child's health care and/or education? For some parents and students, it is hard to maneuver the intricate rules of health care and educational system.

We felt the whirlwind once, and it was not a good experience, but that feeling is what started it all. Prior to giving birth, a mother develops a special bond with the unborn child. As birth draws near, feelings of love, nurturing, and providing protection are the top three thoughts. These feelings in the womb are feelings like no other. An unanticipated complication during pregnancy can make you feel powerless as if you are spinning out of control. It can make you consider giving in to the unthinkable considerations unless you know your rights. This is where it all begins. Well, at least this is when it all began for our family! Parents must know their rights, especially when (or if) they pertain to the right to refuse treatment if they don't understand the treatment.

This is paramount for anyone receiving medical treatment. Knowing that you have the right to appeal a decision and have a second opinion could change the potential outcome of your condition.

In this day and time, you may think that everyone is aware of and understands their rights; however, there are many parents who do not. My family experienced the health-care and education whirlwind firsthand. Our experiences led to assisting parents in similar situations.

The health-care whirlwind actually resembled a true whirlwind, especially due to the speed of decision making and the force of the medical staff. It can be a frightening experience, but once you know your rights whether on Medicaid or privately insured, you can lessen the speed and the force of the whirlwind and take control of the situation.

The education whirlwind, on the other hand, was not anticipated, and it could catch parents off guard. Parents must be prepared for it. The beginning of the new school year is supposed to be an exciting time. But if your child has been unfairly or repeatedly suspended, becoming the target of implicit bias, or is disabled, the start of school is a whirlwind. The education whirlwind is a thirteen-to-fourteen-year reoccurring whirlwind—a confused rush of PTO and other school meetings, understanding policies and laws, and an onslaught of documents to fill out, sign, and return to the school. It hits you with speed and force but starts to slow down as the school year progresses. For some it does not; the whirlwind takes the form of warehousing students in in-school-suspension, teacher's removal of students, and reoccurring out-of-school suspension (push-out). This is true for the regular, gifted, and disabled students of color. This whirlwind causes the very institution charged with assisting your children to become successful in using zero-tolerance policies to push your children out of the classroom. Students of color and students of color with disabilities are being labeled routinely disruptive and hard to educate at the risk of failure, and ultimately they are pushed out of the education system using repeated suspensions.

The education whirlwind closely resembles a small rotating windstorm with a limited effect, lasting school year to school year. This whirlwind consists of a rush of school meetings, suspensions, and learning new staff, new policies, and laws. This lasts from K to 12th grades, a thirteen-year whirlwind, until the students' graduation or when they are pushed out of the education system. In Syracuse, the whirlwind was unexplainable. Like us, parents have prepared in advance and braced themselves in anticipation of the whirlwind each new school year. We could not prove disciplinary measures were disparate and targeted children of color, but once the disciplinary data analysis was given, we had the proof needed to expose this whirlwind. Together, my husband and I decided to share our experiences since it is clear that the same push-out tactics are being used today.

The whirlwind and the chapters dedicated to "How it all started" have two components that are effective advocacy for yourself and your child in the health-care system and the education system. During the time we experienced the health-care whirlwind, we had no idea that our self-advocacy efforts would morph into community advocacy or a community action agency to combat the education whirlwind.

The experiences you and your child(ren) have in the educational system will be a memorable one, whether it is a good or bad experience. The educational setting the teachers and administrators encountered will set the stage for your children's behavior and learning environment. As a parent, your child's experience at school is very important to develop positive social skills, so if the experience for the parent and the child is not a good one, it can impact social development.

The parent of a child with disabilities faces a different set of circumstances. Their experiences are often different from the parents of a regular student. Learning that we have two children with learning disabilities proved that for our family. When the disability is not a physical ailment that can be seen or if symptoms show up in later grades, receiving such news can be unexpected and stifling.

Our advocacy experiences occurred from 1988 to 2007 in an upstate NY school district. While some are great experiences, others are still questionable. The one thing I am sure of is that every parent out there could use someone to help them understand the policies that govern their child's education. Especially close to my heart is advocacy for disabled students of color. There are agencies that address issues of the disabled. However, over the years, I have found that the unique needs of disabled students of color are not addressed by any agency in Syracuse.

Learning the policies and laws associated with students' disabilities in conjunction with attempting to understand school policy can be a tremendous feat. Parents must become intimate with some documents and very knowledgeable about others including individualized education programs (IEP), the code of conduct, etc. In order to combat this whirlwind, a parent must learn how to fight the program and service push-out and understand disability language and definitions. Parents must also understand how to appeal decisions, suspensions, request reevaluation, or independent evaluation and attend every meeting concerning your child.

This book was written to assist you in understanding the complex education whirlwind. It's intended to be a guide for parents that are struggling to maneuver and effectively advocate for their child's success in the education system. The information provided is from personal experiences, community advocacy efforts, and assisting a large number of parents in my own community in understanding their rights as a student and as a parent. NYS Department of Education and the US Department of Education's Web sites are referenced and quoted throughout this book. These two agencies and their Web sites have been the most reliable tools and weapons in our combat arsenal since 2006. I encourage every parent in New York State to use these Web sites as valuable resources.

If you are not from New York State, see the appendix for your state's department of education Web site.

This book is dedicated to my husband Ras Simien (A. Billue) for encouraging/pushing me to document these experiences and to write this book. Thank you for being there every step of this journey with unconditional love, understanding, tolerance, patience, and tremendous support. Your tireless support is the reason I have the strength and motivation to do this work. To my three beautiful and wonderful children: Cimone, Addis, and Mered, you are my world! You are truly my motivation for doing this work. I love you! To my mother, Betty Simmons, for believing that I can do anything! To my niece, Marquisha, for being able to persevere in the face of adversity and for being the smartest child ever! Auntie loves you!

To my sister-in-law, Nina B., for encouraging me to write this book and for being more of a sister than my sister-in-law! To my niece (goddaughter), LaTarra Tie Odom, for always being there ready to ride with me and always having my back. Thank you and I love you!

This book is also dedicated to the future graduates in my family: Marcale, Jeloni, Kamel, Carlos Jr. and Shania Billue, Jaaziah, Akeli and Jacobbi Qhobosheane, Quadir Scott, and every baby child in my family that will attend the Syracuse City School District. Auntie has your backs!

Acknowledgments

I would like to acknowledge those great educators that provided help along the way! Thank you for being great principals, teachers, and paraprofessionals and for seeing what others refused to see and for doing what others were afraid to do: Mrs. J. Brooks, Mrs. Caldwell/Gerald, Mr. Bacon, Miss S. Nelson, Mrs. D. Schoening, Mrs. D. Williams, Mrs. Valerie Escoffery, Mrs. M. Yauchzy, Miss D. Cook, Miss Stewart, Mrs. Braithwaite, Mrs. Wilson, Mr. Gangemi, Mrs. Thornton, Mrs. Turner, Mrs. Hayes, Mrs. K. Vaeth, Mrs. Masingale, Mr. Dowdell, Mr. Neal, Mrs. Flynn, Mr. J. Holm, Miss P. Clark, Mr. J. Smith, Mrs. Wilson (Dr. King), Mrs. M. Wilson, Mrs. Forante, Mr. Pudney, Mr. Caprina, Ms. Brown, Mrs. T. Harper, Mrs. Reed, Mrs. P. Ellis, Mrs. Antoine, Mrs. Shield, Mr. W. Dowdell, Mr. Nolan, Mrs. King-Reese, Mrs. Kerwin, Mr. B. Nolan, Mr. Harmon, Mr. J. Smith, Mrs. Baxter, Mrs. V. Escoffery, Mrs. L. Hunter, Mrs. Brown, Mr. Pam, Miss Johnson, Miss Ranieri, Mrs. L. Newsome, Mr. R. Neal, Mr. Oliver Johnson, Ms. Torrence, Mr. M. Raymie, Mr. G. Jones, Ms. J. Flynn, Mr. D. Jackson, Mrs. Hammerlee, Mr. Brown, Mr. Derrick Williams, Ms. K. Blue, Dr. C Barber, Dr. Z. Barber, S. Barber, Dr. R. Reeves, Dr. Draper, Mrs. E. Williams, Mrs. I. Minor, Mr. T. Cappa, Dr. Jones, Mrs. N. Cappa, Mrs. Young. Miss S. Contreras, Mrs. K. Bradley, and to a host of others (sorry if I forgot anyone) who went above and beyond to treat and teach all students with dignity and respect. These remarkable people do what it takes to provide all children equal access to quality education regardless of their background, neighborhood, or race!

Thank you all!

Family and Friends that continually encourage me to stay the course:
Linda Williams, Talina Jones, Barrie Gewanter, Pam Billue, Chrissie Rizzo, Debbie Wright, Valerie. Escoffery, the Rushing Family, S. Holloway, Mercedes Bloodworth, Tanika Jones-Cole, Lepa Jones-Pullins, Miss. R.

Burke, Mr. and Mrs. G. Bell, Mrs. Deidra. Jones, Mr. W. Dixie, Miss L. Dunbar, Miss T. Richardson, Shawn, Carlos and Carl Billue (aka the twins), Mrs. Sharon Owens, Big Mama Cynt and Deborah, Shalonda, Petty and Bishop Leroy McClain, Mr. P. Fagan, Malusi Qhobosheane, Miss. T. Duff, Mr. and Mrs. Armstrong!

Special Acknowledgments

I would like to acknowledge The Honorable Helen Hudson, Khalid Bey for support, confidence and trusting in my abilities. Dr. Umar Johnson for his time and energy and especially for coming to Syracuse to assist us!

There are also many families that have allowed me to assist them over the years; thank you for having confidence in my ability to get your child's needs met and to allow your voice to be heard at the district level. Thank you!

Introduction

Once students reach high school, the likelihood of them never returning to school after suspension increases astronomically. Some remain out of school for life in their school-aged period. These students have been warehoused in in-school suspension (ISS) since elementary and then subjected to repeated out-of-school suspensions (OSS) once they reach middle school. Once they reach high school, they are labeled as having behavioral problems or being disruptive, thereby discouraging them from returning to school if they are suspended. For these students, suspension is a life sentence.

Suspended education in Syracuse often leads to young people hanging out on the street corners and sadly in the prison yard. Most are not violent students at the time they are suspended, but still they end up in the court and prison system as street education replaces formal education. This group is not suspended for major code of conduct infractions but only for minor infractions.

This group as you will see illustrated by the data contained in this book comprises largely African American males and disabled. However, there is a growing group of African American female and disabled students being affected by suspensions.

Zero-tolerance policies in school discipline have led to the implementation of practices where school administrators rely on law enforcement tactics to guide discipline instead of reliance in the code of conduct.

Every day, hundreds of students are suspended from school for three to five days each week. There are more students serving suspension than receiving valuable instructional time from teachers. The offenses range from making loud noises in the hallway or classroom, being unprepared for class, dress code violations, to insubordination or talking back to a teacher.

Parents, once you understand that suspensions have a more adverse effect on your children's education than socioeconomic factors, you will realize how suspension can become a life sentence for your children, especially for African American students and African American students with disabilities.

According to "Out of School and Off Track," a report by the UCLA Civil Rights Project, "Prior suspensions often lead to students dropping out of school." However, the consequences of dropping out of school are devastating. It's producing large numbers of uneducated, unemployed, and unmotivated young people. In Syracuse, the crime rate is growing, but it is the age of the perpetrator that is particularly disturbing—the thirteen-to-nineteen-year-old age group.

This is a direct correlation to being pushed out of school using suspension and zero-tolerance policies in middle school. The popular term *school-to-prison pipeline* is also an overreliance on law enforcement tactics in the school setting. The environment in some of our middle and high schools is like prisons and very unwelcoming for the students. Students have been subjected to "sweeps-hallways" and "lock downs" (prisons terms), and if caught during these sweeps, they are warehoused in the in-school-suspension classroom or pushed out via out-of-school suspension.

During the 2011–12 school year, parents pushed for implementation of the dignity in schools' protocols (NYS's Dignity for All Students Act, DASA) in the code of conduct. The Dignity Act prohibits harassment and discrimination of individuals on school property or at a school function based upon a person's actual or perceived race, color, weight, national origin, ethnic group, religion, religious practice, disability, sexual orientation, gender, or sex.

However, that did not happen right away. Standing up and demanding change got the attention of our elected officials, but accurately describing the situation and the plight of suspended students caused disbelief and dismay among community members, parents, and elected officials.

The number of suspensions outweighs the number of minority students enrolled at many of our schools, but the practice of disparate suspension for minor infractions continues to grow in Syracuse. What is really happening? Suspension from school can lead to dropping out of school and ultimately a life sentence, i.e., unemployment, crime, and lack of education.

According to the American Bar Association (ABA), "Students that do not finish school are in essence predestined to a life sentence of crime and unemployment," and this seems to be accurate based on the school-to-prison pipeline in Syracuse as identified by the Center for Community Alternatives.

There is a large group of students who, once suspended at the middle or high school level, are assigned to alternative settings. These students largely suspended for behavioral issues are warehoused in educational settings that are chaotic. The positive behavior intervention supports are not school-wide and are less visible in alternative settings; therefore, students often stop attending and eventually drop out. This is the group I mentioned at the beginning of this chapter.

According to a 2005 working paper by the Center for Community Alternatives, "A large segment of the students placed in the Syracuse's alternative programs are poor and minority students who frequently drop out of school and end up in the juvenile justice system."

In Syracuse, the rate of suspensions can give middle and high school students the mind-set that they are (free) from institutional authority and feel seemingly free to roam the streets. However, they do not realize the ramifications or consequences of their actions until they find themselves unable to obtain employment, or even worse, they realize the likelihood of ending up in the court and/or prison system.

Suspension is a life sentence for many students in Syracuse and across the United States, and as parents, we must become informed of the consequences of routine suspension. First, we must understand that the zero-tolerance policies in our schools are the same as the zero-tolerance policies that guide law enforcement to profile African Americans. Once that is understood, we must demand that our school systems eliminate these policies and the practices.

Parents must become familiar with the process of suspension (Education Law 3214 (3) for rules governing suspensions that are:

Five days or less,
More than five days, ten days or more,
Teacher's removals of disruptive students,
Interim Alternative Educational Setting (IAES), and
Any removal or suspensions of students with disabilities.

If you are not familiar with differences in each of these processes, you will not know how to effectively advocate for your children. It will also be harder to determine if your child has been denied due process when he or she was suspended.

Understanding your right to advocacy can make the difference in keeping your child safe from suspension. There are many community organizations just like the Hotep Resource Center that provides advocacy for students, so parents can fully understand how suspended education can lead to a life sentence of unemployment or incarceration.

We must understand that suspension can be a life sentence for many students and we must pay attention to the number of school-aged children standing on street corners and in other places when they are supposed to be in school.

We must understand that alternative schools warehouse student and often deny them access to educational services and individualized support while remaining under the guidance of district-wide zero-tolerance policies.

This is a life sentence for a large number of students, and we must be willing to take action to address racial disparities in school discipline. It is imperative for parents to be involved in all aspects of their child's education. If your child is being warehoused in in-school suspension or being pushed out by repeated out-of-school suspensions, you must become knowledgeable of your rights.

Urgency: How many of us have seen this scenario play out before our very eyes?

For two years or more, during my daily travels, I began to notice a lot of young folks (my children's ages) on the streets, at corner stores, and on the corners during school hours near my home. Some of these children went to elementary and middle school with my own children, but now it seemed they were not attending school.

Some, I remember, were smart and well-mannered; others, I remember, were silly and talkative. Some had attitudes and disruptive behavior, but after all, these students/children were only between eleven and thirteen years of age in 1999–2000. The common denominator was that they were all attending school.

I observed the same students from 2001 to 2005 (now between fourteen to eighteen years old), still occupying the very same street corners and now vacant homes in the neighborhood. None of them was attending school, even though the school was in walking distance. Even more disturbing was that none was graduating. As I began to inquire, the realization set in—most of the faces familiar to me were students who had been suspended or expelled from school for minor incidents. A great number of those suspended and hanging out on those corners were also students with disabilities.

Today, in 2014, I still see some of the same faces on the same street corners, facing the life sentence of unemployment. The faces I no longer see on those corners are either those that face a life sentence of being repeatedly incarcerated or they are deceased. Parents, we must stop allowing suspension to become a life sentence for any student or young person. This is our chance to flex our collective power—parent power—and stop the suspension: life sentence!

If you need assistance, contact us at the Hotep Resource Center in Syracuse NY.

Chapter 1

The Health-Care Whirlwind—
How It All Started

Let me begin by stating I am not an expert in education or disability laws; however, I am blessed with something more precious than being an expert in either of the above. I am a parent! To ensure my children received fair and equal health care and a free and appropriate public education, I had to become well versed in policies and law, especially those pertaining to the rights of persons with disabilities, and it has been well worth it.

The birth of my second child was the single experience that propelled me from the world of self or child advocacy into a world of community empowerment. Being empowered to take control of your own situation when things seem to spin out of control is truly a gift that must be shared.

The Health-Care Whirlwind

I was between twenty-four and twenty-eight weeks gestation, fifth or sixth month prenatal checkup, and I was admitted to the hospital for bed rest due to preterm labor contractions. After a few tests had been conducted, my husband and I were informed that an amniocentesis was needed due to some abnormalities that showed up in the blood work. They explained that the test showed the possibility of blood sensitization.

What?

What I remember was the doctor stating more extensive testing was needed to rule out the possibility of a condition called Rh sensitization, a condition that can occur if your blood belongs to a different type from that of your baby. What? Our heads were spinning!

What? "My blood type was different from the child I was carrying and potentially harmful to my unborn child." What?

I learned when I was younger that I had a rare blood type AB+ with Lewis antibodies prior because of a surgery for a hernia. The surgeon informed my mother that due to the rare blood type, they had to postpone the surgery for a few hours until a match was found. I didn't understand that having these antibodies could cause a high-risk pregnancy and had the potential to harm my unborn child!

What?

The doctors continued to explain that the amniocentesis was needed to see if indeed the Lewis antibodies differed from the antibodies in my unborn's blood, which would place him in potential harm's way.

What?

I guess we said "What?" so many times that we now had a group of medical staff attempting to explain and re-explain the situation. It didn't matter because the only thing we heard was my red blood cells could be attacking my unborn child. In essence, my blood could form antibodies against the baby's own red blood cells (fetal RBCs), resulting in death. In other words, I could be killing my baby. What?

The doctors continued describing the procedure and the potential harm to the unborn child. We felt we were being rushed to make a decision, and we needed time to think about the procedure. The amniocentesis is an invasive procedure that could potentially cause a miscarriage. No one seemed to hear our concerns; they just kept telling us a decision was needed immediately. After about two hours of badgering and the storm of medical staff pushing us to have the procedure, we agreed. It took about an hour, and once it was completed, my husband and I waited another two hours for the results.

Approximately, two hours had passed when suddenly several doctors entered the room together to inform us of the results of the amniocentesis. The test showed no blood abnormality, and we were relieved. As we looked at the faces of the medical staff, there were no smiles; each face was somber. The OB stated that the procedure showed my unborn child had "spina bifida and the ultrasound showed no lower limbs and his lungs were underdeveloped."

The result—he would not survive more than a few days after birth. They reinforced their findings by pointing out these deformities using the ultrasound pictures.

Somehow, it was suggested that we travel to Buffalo for a late-term abortion, and the staff left us to begin making the arrangements. The hospital's social worker entered the room about twenty minutes later and attempted to explain the rationale behind the need for a medically necessitated abortion. She stated that there were "astronomical costs involved with maintaining a child with physical disorders, not to mention the potential for mental and learning defects in the future."

I remember being told that the hospital was a Catholic hospital and that they did not participate in termination of pregnancy. This is where I first learned about the hospital's duty of law. Duty of law states, "The hospital under its duty of law was informing us of appropriate resources for services." It was stated in the leaflet (given at admissions) titled "Patient Bill of Rights," but we did not pay attention to the document; they were just papers.

Now, the reader may think at this point that we got a copy of the document and read it from cover to cover, but this was not the case. This was the first time we felt the whirlwind. It was as if we were actually caught up in a whirlwind, spinning out of control and realizing that great loss and devastation were drawing nearer. It felt as if the room was spinning extremely fast, people and hospital staff whizzing past the room, but we stood still.

Reading the patient bill of rights went right past our thoughts; actually we were so distraught that our only focus was on how to stop the discussion about aborting our unborn child.

We looked dazed as if someone or something had punched both of us in the diaphragm and knocked the breath out of our bodies. My husband and I looked at each other and flat out refused the suggestion of *abortion* of any type!

Pregnancy and birth are supposed to be a beautiful time for parents, but in some cases, it can be stressful. If you tell your doctor or teacher that due to religious beliefs you do not want a certain course of treatment or a second opinion, it should be respected. At least that is what we believed, but that was not entirely true. It was this experience that required my family to become intimately aware and familiar with our rights, our unborn child's rights, and how to take actions if those rights were not respected.

I learned very quickly that you have to become knowledgeable of your rights under the law, and if you did not, it could leave you with very little to no say in medical, educational, and legal matters. There is absolutely no feeling to describe it except as the whirlwind—split-second decisions, medical staff whizzing by, and explanations sounding like in a foreign language. This is how you feel when you have little to no-say or recourse in matters concerning your health, your unborn child's health, or your living children's health. Parents must read the booklets, pamphlets, and documents that institutions provide concerning your rights. They must not be set aside. You must open them up and read the information in order for it to be applicable or effective. If you are uncertain of the meaning of terms or phrases, ask someone to assist you with the interpretations.

Have you ever thrown away or just ignored those booklets and documents that all institutions give you, regarding your rights as a student, patient, client, citizen, etc.? Have you ever been in a situation where you felt your rights under the law were being violated, but you didn't know your rights, so you let it go? This is how the whirlwind started for our family. The bottom line is that it is imperative to be diligent about understanding your rights and becoming informed.

Chapter 2

A Whirlwind of Decisions or Indecision

"They are going to terminate my unborn first male child, no matter what we say!" That is what immediately came to mind! I am a conspiracy theorist, and it seemed as if the doctors were conspiring to kill our unborn first male child. Why is this the main option being given or forced upon us? Was it really because my child would have birth defects? Was it more sinister? Was this a forced medical abortion? What I had thought was a myth or urban legend about young black women forced to have medical abortions because the unborn baby was deformed or would be born feebleminded was proving true for us.

As Dr. Jawanza Kunjufu wrote, was there actually a "conspiracy to destroy black boys?" Moreover, we didn't believe in abortion, morally and religiously!

The suggestion this late in my pregnancy confused us. Then for some reason, it reminded me of discussions I had overheard as a child about forced sterilization and abortions in order to receive public assistance and food stamps. I remember my cousins and I used to listen to the discussions the adults would be having, as we were not allowed in the room when grown folks were talking. Yes, my cousin and I were eavesdropping. I can also tell you sometimes as a child you are not prepared for the content or context of the discussion you overhear.

This discussion was about receiving public benefits, birth control, and abortion for teenaged African American girls. I was puzzled, and we wondered what this meant. Speaking about abortion was never done in our family. If there was talk about abortion, it was in coded messages that only the adult elders discussed. I later discovered there was some truth to the tales when I learned about the "Negro Project" in Harlem NY from 1939 to 1942. I never heard positive discussions about abortions, medically necessitated abortions, or contraceptives, because it seemed the clinics began to target communities of color.

This gave unprecedented access to contraception and medically assisted abortions well before the Supreme Court ruled on *Roe vs. Wade* in 1973. Throughout my years, I had heard stories of forced abortions and medically necessitated terminations of pregnancy. They said these procedures were forced upon African American girls and women, but I still did not fully believe these stories. As a child, it was hard to believe that the government would do something that was cruel to its citizens.

How could all the previous sonograms and blood tests show a healthy baby? We began to question the diagnosis. The little voice in our heads said, "The doctors can't be wrong. They wouldn't make this decision without real proof, and we saw the defects on the ultrasound, didn't we?" We both thought out loud at times, "The team of OB specialists couldn't be wrong, could they?" Something spoke to my heart, and I told my husband I wanted to be discharged. Now I was becoming afraid for the life of my unborn child and for myself. He didn't hesitate and went to find the discharge nurse and the social worker.

While he was gone, I called my mother. I remember sobbing and explaining the situation to her and her resolve. She seemed firm and began to question me about the previous doctor's visits, and she explained the Rh sensitivity and our blood type (AB+ with Lewis antibodies) that she also carried. In the calmest voice, she told me, "I need you to calm down and be the fighter I know you are. Remain steadfast and unmoved." Then she asked for the name of the hospital and my OB doctor and told me to refuse any further care or treatment that I didn't fully understand. My mother ended the call, stating she would speak with me in a few hours.

I hung up the phone still very nervous, but now I knew I had to be steadfast in my beliefs and my refusal to consent to a medical abortion. It was going to be a fight to keep this child alive. I heard it in her tone. We had no idea that she was calling colleagues at the National Institute of Science and the National Academy of Science in Washington DC. At the time, my mother worked for NIS, but earlier, she had worked at the NAS and kept in touch with several medical doctors. My mother literally called a colleague who in turn contacted several colleagues in Syracuse, and from there, everything changed.

I am still unsure of what happened. It seemed as if hours had passed, but it was only approaching one hour since we had indicated I wanted to be discharged. I was waiting to be released, but every half an hour, we had to communicate to someone that we "are not aborting the pregnancy." In fact, the very idea that we resisted the diagnosis and the proposed course of action seemed to irritate the staff. We continued to remain steadfast and communicated, "Abortion is not an option. If this child lives only for one minute, it would be a minute of unconditional love, and it was a minute we were not willing to sacrifice!"

Afterward, there was an onslaught of hospital staff, social workers, and OB specialists, who came and went. Some checked on intravenous medicines while some checked on our current state of mind—"Are they still refusing medical advice?" At this time, we noticed the color of the medical staff giving the explanations. It had changed. Whether consciously or unconsciously done by the hospital, it was very noticeable. On this one day (within a three-to-four-hour period), we had seen and interacted with more African American doctors, interns, and nursing staff than we had seen during the entire pregnancy. There were more hospital staff of color than we had seen throughout our entire three-year relationship with the hospital. I remembered thinking, *So they are sending in African American doctors and nurses to re-explain the findings and the suggested course of action.*

We continued to communicate that abortion was not an option, arguments almost ensuing with the staff! At one point, I remember yelling out loud at a nurse of color, "Abortion is not an option!" The room was cleared, and no one, including the staff, entered my room for at least the next thirty to forty-five minutes.

When the staff returned, all of a sudden, they said, "Whatever you decided is fine, and we are completing your discharge paperwork." We wondered, *What had changed?* Worst-case scenarios suddenly became the best-case scenarios; that is, there were actually cases of children surviving spina bifida, being born without upper and lower extremities. Now again, we wondered what had changed. After dinner, I still had not been discharged, and it was getting late. My husband had to leave and pick up our firstborn. He told me to call him when I was released and that he would return, but it was what happened next that changed everything!

It was approximately 7:00 p.m. when the OB and a new doctor with "Chief of Staff" on his name badge entered the room. I thought I was being discharged home, but the look on their faces made me wonder, *What now?* My OB introduced the hospital's chief of staff, and as he extended his hand to shake my hand, he asked, "Who does your mother work for?"

I was surprised, but I replied, "Why?"

He looked at me and said, "Whoever she works for and whoever she is, she is very connected!" In fact, they had come to inform me that arrangements were being made for me to be transferred and transported to another local hospital's perinatal center for further testing and observation.

At that point, another man entered the room and introduced himself as the ombudsman and told me he was present to ensure a smooth transition.

I specifically asked, "Why?"

The chief of staff told me, "It was out of our hands, but you are not being moved for any termination of pregnancy." I was puzzled, but I knew my mother's hands were all up in this!

I was overjoyed and called my husband to tell him what the proposal entailed. While we didn't know what was next, we felt it was better than the options previously presented. We only knew the abortion option was off the table! The ombudsman indicated the transport to the perinatal center was definitely happening within the hour, a nurse would be in to pack my things, and the ambulance would be waiting downstairs to transport me to the other hospital.

Within an hour, I was discharged from one hospital and transported by ambulance to another hospital where I was admitted to the perinatal center. I called my mother once I was settled, and she told me about the phone calls she had made to her colleagues and about a couple who knew physicians in Syracuse. One person with influence contacted a colleague at the perinatal center right here in Syracuse. We spoke for a while, but before the conversation ended, in a firm voice, she told me to "get a copy of the hospital's patient's rights" and read it tonight. When I did, the document clearly explained and outlined the rights and protections all patients were afforded. To make a long story short, I became intimate with the patient's bill of rights for that hospital that night, referred to it over the remainder of the pregnancy, and still rely on it during patient advocacy matters.

Once I was familiar with my rights, I no longer felt bad about pushing back and asking for a second opinion. I learned that we are entitled to a second opinion under the law, that it is legal to refuse treatment, and that if we do not understand the course of action, the medical staff has an obligation to explain it in layman's terms. Now I was at least minimally informed of my rights, as well as of my responsibilities as a patient!

I gave birth at thirty-six weeks to a healthy, six-pound seven-ounce baby boy with all extremities and no ailments. My husband and I had decided that even if we could only provide this child with our love, human touch, and affection for one minute or for one hour, it was better than the alternative of termination of pregnancy! Just imagine what the outcome could have been because in the back of our minds we thought the doctors and the specialist must be right, but we couldn't give up on our child!

I remember an incident at a clinic when I lived with my great-aunt in Princeton, West Virginia. My aunt had an appointment with the ob-gyn doctor at the clinic to discuss my menstrual cycle; however, the entire appointment turned into a birth control seminar. This was in 1976, and the rationale was that birth control pills would control the frequency of my menstrual cycle. When access to abortion was mentioned, the conversation made my aunt very uncomfortable as it was against her moral and religious beliefs. I remember her telling me to get dressed as if we were going to make a run for it. When the nurse reentered the room, my aunt told the nurse that she needed to talk to my mother prior to granting consent.

The nurse then stated, "I didn't need parental consent for anything at the clinic." We never returned to the clinic. Instead, she told me a sinister story about her pregnancy and the termination of her unborn child in 1939. I found it was a painful story for her and one I really did not want to know about, but it was a story I needed to hear. I didn't know what to believe until Brian Williams of NBC's Rock Center reported a story of an African American woman named Elaine Riddick in 2011. Remember, I did not really pay attention to any of the aforementioned discussions about ulterior motives of birth control, forced sterilization, or forced abortion. After all, the times were different, and I did not have any reason to believe anything foul or sinister was occurring back then or when my child was born. That was before I watched the story of Ms. Reddick. Now I can no longer dismiss the evidence or the facts. It did not dawn on me until that TV program that my unborn child was in imminent danger, that forced sterilization or unnecessary medically terminated pregnancies actually occurred, and that my aunt's story was true. The awe was in the reality: There is really a "conspiracy to destroy black boys," especially black children—male and female alike!

Prior to this pregnancy, I wholeheartedly argued that doctors would not conspire to eliminate African American boys. Eugenics was a myth to me; using birth control to induce abortions couldn't be true because in my head the rule that doctors take an oath to "do no harm" was implanted. Sadly, I was mistaken! Now I needed to know more about the number of spontaneous and medical termination of minority babies, especially those born with birth defects, deformities, etc. Could I be wrong?

I started to realize that what had occurred during my pregnancy was not by accident or chance but by design! I say this because again I gave birth to a healthy baby boy without spina bifida, with all his limbs, fully developed lungs, and no abnormalities. Just imagine if I had been swayed toward abortion; it was a recommended course of action!

This single experience caused me to be overly diligent and conduct research, read all materials, and become intimate with the laws and rights concerning our children. Through advocacy and assisting others, I have been able to share the knowledge with those needing assistance. Self-advocacy or parent advocacy of a student means teaching the parent or student how to effectively advocate for the needs of their child instead of having someone else do the advocacy for them.

Chapter 3

The Infant Mortality Whirlwind— Syracuse Congressional Hearings on Health Care for Pregnant Women and Babies during the First Year of Life

The second time I felt the whirlwind was in 1990. While researching and exploring the issue of infant mortality in the Syracuse, the winds began to pick up speed and force as the issue became public. This whirlwind came out of nowhere and hit Syracuse like a hurricane in a third-world country.

I was on a committee formed by the local chapter of the NAACP, looking into statistics on infant mortality that were about to be published in a local newspaper. First, I had taken CPR during my first pregnancy because of the rise in infant deaths due to sudden infant death syndrome. The infant mortality rate among African American and Latino women in Syracuse was at the rate as that in third-world countries; the topic seemed to be in my self-interest.

I didn't know much about infant mortality rates, but I was eager to become more knowledgeable due to my own experience. Moreover, infant mortality was an epidemic occurring in my backyard, I mean literally in my backyard. At the time this report was released, both major hospitals were located less than one block from our apartment in Pioneer Homes and less than three blocks from our apartment when we moved to Central Village.

Sadly, I was not surprised to learn that my neighborhood or community had the highest rates. What surprised me was that the communities surrounding the three large hospitals in Syracuse all had the highest infant mortality rates in the city. How could this be?

I learned that the public housing apartment complexes we lived in and those surrounding it had some of the highest infant mortality rates in the entire city. During research, we discovered that in several zip codes, infant deaths among African American babies during the first year were preventable. There was story after story of ER visits for choking incidents, head injury from falls, and sleep apnea, which could have been preventable using basic first aid skills.

I learned that an infant could possibly be revived during an episode of sleep apnea if parents had access to those basic first aid skills. Knowing what to do when a child is choking or if they suffer a fall is valuable information. If a parent does not know what to do in these situations, it could lead to the death of the infant. Sudden infant death syndrome incidents were growing in Syracuse, and we had questions. How many deaths had occurred during the infants' first year of life? How many infant deaths were primarily in the African American community? There were stories of bathtub drownings, suffocations, and falls, and in most cases, the parents did not have access to a telephone or know the basic first aid measures.

The committee quickly realized that a lot of parents are not adequately equipped with basic first aid or CPR skills to prevent a potentially life-threatening incident. This became disconcerting, and I reported this, on behalf of the Syracuse Onondaga County NAACP, as a major contributor to the high death rate of infants in the city.

According to the *New York Times* and the Syracuse newspapers, Syracuse learned it had an infant mortality rate rivaling that of third-world nations in 1989. "In 1990 preliminary indications were that infants continued to die at alarming rates the preliminary 1990 rate was 17.1 deaths per 1,000 births. In that year, 53 infants born to Syracuse women died before their first birthdays." This preliminary rate reflected "a significant increase in the rate from 1989 which was 13.9 deaths per 1,000 births, and in 1988, when it was 12.7 deaths per 1,000 births."

In June of 1989, I was invited by Congressman James Walsh to testify before a select senate subcommittee on infant mortality here in Syracuse. I had proposed a program to combat infant mortality within the Syracuse Housing Authority (SHA), particularly at Pioneer Homes and Central

Village apartment complexes. This was not a new program as it was offered to Onondaga County residents—only to county residents that lived outside the city of Syracuse—and the program was free. The county's program involved educating parents who lived outside the city limits, while our program involved educating parents that lived in the 13202 and 13204 zip codes where the rates of infant mortality were the highest. The county's program was titled "Healthy Start," but it wasn't meant as a healthy start for all babies, especially inner-city babies.

At first, we thought everyone would jump at the opportunity to teach basic parenting skills and CPR to those residents most affected by the raising rates. The parenting techniques and basic first aid skills were coupled with a comprehensive case management component with intensive follow-up and home visits. We inquired about delivering this program to inner-city residents but quickly found this was not a program designed for all residents. Boy, was I correct! The program was being offered only to county residents who lived outside the city of Syracuse.

I camped out at the county executive's office for two days during normal business hours. I could not get a meeting with this man, but on day three, I was granted a meeting with his executive assistant. This woman introduced herself, quickly took the written information, and dismissed me. She indicated that the county executive would review it and get back to me as soon as possible. More than a month had passed, and I heard nothing. Each week, I called and left messages for both the county executive and his assistant, but there were no return phone calls.

I wrote a letter to our congressman James Walsh, explaining our findings and our potential solutions to some of the infant mortality issues in Syracuse. I was pleased to learn that the congressman was also concerned about the issue, and he invited me to testify at a select senate committee hearing later that month. Now the findings would be presented to the public at large, but no one was prepared for the infant mortality whirlwind that was developing in Onondaga County. Once I testified and presented the findings, Congressman Walsh made the necessary funding available. This funding came via the county executive's office and was exclusively designated to conduct the pilot program within SHA and two other areas of the city. As a result of the hearings, the program was implemented at the SHA and eventually throughout Onondaga County as Comprehensive Medicaid Case Management (CMCM).I began to see it clearly: The key and the power were in the knowledge, and knowledge was truly powerful! Becoming familiar with data, laws, and terminology that seemed foreign was a necessity for protecting my family as well as my community. I realized at that point that in the African American community there was nobody who would ride in on a white horse to solve our problems. Our problems would have to be approached and solved for us by us! It was not the implementation of our solutions that was the successful feat. It was seeing how the power of knowledge could be used to create a win-win situation in the political arena. Remember, my power also lies in being a parent! This time I did not feel backed into a corner because policy and demographic data were on my side. This time the policy makers felt the whirlwind!

This was a fierce whirlwind indeed, but this whirlwind was not like the ones before. This time it was different: It was my own whirlwind that caught the county executive, his staff, and other local politicians off guard. The ability to interpret policies and laws seemed to connect with our congressional leaders and level the field. I believe this was a key element in being able to gauge their concerns on the issue and find a win-win solution.

Find out who your city, county, state, and federal elected officials are and meet with them. I am sure wherever you live there is a committee on health care as well as education. Take the time to see who is on these committees and the issues they are working on. You should not be afraid to call your city, state, and federal representatives to enlist assistance. At this time, I worked for a community health center in Syracuse, and due to the implementation of managed care in New York State, I became familiar with health-care policies and the laws. There are policies and laws associated with fair and equal health care, as well as access to private physicians under Medicaid managed care guidelines. These same policies and laws are applicable to providing parents and infants access to comprehensive health care during the first year of life. I looked at the provisions that covered our issues and our solutions. I found most had been implemented in the New York City area including access to private doctors, but that was not the case in Syracuse. I realized that there were many policies and laws that I was not familiar with, so I did research and became familiar with the policies and laws.

Understanding policies and laws governing quality health care, including the right to a private doctor even if you have Medicaid, is essential for all parents to become familiar with. Keep every leaflet and pamphlet governing your medical care, education, etc.; you may need to rely on these documents in the future.

Chapter 4

The Education Whirlwind

The next whirlwind was the education whirlwind. This is when I developed this rationale: "Sometimes you must rely on recollections from the past to fully understand the implications of the present."

As a child, from the age of about eight months old, my sons began rocking. The rocking did not worry us or cause us to seek medical attention because this was common. It was common among five out of eight children, especially my husband's siblings. Over the years, the family would recall stories regarding their mother having to purchase a new sofa each year. The cause—the five siblings would "bump it out." All adults now are somewhat successful; none had been diagnosed with any type of learning, physical, or mental disability. There was a visual impairment in two of the girls, but that was corrected with surgery.

When my son was in second grade, the teacher called us because he was exhibiting disrespectful behavior. She asked us to attend a meeting after school. Upon arrival, the teacher told us that every time she spoke to our son, he would "rock back and forth," which she considered a sign of disrespect. I was offended, but we attempted to explain that he had rocked since birth, and this was not a sign of disrespect. We indicated that there was a long history of rocking in my husband's family and it was not a sign of disrespect.

Before we could finish the sentence, the teacher suggested that our child should be tested by our pediatrician for attention deficit (hyperactivity) disorder (ADHD). She continued to tell us that she had already consulted with the school nurse and social worker earlier that day, so she called them to the classroom. Both indicated that rocking was indeed a sign of autism and the alleged disrespect was due to ADD or ADHD, which was affecting his ability to focus. We were absolutely floored by the assessment.

As a parent, even when you are told not to worry, it's normal that you still worry. So to think that we had not already inquired about rocking with our pediatrician was insulting. Even more insulting was that the teacher, social worker, and school nurse seemed noticeably doubtful that we had consulted with our pediatrician and suggested that we have him retested or seen by a neurologist. Again, I thought this was absurd, but I was willing to make the appointment.

I protested the thought that rocking was a sign of disrespectful behavior. I asked all three how they were able to make a preliminary medical diagnosis like ADHD, ADD, or autism without the input of the school psychologist or an MD. No one could answer the question, and silence fell over the room. How could these nonmedical doctors make that assessment? Now the room seemed to turn tense as we questioned the rush to judging and labeling our son's behavior as disrespectful.

The African American male teacher in the classroom called us later that evening at home. My husband spoke with him and was surprised that he indicated our child's behavior "was not disrespectful." In fact, he told my husband that our child's behavior was "no different from the behavior of any other child in the classroom."

The assistant teacher was not sure why our child was being singled out and sent out of the classroom. Then he told my husband what he had noticed. Our child's behavior only became an issue when he requested assistance with classwork and was ignored by the teacher. The assistant teacher indicated that when he "attempted to assist our child," the teacher would tell him to "stop catering to that boy."

After hanging up the phone, we decided to investigate. Why would this assistant teacher contradict the head teacher? Until now, we had never thought to assign race as a detrimental factor to our child's education, but now it was a real possibility.

Was this determination about his mental capabilities and a rush to judgment or was it designed with the stereotypes associated with black boys in mind? These stereotypes and prejudice would lead to bias that would attempt to push him out of the classroom, label him, and encourage him to dislike school so much he did not want to attend, and by junior high, he would be ready to drop out. Was it an attack on his mental psyche?

According to Amos Wilson, "Damage to the psyche is surely as read as damage to the body." Wilson asserted, "It is plainly not true that sticks and stones may break my bones but names or words can never hurt me" (Amos Wilson, 1998).

It was not hard to realize that the same old Jim Crow tactics that were used in the sixties were still being used in 1994 and now in 2013. It was no longer overt as denial to a fair and quality education was for African American students in the sixties. In fact, it was now an overt systemic institutionalized practice (suspension) designed to push out African American students—a whirlwind with the speed and force of a freight train heading straight for your children, spinning them about with disregard as if they were not human beings.

Today anyone, even those on the outside looking in, can visibly see that our school district's diversity does not reflect the diversity of the students. Repeated suspension of the regular and disabled students of color has become the main tool used to push out African American children, especially boys in our school district.

In our case, it was during the 1994–95 school year after a series of meetings with the school nurse, social worker, and principal (who all recommended testing by a physician and neurologist). We were told that our son was either autistic or hyperactive, and we called the pediatrician. This nonmedical diagnosis had potentially the ability to label a student, which could have led to our son being pushed out of the classroom onto the street corner and from there on into the prison system or the graveyard.

The doctor examined him and found no evidence of ADD, autism, or ADHD. Rather, he found a possibility of bright child's syndrome or a gifted child but definitely no autism or hyperactivity. The doctor questioned our intentions, reminding us that she had already indicated he was a normal child. We told her about the school district's insistence, and she told us to trust her as she was the MD. But after our constant insistence, she made a referral to a neurologist. Remember, we still had not addressed the teacher who refused to acknowledge the request for assistance in class work or what the assistant teacher had indicated. We focused on the medical diagnosis until the pediatrician suggested bias or something more sinister—implicit bias—toward our child.

Now the results were in, and both the pediatrician and the neurologist concluded and insisted there were no medical or neurological issues. Both doctors put their findings in writing, suggesting that the district provide a second opinion by a MD, neurologist, and psychologist if they "took issue" with the findings.

What is going on? we wondered. We presented the findings to the school and demanded the Syracuse school district provide a second opinion if they wanted additional testing. Now was the time to address the comments of the teacher, but then the doctor told us something disturbing. Our child indicated to the pediatrician that the teacher "made comments about his hair and called people with hair like him a mop head." She informed us that she was calling the school because he indicated that the bruising on his arm was because the teacher had grabbed him repeatedly.

Now the wind began to pick up the strong force of her words; my child's own words through the voice of our pediatrician were troubling. When the pediatrician told him to tell us, he became worried about his teacher (his words). So the doctor decided to tell us (with his permission) what he felt was occurring. I was devastated and angry! I could see very clearly, and my moves were calculated and designed to get me back to the school. How did I fail my child?

My husband knew that I needed to be calmed down! The fury and the rage became emotions of sorrow for my child and malice toward the teachers. I didn't notice the bruising on his upper arm until he pointed it out to the doctor. Why didn't he tell us? Why did he want to protect his teacher if she was hurting his mental state (psyche) and his physical being (body)?

Dr. Wilson acknowledged, "Psychic violence in which the intended effect of the perpetrator (the teacher in this case) is to inflict mental or emotional harm is continuous with physical violence." Now I needed answers regarding the assistant teacher's comments and the treatment of my child!

If the teacher wanted him tested again, the school would have to arrange it. To my surprise, the social worker requested the second testing without our knowledge. We received a letter, stating that his teacher and the social worker had requested additional testing by the school psychologist. Our child was placed on a waiting list with a three-year backlog because both the teacher and the social worker were sure the doctors were wrong.

This again angered me, and I challenged the district's waiting list and asked them to move him ahead. This was done with a letter campaign. Now I really wanted to prove them wrong. There was no ADD, ADHD, or autism, but for some reason, they believed it.

The principal's involvement was instrumental; there was a change in teacher and classroom for our child. The district was now investigating our allegations of physical and mental abuse, assessing the pictures of the bruising and phone call and letters from the doctors. The principal was very nurturing. Mrs. Brooks provided a space in her office for our child to learn until she could find the right teacher. See, it had to be the right teacher to work with our child's broken spirit. Why? Because I became his watchdog, the pit bull ready to defend and/or attack to keep my family and home safe! I was the guard dog on alert, the lioness hunting the creature that had attacked her cub. The principal spent many a meeting with us, attempting to mend the unmendable fence the teacher had caused to break. There was no repairing the trust lost with this teacher after that incident.

Each month, I sent the district and the Committee on Special Education the same letter for nearly almost nine months, requesting a rush on the testing. Prior to getting a meeting with someone at the administration level, our child had already transitioned into another grade level. My husband and I noticed that our younger son was writing some numbers and a few letters backward and really misspelling words. When we inquired, his teachers told us it was normal and he would grow out of it soon, but still there was no testing.

The next school year, my younger son entered third grade and my elder son moved up to the fourth grade, and that is when the *real* advocacy and activism began! Everyone in the district now knew of the Billues, especially that Twiggy Billue, and that is just what was needed. This district needed to be shook up! We caused a whirlwind that felt like a tornado hitting the school district. What I had accomplished before this was nothing, but I readily accepted this challenge. This time I was fighting for my children and fighting a good fight! Advocating for testing was like a second full-time job; as we fought for testing, we noticed my son was encountering problems with simple math, math steps, and math facts.

We began to see that autism or hyperactivity was not the growing problem for our son. The problem was with written expression. We learned that he could not express his thoughts in written form (on paper), as well as verbally. He was good in reading, but when it was time to put what he had read on paper, he needed assistance. Our son was now able to express to us in the fourth grade that when he asked for assistance he was ignored.

It was during the third grade that his teacher began to identify and describe his behavior as "disruptive." What we did not realize was that this label would follow him for the rest of his school year even if it was incorrect. Once your child is improperly and unfairly labeled by a teacher, it is nearly impossible for the child to dispel the stigma. Teachers talk to other teachers and share these stereotypes about students they view as difficult or hard to teach, which in turn vilifies the student.

During this school year, my younger son suddenly encountered a very identifiable speech problem. His third-grade teacher indicated that he needed speech therapy and she suspected he had a developmental delay. An older African American teacher took issue with the assessments of the previous teachers and contradicted their assessment that he would grow out of it. This was an older African American teacher who treated all the children in her classroom as her children. Ms. Turner was determined to have his problem verified and get him the assistance he needed. This teacher knew the painstaking measures we were dealing with, pertaining to our older son, and she vowed not to let him slip through the cracks, even though there was a two-year testing backlog. Our younger student couldn't roll his "r" or pronounce certain words; he sounded as if he had a cleft palate at times, but he didn't.

Why did the district ignore his speech impediment? Why did we believe the teachers when they said he would grow out of it? Our pediatrician again stepped in and sent our younger student to a speech pathologist. The testing concluded that he was developmentally delayed in his speech by two years, and documentation was forwarded to the pediatrician and the school psychologist. The diagnosis also informed the school district that he needed speech therapy three times a week. We knew this was not going to occur as immediately as the doctor and speech pathologist wanted due to the backlog. He was also placed on a waiting list.

We had private insurance, but our pediatrician and all the specialists she had referred us to stated they found no evidence of ADD, autism, ADHD, or neurological defects in our child, but the school district ignored the MD and the experts and requested its own testing. For our younger son, it was more serious as his speech was delayed by two to three years, and all the teachers told us was that "he would grow out of it." Now we knew that wasn't true!

All it took was a teacher to carefully listen to the child and our concerns to determine, based on their thirty years of teaching, that there was a serious problem with his speech. It took Mrs. Turner all of two months (September and October) to notice his speech was impeded and to advocate on his behalf. Thank you, Mrs. Turner!

Parents, be careful when teachers and nonmedical persons make a medical diagnosis or assessment of your children. They are not qualified to make preliminary medical diagnoses or medical assessments of your child.

There was one good thing in all this: Each time we attempted to use our insurance for therapy or assistive technology, the doctors and the insurance company informed us that the school district could provide the required services and/or therapy for free. Our pediatrician informed us that she had several patients who had received academic assistance and speech and occupational therapy during the school day. She indicated that services and therapy would be administered while they were in school, eliminating a pullout during the school day. This was great news, but getting the school district to listen seemed like a fight instead of attaining the services and assistance to help them succeed.

During the winter break of the 1994–95 school year, I attended a meeting regarding new changes to the school district's code of conduct.

During this meeting, I learned about early intervention programs, Section 504 assistance, and the Committee on Special Education. The focus of the meeting was making sure the code of conduct mentioned all the above, but I really attended to learn the district's appeal and grievance processes.

This was a chief complaint among parents as the process was not clearly defined or outlined. I was surprised that only five parents attended the meeting when the facilitator explained verbally how a parent could appeal certain decisions. There was no written material or information distributed, but this was when I learned how to effectively use this policy (the code of conduct) to advocate for my children's needs.

Using the code of conduct, I began a letter-writing or phone-calling campaign to the district's Committee on Special Education, the 504 Committee chair at the school, school administration, and Onondaga County Department of Health to push for immediate testing. I referenced Individuals with Disability in Education Act (IDEA), Section 504, and the New York State Education Department's office of special education. Remember, the doctors had already proven the teacher, nurse, and social worker's assessment or preliminary diagnosis as incorrect, but the social worker wanted additional testing.

We were ready to have them tested! Really we wanted them to see how they all had wrongly assumed that our child had ADD, ADHD, and autism! After I was sure the letters had reached each destination, I scheduled meetings with all the entities. Now I was armed with a letter from our pediatrician and neurologist, stating he had no autism, ADD or, ADHD, but there was great evidence of bright child's syndrome or a gifted child. The letter even recommended that he should participate in the district's gifted program at the Center for Inquiry.

This pediatrician had been our children's doctor since birth, and she had always noticed that both excelled, but she was puzzled by the suggestion of autism, ADD, or ADHD. Above all, she was puzzled by our resistance to her diagnosis.

We explained it was because of the insistence of the teacher, the school social worker, and the school psychologist. Really it was, but it was more than just that; it was the whirlwind of meetings and discussions. It was the whirlwind of accusations and allegations. It was the whirlwind of labels and ridicule, and the aftermath negatively impacted our sons' education. It was the whirlwind of assumptions and medical diagnosis by nonmedical professionals. It was the whirlwind of assumed economic condition as the social status that allowed the stereotypical behavior to be projected on our son. It was the whirlwind of whom you believed.

Once we finished our explanation, the pediatrician felt compelled to pen another letter to the school nurse, the social worker, and the school board office. In this letter, she sternly stated her medical opinion and identified that she was aware of potential abuse and that she was informing child protective services of the bruising incident. The letter strongly suggested the emphasis on behavior and neurological issues should be dropped and the school should conduct its own research-based testing to see if he had a "specific learning disability" as her results were final.

The pediatrician sent the letter from her office and copied us. We also penned our own letter (attaching all the letters from medical doctors) to the superintendent of schools, the director of special education, Syracuse University's School of Law, and the Onondaga County Department of Health. The letters outlined the issues and included the school district's policy "to identify/assist a child with special needs." I again referenced the federal policy, defining our son's entitlement to services under Section 504 under "the hidden disability." Within two weeks of these letters being sent, both children received the testing.

First testing concluded the following:

Elder Son: Learning disabled in written expression and math. The psychological review concluded there was no evidence of ADD or ADHD. The district's physician and psychologist concluded that there were no signs of autism but that he was gifted. Both concurred with the recommendation of our doctor and the specialist to enroll him in the gifted program at the Center for Inquiry. The neurological report was also entered as evidence by the district's psychologist—"no evidence of ADD, ADHD, or hyperactivity."

At the end of the meeting, we received an IEP for both children, stating what services and resource each would receive. The testing modifications, assistive services, and access to the resource teacher as needed were identified on this document. All services were to be implemented four times a week with additional tutoring for both at Beauchamp Library over the summer. It was also recommended that he be transferred to another school with smaller classrooms at the new Solace School located on the eastside of Syracuse. It was also recommended that he attend the Center for Inquiry in the beginning of the next week.

The school district's speech therapist also agreed with the findings of the speech pathologist, but we had no idea that this son also had a learning disability and needed occupational therapy to develop motor skills.

Younger Son: Learning disabled in written expression and math. What was more surprising was the experienced African American teacher's assessment was correct! He was developmentally delayed in speech by three years—a problem that would not correct itself. The IEP indicated that he needed assistance with increasing cognitive skills and fine motor development. The recommendations included speech therapy, occupational therapy, and academic intervention via resource four days per week. This also included testing modifications and tutoring during the school year.

Wow! No behavioral issues! I wanted to say out loud, "I told you so!" I couldn't! I now wondered, *Why the aggressive push toward disruptive or disrespectful behavior?*

There was no evidence of ADD, autism, or ADHD; in fact, both our sons were "learning disabled." We needed answers, and we needed them now. Why was the possibility of LD ignored until the doctor became insistent? Why was the emphasis on behavior, autism, ADHD, and ADD? The problem was "frustration in learning," a classic sign of the learning disabled. Why was it interpreted as attention deficit disorder? Why was rocking considered disrespectful? Why were his requests for help ignored? Why didn't the teacher look at the possibility of a learning disability instead of behavioral or mental issues? If your child is learning disabled in written expression and math and their actions were interpreted as disrespectful behavior, how would you feel? If your child is able to speak well verbally to compensate for the learning disability, why is that considered disrespectful behavior or a smart ass? Parents, you have to make sure your child's disability doesn't become his label of ridicule or interpreted as a behavior problem. Do this right at the start of any issues as this indecision may hamper the assistance instead of providing the needed assistance.

Finally, we found the answer, at least, that is what we thought.

For some reason, we never concluded that our pediatrician and other specialists were correct in stating there was no medical problem with our child. Was it the experience of the health-care whirlwind? Was it the fact that we assumed that teachers would not injure our child? Why didn't we push for early intervention? Simply put, we were fooled and caught in the whirlwind. We refused to believe something sinister was occurring. There is no way a teacher would misinform a parent or miseducate a student. As educated as we were, we had never heard about anyone experiencing what we experienced, so we pushed the sinister thought of "a conspiracy to destroy black boys" to the back of our minds. Although we didn't believe the assessment of the teachers, the school nurse, and the social worker, we also denied the factual diagnosis of potential learning disabilities from the medical doctors. It was the whirlwind to prove everyone wrong that clouded my judgment! Who would ever believe that the school would mislead parents and miseducate our children?

We had to continue to watch the situation all the while, becoming intimate with the school district's code of conduct for every school year, as well as state and federal policies regarding rights for people with disabilities and laws governing special education. We also learned the eligibility requirements and how to request programs such as early intervention and the 504 plan and how to interpret other documents including the IEP.

· However, we did not know we would have to rely on all this information within six months of the initial testing.

This "conspiracy to destroy black boys" was becoming more real for our sons and us as each school year approached. Dr. Kunjufu asserts, "You cannot teach a child you don't love, you don't respect and that you don't understand," and this assertion was profound as it guided me to my next questions (Kunjufu, pg. 53). "Why are African–American boys labeled with a behavioral disorder?" Then my heart began to race as I read the next questions in his book *Countering the Conspiracy to Destroy Black Boys, Volume 2*:

1. "Is there any relationship between female teachers and black boys being labeled a behavioral disruption or suspended?"
2. "What are the differences between black and white female teachers as they relate to black male children?"
3. "What are the differences between black and white female teachers in their impact on black boys?"

I was stunned and in awe that Dr. Kunjufu had the courage to ask the tough questions in 1986. It was now 1994 and these questions were still relevant. Dr. Kunjufu also noted, "Black males lead the nation in suspensions." There was one area of concern for us—his emphasis on the number of black children receiving special education: "85% over half are black boys."

Now we began to wonder if special education was a precursor to sentence of suspension instead of leading to acquiring needed assistance. We knew we had to become actively involved and get up to speed on policy. If there was a conspiracy, we would be read to combat it. We didn't know that defense would occur within the next few months at the first review meeting. We also didn't know that gifted programs were not for children of color, but we learned about this quickly.

Chapter 5

Beware of Gifted Programs

Services had started, but a new dynamic was taking place. He was testing out of services. No one seemed to have read the IEP or was ready to implement the services. Instead, the label or designation was being used to send him out of class. Teachers and administrators told him to stop faking and that there was nothing wrong with him. It was actually being used against him instead of working to make him successful. Our son wrote a student grievance (with my assistance) and handed it to the building principal, requesting a meeting.

Remember, this child could communicate well verbally, but the problem was written expression. We also advocated for both children to receive assistance in note taking. Assistive technology and/or a scribe were covered in state and federal policy and could be integrated into the academic and testing modifications. This assistive technology he used was called the Dreamwriter, and we were given Kurzweil voice to text software to use at home. We also noticed one great virtue about our children: They were not afraid to advocate for themselves.

By now, the reader should realize that we engaged our children in understanding the need to advocate for themselves. I remember holding family meetings, reviewing the code of conduct with our children and informing them:

1. They possessed the power to advocate for equal treatment.
2. They were not to be afraid to call it out, especially when a teacher singled them out and made fun of their disability.
3. They had the right to due process according to the code of conduct. The due process is the grievance process for students and parents.

We indicated that taking advantage of the information in the code of conduct would change how they were being treated. It definitely worked; the teacher who had singled him out was no longer at that school.

Remember, the psychologist recommended his transfer to Solace School, the new innovative teaching school. Now the recommendation was to discontinue services that had just started, which seemed absurd, but the school district was serious!

I was able to investigate on my own, prior to the meeting, and found that "the new teacher was uncomfortable" around my son. When I asked her why, she just shrugged her shoulders as if to say "I don't know why." This was a new dynamic, but this time the principal overheard the comments and immediately intervened. As an African American woman with a black son, she was offended by the terms used to describe our son, and she took issue with it without hesitation. Mrs. Schoening was actually surprised how our son's behavior was still an issue even after report after report indicated he was a normal functioning child without behavioral issues. What was going on here? The principal scheduled a meeting among the three of us, regarding a plan for our son, but that meeting turned into another story of another teacher not being accustomed to teaching inner-city students.

What was really going on?

I was getting tired of that excuse, so I decided to drop in without notice. I would sign in at the office and proceed straight to the classroom, sitting in the back. Of course, my child had very good behavior when I was in class. He got one-to-one assistance from the teacher, but when or if she thought I would be absent, it was a different story. I would stand outside the classroom almost invisible to anyone inside the classroom and hear how he was treated. It only took that one instance to hear my child insulted, mimicked, and yelled at by an adult to raise my level of concern. I entered the classroom, and this woman was face-to-face with my son and was yelling and pointing her finger at his face. My level of alertness rose, and the lioness jumped out, and I was ready to pounce. I circled the teacher, but I quickly realized I needed to go get the principal.

Looking back, the expression on the teacher and the teacher assistant's face was that of total shock and horror as if they were the prey the lioness had cornered just before the kill. I really wanted to yell at her, get in her face as she did my child, and yell back, but I did not. I calmly walked over to my son and told him to get his things, and we walked straight to the principal's office. The next day, Mrs. Schoening placed a call to Darlene Williams, and another change took place. I think this was when the principal discovered that my child was being unfairly singled out, and she immediately instituted corrective measures.

Now remember, he was also in the gifted program and excelled, but the classroom teacher's assessment was that he no longer needed services. This was a new school with staff that was not familiar with our son, so whatever was indicated in his file by his previous teachers and written in the IEP (positive or negative) was the only description this new school had of our child.

You see, I have known for a long time that because of our son's intelligence and justice orientation "he could be considered a smart child or a smart-ass child" to the person attempting to belittle. He truly was blessed with a gift in addition to his ability of advocating for himself. When his efforts failed, he now knew that he had to tell Mommy to investigate!

The medical doctors, including the neurologist, told us to have the school district's psychologist test his IQ and suggested he may be gifted—bright child's syndrome, even though he was not a late speaker. But we had no idea of the hidden restriction on African American boys in the gifted program. They were not allowed, and it was a white, middle-class student program. We definitely did not fit this profile. The recommendation to the program was from the doctor and specialist, and it was written on a prescription pad. This teacher actually suggested that he was not gifted and discontinued his transportation to the gifted program. The Center for Inquiry's principal was another African American woman that stood her ground—Mrs. Harper. We had no idea that he was being prevented from attending the Center for Inquiry until Mrs. Harper called to inform us that he had missed several days. We contacted the principal, and a meeting was scheduled for the next day.

The principal informed the teacher that the school had to follow the IEP and the medical recommendations. "No one could discontinue services, except the Committee on Special Education."

I remember the statement clearly: "Contrary to popular belief, this child does not have a behavior problem and is not autistic or hyperactive." This was when we learned that he needed more time to achieve benchmarks on his IEP, prior to the teacher recommending discontinuing any service, including the gifted program. The next week, my husband also reached out to Principal Williams, and he was transferred immediately to our neighborhood school. We knew all schools in black neighborhoods predominately had failing test scores, but we didn't want him bused across town any longer. We wanted him near and in our sights as we realized there was a "conspiracy to destroy black boys."

The triennial review was scheduled for both children; it was implied that the district would only continue their services for the rest of the school year, but that decision would be made at the annual review at the end of the school year. Now it was the beginning of sixth grade for our elder son and the fifth grade for our younger son. Official notification was sent, indicating that services would be discontinued at the end of the school year and the date for the upcoming annual review. There was also a recommendation to discontinue attendance at the Center for Inquiry, the program for gifted children.

I wrote the letter, appealing to the decision prior to the meeting, and mailed it to the Committee on Special Education. What I didn't know was that Ms. Brooks, Mrs. Schoening, and Mrs. Williams had all decided to come to this review, and the CSE was not prepared.

It was the best decision I made! We already knew he had high, very high, IQ scores, but how could this compromise his ability to receive additional services for his learning disability? Our son was gifted, but I knew nothing about policy or laws regarding gifted students.

I started doing research and came across the Javits Gifted and Talented Students Education Act of 1988. This act was originally passed by Congress in 1988 as part of the Elementary and Secondary Education Act to support the development of talent in US schools.

Then I remembered, "The intellectually gifted program is not for black boys," but what did this mean? Is this why the recommendations to end services and access to the Center for Inquiry were being pushed? Was I being naive again? Did we fool ourselves into believing that we would be allies with the school district in the aftermath of the previous battle?

This time we did not feel like we were in a whirlwind. This time we knew what to do—become familiar with the rules and regulations that applied to gifted programs, special education, request or appeals for additional testing, etc., to maneuver this complex system. What we didn't anticipate was having to rely on all these documents at the review.

Once again, we made calls and wrote letters to the school district's CSE, Syracuse University's Office of Clinical Legal Education, and the NYS Department of Education. We engaged principals, a few teachers, and the occupational therapist to write letters and/or attend the meeting. We also brought the matter to the attention of the Committee on Special Education and the Board of Education by attending monthly meetings and asking the following questions:

1. How can you measure if the new methods of instruction implemented actually worked in such a short time?
2. How could milestones be met and major objectives be achieved in less than a year?
3. Can you show us in writing based on the work completed in the class and the IEP that all the goals and objectives identified in the IEP had really been achieved?

School district administration, especially the director of special education, seemed agitated when we attended committee meetings, called his office, or mailed letters to his office. I am sure it was because we asked the same questions, and he didn't have answers. We didn't hear anything from anyone at the district, prior to the date of the annual review. We attended the review, accompanied by a friend who held a master's in special education and is currently teaching inclusionary education in the school district. We had a copy of the appeal letter in hand to submit, just in case services were denied.

No one in that room knew that I was prepared to cause trouble to keep services in place. I was preparing to cause a powerful whirlwind within the school district. The legislation that I was most familiar with was US Constitution's Fourteenth Amendment. The "equal protection" clause covered the right of children with disabilities to be educated. Then there was Public Law 94-142, which covered the "education for the handicapped," now covered by the IDEA. This law had a provision that stuck out to me "to improve how children with disabilities were identified and educated, to evaluate the success of these efforts, and to provide due process protections for children and families."

Due Process Protections: Now it hit me that everything we encountered was by design. I could no longer ignore the fact that we had been misled and our sons miseducated. We realized that none of the protections below had been followed to determine if they had a disability or if that protected their right to receive services.

At this point, we learned about determining if services are needed:

1. The evaluation for special educations services is more than a single test; it consists of information from the teacher and others who have worked with the student.

2. The assessment must be in all the areas that may be affected by the suspected disability. The school must evaluate your child at no cost to you if the school thinks your child may have a learning disability.

3. Teachers or other professionals can recommend that your child be evaluated, but the school must get your explicit written consent before any part of the evaluation is started.

4. If the school can't evaluate your child, they must explain the reason in writing and must also provide information about how to challenge the decision.

5. The evaluation process cannot discriminate against your child because he or she is from a different racial or cultural background.

6. The parent has the right to be a part of the evaluation team that decides what information is needed to determine whether your child is eligible.

None of the above was followed, and we realized we had been denied due process protections. We had the right to obtain an independent education evaluation from a qualified professional and challenge the findings of the school evaluation team, but it was the reverse in our sons' cases. We were directed by the school to have our pediatrician and a neurologist test our son for ADHD, autism, and ADD. Learning disabilities were never discussed as a basis for testing only behavioral issues. Now the testing indicated no neurological or medical issues; instead they both had "specific learning disabilities," and the district wanted to end the services.

There was a backlog, a three-year waiting list, our district's CSE indicated, but due process protections state your child's evaluation should be completed within a specific time frame—sixty to ninety days after receiving parental consent. It was almost nine months later when the district scheduled the testing, and it was completed over four months clearly after the timeframe.

Now we were faced with keeping services in place and knew the following information created the whirlwind on the Committee on Special Education.

Parents have the *right* to attend and participate in meetings to design the IEP. The meeting must be held within thirty days of being eligible for special education services. An IEP should set learning goals and state the services that the school district will provide.

What stuck out was how all the above simply stated the following:

1. The parent has the right to participate in the development of the IEP as a member of the team.
2. The parent can request an advisor to assist you in understanding your rights and responsibilities and request that this person be present at meetings.

Due process protection means you have the right to challenge any school decisions concerning your child. If you disagree with a decision or if an agreement can be reached, use the law. During this time period, the law or policy used is Public Law 94-142, now called IDEA.

This law provides the means for us to fight the decision to remove services. Today, the law is stronger than when we relied on its usage.

From the beginning, special education law and policy has been stating that parents and teaching professionals must work together, but we were not aware of the provision until we did our research. Parental involvement is encouraged to enrich educational opportunities. What happens if a parent is not aware of the right to participate? What if you want to participate but the school does not encourage parent participation?

The school was under a mandate to report progress "to parents of children with disabilities as frequently as they report to parents of non-disabled children," but it never occurred. If progress were reported, at least monthly ending services would not be an option. There had not been time for any benchmarks or goals to be reached because the teacher was "uncomfortable" around our child.

By the time we finished the annual review meeting, both children had received designation with services through the twelfth grade granted by the committee! Now I was recognized as a special education advocate as word spread around the school district. It became known that I was an agitator that held the institution accountable.

What they didn't realize was that I used their own policy to get our needs met. I attended every meeting and committee meeting from that point forward. It was still a battle to undo the miseducation, but we stayed the course.

I guess this is best summarized in the following Psychology Report (2004):

> "The problem, in retrospect, with this yes-no decision making as to whether A_____ has an educational disability has been an over-reliance on a discrepancy-based definition of learning disability. Politics appears to have governed in what should have been a research-based, data-driven decision making process."
>
> "He was able to draw on extensive knowledge and understanding of topics that goes beyond most high school students. A_____ demonstrated superior language skills when his struggle with text-based tasks did not interfere with his performance."

This report actually confirmed that for years our child was considered disrespectful and disruptive by teachers although he was not. Our son was unfairly disciplined when in fact he was learning disabled in reading and written expression and showed difficulty in math, English, and social studies. Our son did not have medical or behavioral issues; he had a specific learning disability or "hidden disability" as you will later learn about. How many other students and parents experienced this? His frustration in learning and his emotional response to not getting help when needed was also misunderstood. See below:

> "There is an emotional overlay (seen only at times, less frequently or consistently more recently) that comes across as his being disruptive, off task or unmotivated depending on his ability to cope with the academic demands of the situation. Based only on his interaction in the testing sessions, it appears that A_____ copes well when his limitations are acknowledged and accommodated, and he is recognized for his successes."

There were no neurological or medical problems, but a learning disability had been interpreted as behavioral issues because he became "frustrated in learning." What kind of teachers are these teachers?

Now the alert level rose and remained like that until both finished school. We had decided that the school district needed to be watched. I was willing to be that watchdog, not just for my children but for all children! This time the truth and proof were put in writing, which now was undeniable:

"There has been some indecision as to whether A____ qualifies for special education services." "The case is unequivocal that he in fact has a learning disability." There is also a pattern of his parents advocating for him. This pattern has been necessary as SCSD has not always provided sound decision making, or teachers that have been able to sort out whether behavior problems have been the result of a lack of social skills or a reaction to frustration in learning. His parents have acted summarily to change his program when they saw a need. These parent-initiated changes appear to have been in A____'s long-term interest. A____ remains well motivated to achieve when adults in school are able to find a common ground with A____'s parents' expectations for his learning.

In 2004, removal of services was suggested by the new director of special education and the Committee on Special Education, but as you see above, both children continued to receive services and the indecision was finally exposed. The new staff and teacher will only learn about your child through the school record and/or the IEP, so make sure you are involved. We continued to monitor the teachers and closely watched the school district's decisions and determinations until both graduated.

This means visiting the schools so much that people start to think you work there. I also had the luxury to be assigned to work in the high schools and was able to see firsthand how unfair the education system could be for children of color. Our sons graduated high school in 2006 and 2007 with Regents Diplomas, but I continued to work in the schools for all children and their parents.

During the graduation party, my son made a speech, thanking me for not giving up on him in the womb and when things got rough, especially in school. I cried as he recounted how he had felt in the fourth grade when we were told "not to expect much academically and he would never do work above a D." The social worker indicated that he would only graduate with an IEP diploma, not a regular diploma. He was in the fourth grade, and these words stayed with him. I was saddened to know this stuck with him and that "really words can hurt you." That's why I challenge the saying "sticks and stones may break your bones, but words can never hurt you."

Then he said in an excited voice, "My mother has my back, and I can always count on my parents!" He told the crowd, "You don't know how long my parents had to fight and defend me and protect my rights when I was in school! My mother is not afraid of anyone. Standing up to prejudice and fighting discrimination associated with my learning disability is what she is good at. My mother learned policies and laws, not because she wanted to but because she had to protect us. She is the most intelligent person I know! My dad is fearless. He doesn't back down, and everyone knows the battle gets tougher when my dad shows up. The schools know that the Billues fight for their children, but they are never ready for my parents! Mom and Dad, thank you for fighting a long and tough fight without giving up!" He concluded by stating, "Now look at me . . . a Regents Diploma!"

My children have a habit of telling their friends to "call my mom." Over the years, this has morphed into assisting and organizing parents and students in understanding the education system and their rights. The call to action was from my own children. If any of their friends were facing the same issues, regardless of their race or ethnic background, I was called to act.

I will state here that I have never been called to assist a parent whose child was not entitled to receive due process or services. It was the opposite in each case; the denial of due process and/or services was actually services the student was entitled to receive, according to the school district's own policy and state and federal laws. This is where our self-advocacy actions morphed into community action.

Chapter 6

Suspended Education—
African American, Latino,
and Disabled Students

"You can't teach them if they are not in the classroom!"

One evening in early May 2013, two African American politicians contacted me by phone. They wanted me to review and give my thoughts on a report regarding very high suspension rates in the school district in the timeframe of the 2010–11 and 2011–12 school years, especially among African American and Latino students.

Both seemed very agitated and indicated that a Syracuse newspaper reporter would release the report in a couple of days. I notified the president of the local chapter of the National Action Network, as this was the venue they used to request this review. We all ended up on a conference call regarding the report, and I was formally asked to examine the document and present the findings.

Each shared their concerns, but the most disturbing aspects of their concern were that at least 5% of all K-1 grade students had been suspended and that nearly ten thousand students, predominately students of color, had been suspended during this time period.

I was not familiar with the report, but I was familiar with the disproportionate suspension of students of color. I also had no idea that such data existed, even though it had been requested in the previous year, and the district indicated it was not available. I was not aware or notified about the matter at hand. I knew that the very same politicians didn't think the issue was a matter of great urgency until NAN brought it to the forefront. I wondered why there was urgency now. Being unfamiliar with the suspension rates, I was unwilling and hesitant to give any opinion until I became familiar with the data and the document containing the data. It was agreed that the document would be forwarded to me for review, but it was noted that the document needed to remain confidential among the four people on the call, and I agreed.

My volunteer work in recent years has been in connection with disproportionate and disparate suspensions among students of color, academic ineligibility, and school resource officers (SRO). I have held the roles of co-chair of the criminal justice committee (2010) and currently (2013) co-chair of the education committee for the Syracuse chapter of the National Action Network. I am currently involved in documenting suspected disparities in suspensions of African American students.

This documentation also consisted of attending meetings with parents and students, collaborative initiatives with the NAACP, the NYCLU, the district's superintendent, and the US Department of Justice Conciliation Unit. More recently, the New York State attorney general's office reviewed our allegation of disproportionate suspension among students of color in Syracuse.

Upon the first review of the data, I immediately noticed that indeed almost ten thousand students had been suspended during the identified time periods and that suspension rates for minorities were sky-high! (See Table 1.)

As I continued to review this document, page six startled me, so I began to take notes to effectively process the information. I started over again, attempting to see if I had missed something, but the awe remained. Over the next five hours, it seemed disparities based on race were on every page! There were seven pages of handwritten notes, and every page of the document contained handwritten notes. I had to take a break; this could not be this evident, and there must be some sort of mistake. *Why would the district put out a document this incriminating?* That is the thought that plagued me.

Something told me to take a look at the district's demographic profile; this information was provided in the 2012–13 calendar. Again, I thought I must not be reading this document correctly. The school district would not dare admit there was disproportionate suspension among children of color, and it must be a mistake. The numbers actually reflected that nearly ten thousand students were suspended out of school during 2010–11 (9,545 students suspended) and 2011–12 (9,988 students suspended) ; the demographic data suggested something much different was going on.

Table 1 Disciplinary Data Analysis (Page 4)

Out-of-school and In-school Suspension Summary

	2010-11	2011-12
Total number of out-of-school suspensions	9,545	9,988
Total number of students suspended out-of-school	4,167	4,210
Total number of in-school suspensions	13,967	12,135
Total number of students suspended in-school	4,539	4,305

The numbers for K-2 grades were very troubling because you wonder what the actions could have been that resulted in suspension for this age group if it was not a violent disruption.

Figure 1 Disciplinary Data Analysis (Page 6)

Over the past two years, changes in the percentage of students suspended out of school varied by grade

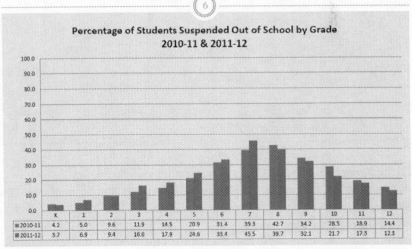

Percentage of Students Suspended Out of School by Grade
2010-11 & 2011-12

	K	1	2	3	4	5	6	7	8	9	10	11	12
2010-11	4.2	5.0	9.6	11.9	14.5	20.9	31.4	39.3	42.7	34.2	28.5	18.9	14.4
2011-12	3.7	6.9	9.4	16.0	17.9	24.6	33.4	45.5	39.7	32.1	21.7	17.3	12.3

Now I really felt compelled to look at the district profile against the demographic data contained in the report. The numbers did not add up to the district's ethnic breakdown, especially when the suspensions in this report indicated that half of certain ethnic populations had been suspended. Of course, I had a copy in hand, on my kitchen wall.

District Demographics/Profile
Student Information

- 19,720 K-12 students
- 1,310 prekindergarten children (including Universal, Experimental, and other Pre-K programs)
- Services to students speaking 77 languages
- 10,000 breakfasts and 14,200 lunches served daily
- 10,569 total public school students transported daily
- 1,698 total non-public school students transported daily to 35 non-public schools
- Free/Reduced Lunch 85%
- Special Education 20%
- English as a Second Language (ESL) 14%

District Demographics/Profile
Ethnic Breakdown

- Black 50%
- White 26%
- Hispanic 13%
- Asian 7%
- Multiracial 3%
- Native Americans/Alaskans 1%

http://www.syracusecityschools.com/tfiles/folder514/SCSD-School-Calendar-and-handbook-2012-13.pdf

The concern grew after reviewing the ethnic breakdown of students as provided by the school district against the percentage of students suspended under OSS by ethnicity—well, it was actually after figuring our district was not accurate in reporting the data.

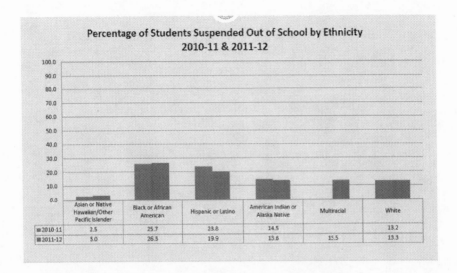

Percentage of Students Suspended Out of School by Ethnicity
2010-11 & 2011-12

	Asian or Native Hawaiian/Other Pacific Islander	Black or African American	Hispanic or Latino	American Indian or Alaska Native	Multiracial	White
2010-11	2.5	25.7	23.8	14.5		13.2
2011-12	3.0	26.3	19.9	13.8	15.5	13.3

How could these numbers (suspension data) be correct when compared with the school district's ethnic breakdown? African Americans make up 50% of the student population, but 25.7–26.3% of that ethnic group was suspended. That is half of the entire African American student population.

Even more disturbing was that there was no data for students with disabilities, and that prompted the following questions:

1. Where is the data on children with disabilities?
2. Where is the data on children sent home without being formally suspended?
3. Where are the demographic breakdowns for Middle Eastern students, African students, or the overall student population for refugee and immigrant students?

They do not fit the multiracial category, and this seemed to indicate that not 100% of all ethnic populations are included in the demographic breakdown. It led me to believe the numbers of suspension as it related to the ethnic breakdown listed in the disciplinary data analysis are not accurate. My suspicions grew stronger, so I needed to verify some items and get a second or third opinion or set eyes on taking a blind look at the disciplinary data analysis document. What was particularly disturbing was the middle school data, indicating that some schools had suspension rates above 50%:

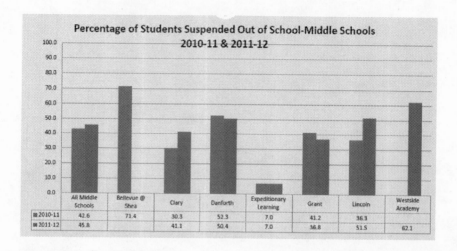

Percentage of Students Suspended Out of School-Middle Schools 2010-11 & 2011-12

	All Middle Schools	Bellevue @ Shea	Clary	Danforth	Expeditionary Learning	Grant	Lincoln	Westside Academy
2010-11	42.6	71.4	30.3	52.3	7.0	41.2	36.3	
2011-12	45.8		41.1	50.4	7.0	36.8	51.5	62.1

While I contemplated on who would assist me with this endeavor, I wondered if anyone else would see what I was seeing. I needed to put the series of undocumented or illegal suspension complaints I was working on for NAN into the context of this report.

Chapter 7

What Every Parent Should Know about Suspensions and Illegal Common Practices

There is a common practice of undocumented out-of-school suspensions (among administrators and teachers) in this district. This type of suspension is an illegal suspension. This is a practice where the classroom teacher, or other school staff, sends the student to the office. The principal or his or her designee decides to send the child home for the day (or a couple of days) to cool off or calm down normally for disruptive or routinely disruptive behavior, which is also termed as low-level acts of violence. The parent(s) pick up the student and are told by the administrator that the student will be allowed to return to school when they have "calmed" down. The parent follows the instructions and returns the child to school on the day set by the administrator. There is no written documentation provided or given to the student or parent.

At this point, I want to provide the definition for disruptive student according to the code of conduct for the SCSD:

"A disruptive student is a student who is substantially disruptive of the educational process or substantially interferes with the teacher's authority over the classroom."

Knowing this definition would mean that you understand there is no difference between your child being sent home and suspended. Teacher removal and sending a student out of class are "considered time-honored classroom management technique" instead of being viewed as missing valuable classroom instruction.

Remember, you can't teach them if they are not in the classroom!

How would you know if your child or disabled child was suspended fairly or with due process? Do you know the laws regarding a student's discipline or discipline for student with disabilities?

I mentioned this because parents of both the regular student and the disabled student must be familiar with the code of conduct, as well as state and federal laws. Parents must also become familiar with the suspension process so they can recognize and combat the undocumented or illegal suspension (a common practice) when it arises.

Why was there no data on undocumented suspensions? Why don't they provide it as well since it could be no more incriminating than the disciplinary data analysis? After all, it was a time-honored practice to send students out of the class or home with parents without documentation. Why the secrecy now? I wasn't surprised it was not included as the district refused to acknowledge such a practice was occurring. This practice among teachers and administrators had been brought to the attention of the board and the superintendent but had not been addressed.

Parents believe it's true, so it should have been looked into, but since this practice has been occurring among African American and Latino students, it was easy to ignore until now. Addressing it would prove that disproportionate numbers of students of color are being pushed out onto the street corners. To make the long story short, the problem was not being addressed.

Definitions Parents Must Know:

1. Undocumented Suspension: Low-level instances of disruption, where the student is sent to the school's administrator(s) and a decision is made to call the parent(s) to pick up the child for the remainder of the school day or for two to three days. No documentation accompanies the child or is given to the parent when the child is picked up. No documentation is mailed. The student is returned to school when the administrator indicates it's OK for the student to return. This is an illegal suspension!

2. Documented Suspensions: Student suspension for any allegation, where documentation of the alleged act is identified, course of action identified, and your right to appeal suspension is provided. This documentation either accompanies the student home and/or a copy is mailed to the parent(s)' address on file.

Parents, and significant others, were arriving to pick up their children in numbers I had never seen in previous years. Parent after parent also expressed dismay that their child was missing valuable classroom instructions. Some indicated that their child was being sent home almost on a daily basis. During the 2011–12 school year, several parents requested my assistance, which always involved accompanying them to informal meetings and formal hearings, but what was noticeable was the outcome of the meetings or the hearings. The outcome always resulted in the child remaining in school. Once we suggested positive behavioral interventions were put in place, the calls for these particular parents eased up, and there was no need for the undocumented suspension. We updated the superintendent's office about each case we encountered since this practice was denied by district officials, but we did not hear anything regarding the matter.

The important factor here is that you have to know a little bit about how federal and state laws guide your district's suspension process. The written policy is in the code of conduct. Knowing just a little about these policies will help you assess if your child has been unfairly (without due process) or illegally (undocumented) suspended. Over the years, experience has taught me that most parents are not aware of the process, so let's take the time here to do a review. Start with the code of conduct and the State Department of Education's guidelines for suspension. If your child has a disability, IDEA will define the process. This is where you will begin to recognize the differences between legal and illegal suspension of a regular student and suspension of a disabled student, including additional rights students have under the law. While conducting some research, I found an article on student discipline and disabled students that directed me to IDEA. I will share it now before we cover the suspension process as some of the information is disturbing.

In 1998, Volokh and Snell asserted that "the civil rights movements changed the way a school district could discipline students but the biggest win was for disabled students when Congress passed the Individuals with Disabilities Education Act (IDEA) in 1995." The IDEA guarantees a "free, appropriate public education" for children with disabilities. The

Volokh report also indicated something very disturbing: "There were three primary classifications of education for difficult-to-educate students:

1. Special education for students with disabilities,
2. Education for at-risk students, and
3. Correction's education" (Volokh and Snell, 1998).

"Education for difficult-to-educate students!" What did this mean? I felt a need to find out more, especially about the category "at-risk students." The reason is that, to my understanding, only poor and inner-city youth and students are defined as "at-risk."

Then the lightbulb came on, and I knew it was a catch phrase: "Education for the difficult to educate." So I did a little more research and found another report on the term as given in the following definitions:

Rossi and Stringfield acknowledged that the term or phrase "at-risk students" identified those living in poverty and students of color. "At-risk" and the "difficult-to-educate" are "identified as students living in poor housing conditions, free-lunch recipients, students subjected to drug abuse by a caregiver or on drugs themselves." Plain and simple, the students usually identified as at-risk are poor children and children of color! This report suggests that the numbers are growing so rapidly that they indicate that "by the year 2020, the majority of students in America's public schools will be living in circumstances traditionally regarded as placing them at risk of educational failure." Is this difficult to digest? In addition to "misunderstandings and insufficient resources," there was a "lack of regard for individual differences and capabilities," suggesting that at-risk students are "treated harshly by the very institutions that seemingly were created to help them" Rossi and Stringfield, 1997).

Parents, stay on top of identifiers and monitor phrases commonly associated with your children. In most cases, I have found there is no watchdog group for students of color with disabilities, so parental monitoring becomes essential.

Understanding the Suspension Process

If your child has been or is being suspended, you should receive oral and written notice of the accusations facing your child. If you do not, call the principal immediately and request written explanation of the suspension, referral, or other disciplinary actions.

The suspension notice should include the following:

1. The specific act involved
2. The evidence the suspending authority is basing its decision on
3. The number of days suspended, i.e., when the suspension starts and when the suspension ends
4. The process for requesting an informal meeting or conference with the principal or the principal's designee
5. The process for appealing the suspending authority's decision

I suggest that every parent should request an informal hearing if your child is suspended out of school or gets in-school suspension. This is when you will learn that if an investigation of the incident occurred whether there were witnesses and their statements, and it will give you and your children a chance to present your own evidence to the principal or his or her designee for further investigation. Due process means not rushing to judgment.

Parents, please note that if the behavior or conduct your child is displaying is perceived to "present an immediate danger or disruption to the academic process," your child can and will be immediately removed from the school. Yes, without any advance notice to you, parents, your child can and will be removed from the school. However, that doesn't remove their obligation to notify you orally and in written form as soon as possible.

It is important to become familiar with the suspension and appeal process in your district. Become familiar with the differences between short-term suspension and long-term suspensions, as well as the difference between in-school and out-of-school suspensions.

Suspensions can become a part of your child's permanent record, so understanding the process is in your self-interest. Below are some common terms and their definitions often associated with or used during suspensions in our district. While I am sure the terms vary from city to city and state to state, these definitions are taken from the SCSD's code of conduct.

It is a lot to take in at once, so you may have to create an outline with terms and important facts in order to get a comprehensive understanding of the process. Parents in Syracuse didn't take advantage of the appeal process because there is no clear process outlined in the code of conduct.

Suspension Terms and Definitions:

1. Suspending Authority—Superintendent or principal (any teacher can recommend suspension)
2. Short-term Suspension—Five days or less
3. Long-term Suspension—Five days or more; the principal may recommend to the superintendent or the superintendent's designee for student behavior when a suspension of more than five days is warranted.
4. IAES (Interim Alternative Educational Setting)—A temporary educational placement for a period of up to forty-five days.
5. Notice—Notification of the suspension; the notice shall provide a description of the charges against the student and the incident for which suspension is proposed and shall inform the parents or guardians of the right to request an immediate informal conference with the principal.
6. Student Notice—The student must be notified immediately, orally.
7. Parent Notice—Within twenty-four hours after the student's removal, the principal or another district administrator designated by the principal must notify the student's parents or guardians by telephone and in writing that the student has been removed from class and the reason(s) why.
8. Written Notice—It must be postmarked within twenty-four hours of student's removal to the last known address.
9. Telephone Notice—The notice (which can be done through telephone) and opportunity for an informal conference shall take place before the student is suspended unless the student's presence in school poses a continuing danger to persons or property or an ongoing threat of disruption to the academic process.
10. Danger to Self or Others—If the student's presence does pose such a danger or threat of disruption, the notice and opportunity for an informal conference shall take place soon after the suspension as is reasonably practicable.
11. Informal Meeting—The parent has the right upon request to meet informally with the principal or their designee to discuss the reason for the removal. At the conference, the parents or guardians shall be permitted to ask questions about complaining witnesses' statements under such procedures as the district may have established.

12. Principal's Decision—After the conference, the principal shall promptly advise the parents or guardians in writing of his or her decision.

Appeal Suspension

1. Step One
   The principal shall advise the parents or guardians that if they are not satisfied with the decision and wish to pursue the matter they must file a written appeal to the superintendent within five business days, unless they can show extraordinary circumstances precluded them from doing so.

2. Step Two
   The superintendent shall issue a written decision regarding the appeal within ten business days of receiving the appeal. If the parents or guardians are not satisfied with the superintendent's decision,

3. Step Three
   File a written appeal to the board of education with the district clerk within ten business days of the date of the superintendent's decision, unless they can show extraordinary circumstances precluded them from doing so.

4. Appeal to the NYS Education Commissioner
   Only final decisions of the board may be appealed to the commissioner within thirty days of the decision.

Now that we have covered our bases with terms, definitions, short-term suspensions, and appeal process for short-term suspensions (in-school and out-of-school), we can move on to suspensions that are longer in duration, five days or more.

Myth: Most parents believe that the teacher initiates the suspension. That is far from the truth of the matter.

Reality: Only the principal, vice principal, or his or her designee can recommend or impose short-term suspension. Long-term suspensions are requested by the principal and imposed or granted by the superintendent or his or her designee on behavior.

Dispel the myths by becoming familiar with the code of conduct as it outlines the process. It may not clearly or easily outline the process, but it's an important starting point.

Long-term Suspensions

Now let's take a look at long-term suspensions. This information is contained in the code of conduct, but it is not easy to follow. So just like short-term suspensions, we learned to use the code of conduct to create a clearer process to follow and felt compelled to share it with other parents. Highlighting the important parts of the code and creating an outline was a key element in developing a good understanding of procedures and processes.

Long-term Suspension—Five Days or More

1. Suspension for five days or more—Principals generally request this type of suspension. It must be granted by the superintendent or their designee for student behavior.
2. Notice—Suspension for more than five days: When the superintendent decides a suspension for more than five days is necessary, notice is given to the student and the student's parents including their right to a fair hearing in a reasonable time frame.
3. Fair Hearing—For long-term suspensions, your child has the right to a fair hearing. At the hearing, the student shall have the right to be represented by counsel, the right to question witnesses against him or her, and the right to present witnesses and other evidence on his or her behalf.
4. Hearing Officer—Suspension longer than five days and formal hearings require an official hearing officer. The superintendent shall personally hear and determine the proceeding or may, in his or her discretion, designate a hearing officer to conduct the hearing.
5. Official Record—A record of the hearing will be maintained either in writing or the hearing will be taped and the tape recording of the hearing will serve as the official record of the hearing.
6. Decision—The superintendent or their appointed hearing officer shall make findings of fact and recommendations as regard to the appropriate measure of discipline.

Long-term Suspension Appeal Process
Appealing the superintendent's decision, if you are not satisfied with the decision:

1. Step One
   An appeal of the decision may be made to the board; appeals to the board must be in writing and submitted to the district clerk within ten business days of the date of the superintendent's decision, unless the parents can show that extraordinary circumstances precluded them from doing so.

Appealing the board of education's decision, if you are not satisfied:

2. Step Two
   Appeal to the Board—The school board may adopt in whole or in part the decision of the superintendent. Final decisions of the board may be appealed to the commissioner of education within thirty days of the decision.

According to NYSED, "Prior to the IDEA Amendments in 1997, discipline policies allowed school personnel to remove a child to an IAES-interim alternative educational setting for up to forty-five days if the student brought a gun to school." That changed to include "disruptive incidents" as well as violent behavior and is reportable to the State Department of Education via the VADIR.

These amendments to IDEA in 1997 included regulations and guidelines on discipline for students with disabilities that stated the following:

1. "Schools could remove a student for up to ten school days at a time for any violation of school rules as long as there was not a pattern of removals."
2. "A child with a disability could not be suspended long term or expelled from school for behavior that was a manifestation of his or her disability."
3. "Special education services must continue for students with disabilities who are suspended or expelled from school."

Today this provision is powerful in the context of the disproportionate suspensions and in lieu of the disciplinary data analysis.

Now there is a new dimension to student removals in January 2006; *Teacher Removal of Disruptive Students* was added.

Teacher removal of a disruptive student is a faucet of classroom management. If your child's "behavior is deemed disruptive and interrupts the learning environment and the ability to teach and control the classroom," your child will be removed from the class. The strategies used here are zero-tolerance strategies, meaning that in most instances the student is sent out of the class or home for a full day or a day or two. That classroom management technique is really a form of institutional bias designed to systemically push out students of color.

Systemic Push-out: Students of color are pushed out of the classroom onto the street corners and in some cases into the prison yard or the graveyard.

Parents are not aware that since this practice is considered a "classroom management technique," the removal does not constitute a disciplinary removal such as out-of-school suspension (OSS) or in-school suspension (ISS).

Teacher removals are defined as *the teacher directing a student to briefly leave the classroom to give the student an opportunity to regain his or her composure and self-control in an alternative setting.*

Such practices may include, but are not limited to, the following:

1. Short-term time-out in an elementary classroom or in an administrator's office
2. Sending a student to the principal's office for the remainder of the class time only
3. Sending a student to a guidance counselor or other district staff member for counseling

The above information and definitions are from the SCSD's code of conduct (2012–13). However, this is the process and procedure I encourage parents to follow as it is more comprehensive than the procedures and process identified in our code of conduct. It was taken from the most defined process I have found in NYS under Project SAVE in the Glenville NY/Clifton Park area of NYS.

Teacher Removal of a Disruptive Student Procedure and Process

The teacher makes a judgment that the student's behavior is not in compliance with the classroom rules and the code of conduct.

1. Short-term Removal—One Period
   The teacher will send the student to the designated alternate area or classroom with a referral form, stating the nature of and the reason(s) for removal from the class.
2. The teacher should notify the principal and/or his designee verbally or in person that the student has been removed and sent to a designated alternate area or classroom.
3. Students have the opportunity to initiate the first steps of due process protections as the teacher must be available for an informal conference regarding the removal.
4. The teacher or the school must orally notify the student's parents of the removal from class and state the reasons within twenty-four hours of the removal.
5. In addition, due process protections give the parents and the student the right to a meeting or conference within two days of the removal to discuss the reasons for the removal, if requested.
6. The building administrator or his or her designee will determine if the misconduct that warranted the removal is subject to further disciplinary action beyond the one period removal.
7. The principal must notify the parents if they determine the misconduct needs further disciplinary action than the one-period classroom removal.
8. Students are responsible for making up all missed assignments during the removal period.

What I didn't realize prior to finding this document on the Burnt Hills-Ballston Lake Central School District Web site was that there was actually another dimension to "teacher removal of a disruptive student"—a long-term removal dimension.

The Burnt Hills-Ballston Lake Central School District policy defines long-term teacher removal of a disruptive student as follows:

Long-term Removal—More than one period or class:

The first six steps are the same as the short-term removal steps, but it differs in this way:

1. The teacher, the principal, and/or his designee together will determine if the removal from the class should be extended beyond one period, for the remainder of the school day, or for one full school day.
2. Removal may not last more than five consecutive days.
3. The parents of the student must be notified of the removal by the principal and/or his designee.
4. The teacher and the student will be responsible for other academic activities during the removal period.

Appeals and Waivers

The parent and the student under due process protections have the right to appeal all decisions regarding any removal from the classroom as per New York State Education Law #3214 and Project SAVE Legislation.

NOTE: The principal and/or his designee cannot set aside the removal imposed by the teacher unless the following conditions are met:

1. The evidence does not support the charges against the student.
2. The removal is in violation of the code of conduct or any state or federal laws.
3. The conduct warrants suspension from school pursuant to Education Law #3214.
   Students are able to return to class once the period of removal expires, or the teacher agrees to an alternative disciplinary arrangement, or the principal or his designee renders a final decision.

Parents, do we understand the implications when your child is deemed disruptive and removed from class by a teacher? Is the behavior or conduct of your child so terrible that he or she needs to be removed? These are questions every parent should ask, especially if your child has been or is being suspended or removed from class for disruptive behavior.

The reason this process is outlined is because not one parent I had worked with understood the definition of a "substantial disruption" routinely disruptive, teacher removals, suspension process, or how to appeal decision on discipline.

During the 2009–10 and the 2010–11 school years, the majority of the parents I accompanied on school meetings had students who were learning disabled and/or were diagnosed with ADHD. Some students even had IEPs with behavioral plans in place and were on medication, and the parents did not know about due process protections. In the majority of instances, their behavior consisted of behavior that was consistent with the symptoms of the disability or the learning-disabled student in their attempt to mask the disability when facing "frustration in learning." It means the student could not or did not comprehend the assignment.

I realized something that just as it was with my own children, this removal or suspension practice had remained the same. Zero-tolerance practices were still occurring in 2013, still stereotyping children with ADHD and specific learning disabilities as having disruptive behavior. Why didn't anyone consider the behavior of these disabled students as behavior caused by the disability? Was it as open and clear as Rossi (1995) who acknowledged that "at-risk students are treated harshly by the very institutions that seemingly were created to help them"?

All parents must become familiar with the terms *disruptive student*, *teacher removal of a disruptive student*, and *substantial disruption*. If your child is deemed routinely disruptive and if you have picked your child up from school due to disruptions, you must become familiar with the implications of the terms and consequences for a disruptive student and a substantial disruption.

According to NYS Law Section 3214(3) (a) and the code of conduct for the SCSD (July 2011), a disruptive student is "a student who is substantially disruptive of the educational process or substantially interferes with the teacher's authority over the classroom."

Substantial Disruption—"A substantial disruption of the educational process or substantial interference with a teacher's authority occurs when a student demonstrates a persistent unwillingness to comply with the teacher's instructions or repeatedly violates the teacher's classroom behavior rules."

Teacher Removal—"A classroom teacher may remove a disruptive student from class."

Duration—The duration shall be determined by mutual discussion between the principal and teacher, and the removal will not exceed two days (forty-eight hours). If a mutual consensus is not reached, then the student will be removed for one day (twenty-four hours).

Note: Removal from class applies to the class of the removing teacher only.

Once you have an overview of the suspension and removal process, you will be able to maneuver the process. You must be able to determine if your child has been afforded due process or is being suspended via the zero-tolerance practice using undocumented suspensions as the hidden weapon to push out children of color.

Parents must be familiar with the appeal process as sometimes it is not clearly outlined. Putting the disciplinary data analysis into context meant obtaining data on undocumented suspensions and teacher removals (referrals); this information was not clearly identified in the district's analysis.

Getting data on suspensions or acknowledgment of undocumented removals from the school district was virtually impossible. We knew attempting to obtain more information would also be impossible and would create an adversarial tension and that wouldn't help matters. Questions about the number of undocumented suspensions and teacher removals was requested in earlier years, but now it seemed to me that the data was purposely left out of the disciplinary data analysis.

I stood in awe of the disparities in suspension among race and gender. I thought the district's numbers were inaccurate due to the demographic data, providing the ethnic breakdown of student populations. It was going to take a little more time for me to prove the point. We knew mentioning to the board would cause tension on top of the other questions posed, as we still needed the numbers on the undocumented suspensions.

Even though the question had not been received well, we asked it anyway. The tension we had wanted to create was bringing the board to accountability for the issue and for ignoring our previous requests for information. I was still waiting for clear explanations regarding the data provided in another disciplinary report, the NYS VADIR, particularly a section of that document on "other disruptions," as it was the next set of data I would use to interpret the disciplinary data analysis. Although we requested additional clarity to understand the document, that clarity was never provided by the district.

Parents, to adequately protect your or your child's rights, you have to be familiar with the policies and processes used to address your particular situation.

Any undocumented removal or suspension denies the student and the parent their right to due process. The excerpt given below is taken from the SCSD's code of conduct:

Disciplinary Penalties, Procedures, and Referrals
A. Guidelines for Penalties

"The amount of due process a student is entitled to receive before a penalty is imposed depends on the penalty being imposed. In all cases, regardless of the penalty imposed, the school personnel authorized to impose the penalty must inform the student of the alleged misconduct and must investigate, to the extent necessary, the facts surrounding the alleged misconduct. All students will have an opportunity to present their version of the facts to the school personnel imposing the disciplinary penalty in connection with the imposition of the penalty."

When a parent is not notified of a suspension orally or in writing, your rights are being violated. If your child's school code of conduct states the first intervention is contacting a parent, you must make sure the policy is followed. According to our district, "Notifying the parent/guardian is always the first intervention and part of any consequence." However, that is rarely the normal course of action.

Chapter 8

The VADIR—NYS Violent and Disruptive Incident Report: Syracuse Schools

The NYS Violent and Disruptive Incident Report is a large report that identifies the schools that are "persistently dangerous." VADIR has terms that every parent should know. In previous years, parents had not fully comprehended that "disruptive behavior" was now considered a prohibited act.

In fact, the only reason I am familiar with the reclassification is because during the 2010–11 school year, I was a newly appointed member of the School Leadership Team and the Superintendent's Parent Council. These meetings are venues where VADIR, suspensions, alternatives to suspensions (PBIS), and other issues of behavior were discussed in addition to academic and other school needs.

The excerpt below is from the SCSD's code of conduct and the No Child Left Behind Act. It is highlighted here because of the change, indicating "prohibited conduct now includes disruptive behavior." These new terms are being applied and new discipline measures are being put into place regarding nonviolent student behavior. This is in our district's code of conduct as per Project SAVE:

What is prohibited student conduct?

Project SAVE considers students to be equal partners in keeping themselves, their friends, and schools safe. They have an obligation to report violations of the code of conduct. Student discipline is expected to be self-imposed. Students are to assume and accept responsibility for their own behavior. Expectations of student conduct extend from the classroom to the school bus. *Prohibited conduct now includes disruptive behavior,* misuse of computer/electronic communication devices, insubordination, violence, any conduct which endangers the safety, morals, health or welfare of others, and academic misconduct (example: cheating).

Project SAVE

The Safe Schools Against Violence in Education Act was passed by Governor Pataki on July 24, 2000. The law requires school districts to "record information on violent and disruptive incidents beginning with the 2001–02 school year." It also requires a school district in NYS to "develop an expanded code of conduct that students, parents, teachers, administrators, and other school personnel are involved in revising all aspects of the document." Now it was clear that previous versions of this law did not consider "disruptive behavior" as "prohibited conduct." This began occurring during the 2001–02 school year; however, I never noticed "prohibited conduct *now* includes disruptive behavior" until the 2004–05 school year.

Prior to the May 2013 release of the disciplinary data analysis, a local report directed me to the Web site of UCLA's Civil Rights Project. The Web site had published suspension rates for twenty school districts across the USA. The data was compiled using the 2009–10 school year data, and the report suggested there was zero tolerance for disruptive behavior in this district. I saved and printed but did not intimately review it until after that May phone call from the African American politicians. I was not ready for what this report revealed, and the finding caused more suspicion to grow around the disciplinary data analysis for 2010–11 and 2011–12 school years that our district had released. Didn't our district know about this report?

Now I could see it clearly: Suspensions are routine and the main choice for enforcing minor school infractions in this district. There are zero-tolerance suspensions for dress code violations, skipping school, tardiness, unpreparedness for class, bringing cell phones to school, and disruptive behavior or disruptive acts. Violent and weapon-related infractions are serious and require suspension or even the involvement of law enforcement, but repeat suspension of students of color for minor infractions is an extremely harsh discipline policy.

Suspensions push out students and increase the number of disenfranchised unengaged youth that would rather hang out than attend school. Push-out has long-term economic and societal costs for families of color, including unemployment, incarceration, or death.

Now I needed to review the UCLA 2009–19 analysis below along with the VADIR for three years instead of the two school years that the district had analyzed.

SYRACUSE CITY SCHOOL DISTRICT, NY (2009-2010)

Suspension Rate K-12 for All Students:	20.5%
Suspension Rate for All Secondary School Students:	30.8%
Number of Students Suspended One or More Times:	4,385
Number of Secondary School Students Suspended One or More Times:	2,520

The rates are high, but what was really disturbing was that separation by school level, race, and disability status found profound disparities in the risk for out-of-school suspension. Look at the males with disabilities at the secondary level or high school in the graph given below (the dark and light blue lines).

They are at the greatest risk for out-of-school suspension (OSS).

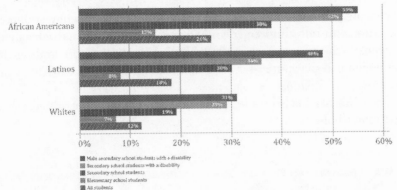

Figure 1: Risk for Suspension at the Elementary and Secondary Levels by Selected Subgroups

There were answers from previous years that NAN and I had requested. This was the first time that the data included suspension by gender and disability, and it was just as startling as the new disciplinary data.

How is it that the director of special education, our board of education, and the superintendent of schools were not familiar with the data on their own district? Why did they indicate they did not have data on suspension of students with disabilities? UCLA's Civil Rights Project acknowledged, using the "U.S. Department of Education data on over 26,000 U.S. middle and high schools to reveal disturbing racial disparities and the increased use of suspensions." This is the data reported to the US Department of Education by NYSED from our school district and reported in the VADIR.

For Parents and Children's Advocates

1. Request data on discipline from your school and district, especially for middle and high schools, and seek policy changes that require annual reporting of disaggregated data on school discipline down to the school level, if not already required.
2. Bring your concerns about large racial, disability, and gender disparities and the frequent use of suspensions to local and state boards of education.
3. Provide support for teachers to receive the training and assistance they need to be effective with diverse learners.
4. If necessary, file an administrative complaint with the U.S. Department of Education's Office for Civil Rights.

VADIR is the reporting system used to document violent and disruptive incidents. I was not sure that parents were making the connection to VADIR and the disruptive behaviors outlined in our code of conduct. The connection is that disruptive incidents are also defined as reportable acts in the NYS Violent and Disruptive Incident Report.

What is even more disturbing is that these disruptive incidents are also known as the symptoms for the medical diagnosis of disruptive behavior disorder (DBD), which includes oppositional defiant disorder (ODD), conduct disorder (CD), anti-social personality disorder, ADHD, etc.

Parents, I urge you to pay close attention to the behavior labels associated with our children, regular education, and special education, especially to the reports such as the VADIR and school report cards as the information is concerning your child and potentially your child's learning environment. *Remember, you can't teach them if they are not in school!"*

The following has been taken from the UCLA Civil Rights Project Web site 2009–10 report:

In the Syracuse City School District, the risk for suspension grew from elementary to secondary school as follows: 12 points for Whites; 22 points for Latinos; and 23 points for Black students. However, for each racial group it was males with disabilities enrolled at the secondary level that were most at risk for suspension.

Table 1: Students with Disabilities Compared to Students without Disabilities by Race and School Level

Syracuse City School District	Elementary School Students Without Disabilities	Elementary School Students With Disabilities	Secondary School Students Without Disabilities	Secondary School Students With Disabilities
White	7%	10%	16%	29%
Latino	8%	9%	28%	36%
Black	14%	23%	35%	52%

Note: All numbers rounded to the nearest whole number; only included if 100 students enrolled in subgroup were enrolled.

Now the VADIR!

You must take the time to look at the VADIR and any report on discipline because the categories are similar to reportable "prohibited interactions." These acts can be used to label your child a disruption, especially by engaging in the behaviors while in school even if they are a manifestation of a disability. These incidents are required to be reported to the NYS Department of Education using the VADIR.

The following has been taken from the SCSD's code of conduct:

Reporting Violent and Disruptive Acts

The New York State Department of Education, under the No Child Left Behind legislation, requires all schools to report Violent and Disruptive Incidents for an entire school year in a Summary Report format.

Reckless endangerment, minor altercation, intimidation, harassment, menacing, or bullying are recognizable forms of disruptive behavior, but it is the hidden or undefined meanings that you must pay close attention to! Become familiar with the VADIR. The VADIR has a category that has been difficult for our district to clarify, and while attempting to explain, it has caused the most arguments in suspension data meetings in the category of "other disruptive incidents."

We believe there are uncounted suspension incidents that our district did not include in the 2010–11 or 2011–12 suspension data. We believe by adding the VADIR's "other disruptive incidents" numbers to those reported, more students were suspended than the district reported, especially when you add the VADIR numbers and the data on illegal undocumented removals. There is a dramatic increase if other disruptive incidents reported to VADIR consist of violent and disruptive incidents not included in the district's report, especially since VADIR requires reporting any disciplinary incident that leads to referral or disciplinary action.

The VADIR Definitions

VADIR describes other disruptive incidents as "other incidents involving disruption of the educational process and that rise to the level of a consequence listed in the *Summary of Violent and Disruptive Incidents Form* (columns j–o)." "Reportable incidents are limited to those resulting in disciplinary action or referral."

Parents, please note the last sentence of this definition: "Reportable incidents are limited to those resulting in disciplinary action or referral." Hmm? So again the question arises: How is the common practice of removal from the classroom (undocumented or illegal suspensions) excluded from the disciplinary data analysis report, especially since most resulted in out-of-school suspensions? They are required to be reported since they are considered referrals and disciplinary actions.

I made this statement publicly in prior years, and it was not received well. I took a chance, mentioning it again at a meeting a few months before this report was released. It was around November or December 2012 during a meeting with the district about understanding the VADIR. The Department of Justice' Conciliation Unit requested that the school district provide the community with clarity and understanding on the categories listed as reportable to VADIR. This was the component of a signed mediation agreement that was not being regarded. The mediation agreement was entered into due to the conduct of police in our schools.

The Director of Pupil Services put together a two-hour presentation, explaining the purpose of the VADIR. However, that was not the purpose of the meeting and not why the group called for the meeting using the assistance of the DOJ to ensure it happened. The group was having trouble in understanding VADIR's reportable incidents in relation to suspensions and removal from class or school building by teachers, school staff, and SROs instead of the principal. The other disruptive incident's category stifled the group and the DOJ Conciliation Specialist.

NYS's Violent and Disruptive Incident Reporting requires school districts to record incidents and report them each year to the State Education Department, who, in turn, uses the data to determine the safety of a school's environment in that district. This is how VADIR is used to assess the climate or the safety of the school.

Parents, when referrals and suspensions are undocumented, it hinders the ability to adequately address the issue. Instead, suppression becomes the norm so that the school is not considered persistently dangerous, and the parent has in some cases no knowledge of the referral or suspension (especially if it's ISS or OSS less than three days).

At this meeting were the signers of the mediation agreement with our school district: the chief of police, the superintendent, the school district's chief of staff, a deputy superintendent, the National Action Network, the NAACP, the Spanish Action League, and a conciliation specialist from the US Department of Justice.

An hour had passed, and the director of pupil services had not answered one question we had posed in previous meetings and e-mails. In fact, the questions we posed and the real purpose of the meeting were ignored. Suddenly, I interrupted the director of pupil services by asking, "When are you going to provide the clarity and the answers to the questions that we posed?"

Silence fell across the room, and again I stated, "We were asked to send our questions to the district, and this meeting was set to hear answers. We are ready for those answers." The director of the NAACP agreed that the purpose of the meeting was to answer the questions about the categories, especially "other disruptive incidents," not for a thorough explanation of the purpose of the VADIR.

Everyone, with the exception of the chief of police, added a comment, but our questions were never fully answered. The VADIR states that other disruptive incidents are covered in columns j–o of the 'summary form'; however, this was unknown to the group. The summary form had not been included in the information provided to the group regarding the VADIR. The meeting was rescheduled until the district provided the form and clarity, which would be at our next meeting; that meeting never occurred.

The VADIR and the Disciplinary Data Analysis for 2010–11 and 2011–12 School Years

Now back to deciphering the most recent disciplinary data. The task before me seemed huge. In January 2013, I obtained a copy of the form from the NYS Department of Education's Web site and reviewed it with the education committee members the following week. I noticed the suspension rates and realized that the VADIR was the information used by UCLA. It was the data NYS Department of Education had reported to the US Department of Education based on what individual school districts reported. It became clear that the columns on violent and disruptive incidents were directly related to the information reported by our school district. Why would district officials play games with parents and taxpayers? Now that I knew the definition of other disruptive incidents, I could use the VADIR to interpret the new data.

Other disruptive incidents are referred to on the summary form as follows:

"School Safety and the Educational Climate—Data Collection: Early Summary of Violent and Disruptive Incidents"

How many enrolled student offenders were assigned or referred to: (Report all consequences)					
Counseling or Treatment Programs (j)	Teacher Removal (Section 3214) (k)	Suspension From Class or Activities (l)	Out-of School Suspension (m)	Transfer to Alternative Alternative Ed Program (n)	Law Enforcement or Juvenile Justice (o)

Source: http://www.p12.nysed.gov/irs/school_safety/2013/School_Safety_Summary_Form_Complete.pdf

The "Early Summary of Violent and Disruptive Incidents July 1, 2012–June 30, 2013" describes the consequences listed in columns j–o.

Now this leaves the layperson or parents to conclude that any prohibited act or disruptive behavior listed in the school's code of conduct matches these columns and that results in referral or disciplinary actions are reportable to VADIR. So why are the undocumented out-of-school suspensions, the common practice of sending a student home for the above, not included in discipline data? Undocumented suspensions are considered reportable, according to NYS VADIR, so this leaves one to wonder: "Why did our school district have so much hesitation and discernment in discussing these columns of consequences on the VADIR with our group and with parents? Why was the VADIR or SAVE policy hard for the school district to explain? It's education policies and laws, isn't it?"

Or was it that VADIR describes these columns as a consequence for incidents resulting in disciplinary action or referral and also states that teacher removals are reportable? If the student was disabled, the teacher removal, if repetitive removal was occurring, could constitute a change in placement for the students with disabilities.

Here is how the NYS VADIR defines disruptive incidents:

---

(20) ***Other Disruptive Incidents:*** Other incidents involving disruption of the educational process and that rise to the level of a consequence listed in the *Summary of Violent and Disruptive Incidents Form* (columns j–o). Reportable incidents are limited to those resulting in disciplinary action or referral.

It was taken from the NYS Education Department's Web site section "Definitions."

Teacher removal of students, transfer to alternative setting, and suspension from class or activities are all reportable on VADIR. It was weird because students were being removed by the teacher and sent home with a parent by the principal (suspension), but the school did not document the incident. Students were actually suspended for reportable (VADIR) infractions (teacher removal) without documentation, and the district did not have any data on the number of teacher removals where the student was sent home for the day or a day or two. Now I began to wonder if parents knew that teacher removal was considered a suspension and reportable to NYSED as violent and disruptive incidents. Did they know about "other disruptive incidents" and what they meant?

I knew parents were not privy to the early summary form if they didn't know it was needed to understand VADIR categories, especially the "consequences listed in the *Summary of Violent and Disruptive Incidents Form* (columns j–o)." How could we get copies of the VADIR and the summary to communicate this information to parents?

These were more questions that needed answering. At this point, I didn't care if the questions frustrated the superintendent and the school board. The frustration was needed because they are responsible for ensuring policy is followed. The fact that the board and the chief administrator could not readily answer our questions or provide answers on the district and NYS education policy or law angered NAN Education Committee members.

Sometime during the 2011 school year, the superintendent was authorized to establish a research unit to gather statistics on disciplinary actions and other statistics the district wanted to analysis. We believed it was established to disprove parent concerns regarding the disproportionate suspension and undocumented teacher removal of students of color, particularly African American and Latino students. Now that it is here, the reader will realize the establishment of the research unit has opened up a can of worms.

The NAN Education Committee in Syracuse was not originally looking at disproportionate suspension or even suspension disparities. Our focus was to understand the VADIR and the code of conduct, making sure both documents were understood by parents and implemented accurately by the school district.

The release of the disciplinary data analysis (the basis of this book) caused us to ask more questions and in turn pushed NAN to the forefront of the suspension issue in Syracuse. This whirlwind was needed; it was time to shake up the data this time based on the district's own assessment. The mere fact that we had questions instead of just accepting the data and becoming outraged was not OK with district officials. I didn't see the document as the true depiction of what was really going on in Syracuse schools. The UCLA report for 2009–10 was the reason, as it was not referenced once by district officials, and that made me suspicious of the disciplinary data analysis for the 2010–11 and the 2011–12 school years. There was also an unusual tension between the district officials and me regarding my usage of the VADIR to interpret the disciplinary data analysis.

I did not find this out until we informed the district. I used the VADIR to interpret the disciplinary data analysis. I also needed to know how many suspensions were repeat suspensions or how many students were routinely suspended. I thought the new data could have encompassed repeat offenders, and this is when I realized that the same data must have been used to compile the district's report and the UCLA report for the 2009–10 year. The referral or disciplinary action was recognized as reportable data on the VADIR.

According to the New York State Education Department and the VADIR, "Offenders and victims must be counted each time they were involved in an incident," but the disciplinary data analysis the district provided did not include repeat suspensions. Or did it? If not, how could this be possible? http://www.p12.nysed.gov/irs/school_safety/2013/ Early_VADIR_Summary_Form.pdf

I continued to review the disciplinary data analysis against the VADIR and VADIR definitions, and more questions arose. If UCLA reported students by gender and disability in 2009–10, why didn't the district's report include students with disabilities?

I considered that I could be wrong! Maybe my findings were inaccurate. I had come too far to stop now, and I needed to know at this point either way. All the information was provided by either New York State Department of Education/SED or our district, but I found out that questioning the school district's own data was not OK with our school district.

I found this out after we posed some preliminary questions to the district's chief of staff at the June 2013 mediation agreement signers meeting held at the local NAACP office. The initial reply was that we could not use the VADIR to interpret the disciplinary data analysis, but once I posed the question about inaccurate district data, the tone of the meeting changed. This was not our definitions; it was VADIR's definition of categories. The definition was found on the VADIR Early Summary Form in columns j–o. This was when the cordial meeting turned very adversarial.

On the evening of June 6, 2013, the VADIR tension came to a boiling point. At this time, I knew we were on to something big! An hour prior to a community meeting to discuss the suspension data and the code of conduct, I accepted a phone call from the superintendent's chief of staff. I thought the call was about picking up copies of the code to distribute at the meeting, but I was wrong, very wrong.

The call was directly in relation to the VADIR being used in conjunction with or to interpret the new disciplinary data. This brief call turned into a thirty-minute loud, very argumentative conversation. The chief of staff took a stand and stated, "You cannot use the data and numbers in the VADIR to interpret the numbers in the disciplinary data analysis" because the reports are different.

I was offended and angry that she did not respect our ability to interpret statistics or see the connection between the two. In fact, I told her just that! She attempted to interject, but I boldly continued talking, stating that UCLA's Civil Rights Project in the 2009–10 data was provided by our school district. The data was collected using two means: NYS VADIR and a survey administered by the US Department of Education, Office for Civil Rights (OCR). It was data and information provided by our district regarding disruptive incidents reportable on the VADIR.

Now I wondered if district officials, including the chief of staff, the board, and the superintendent, had actually reviewed the entire VADIR for our schools in comparison with the disciplinary data at all.

If not, the challenge was there; just do it!
There was no answer.
Then I told her the catch. You also have to use the UCLA 2009–10 report, the code of conduct's prohibited act or disruptive incident sections, and the reportable incidents in VADIR to get the full picture of what we had found. If she did this and did not come to the same conclusions, I would stop my insistence that the data was inaccurate. I would also stop insisting that the disciplinary data analysis be reviewed in conjunction with the 4,000+ other disruptive incidents listed in the VADIR.

This would be an easy challenge for this district official, but it was not. I further stated that since the reportable categories of VADIR were considered disruptive incidents by our code of conduct, especially teacher removals, why were they not documented and/or counted as referral or disciplinary action that consistently led to suspension? I thought she would have welcomed challenges, a chance to shut me up, but our district does not like to be challenged.

So now I took the hard stance; I challenged her to do research and then we could sit and talk afterward, but until then my questions remained! She did not take the challenge! Data suppression and/or making it hard for parents to understand data and documents speak volumes in an arena of distrust and when you can prove the educational system is unjust for students of color. This call caused NAN's suspicions to grow and created more distrust and a need for accountability at the board level.

I really wanted the school district to do the work; well, I really wanted her to do the work, not to rely on what was being told to her by the staff but for her to do her own research. Defending skewed information does not gain public trust or prove the district is transparent.

Parents, remember the key is using the code of conduct, district demographics, and NYS VADIR together if you are attempting to interpret any school-district-generated analysis on disciplinary data. You must be willing to do the work as it is very labor intensive, but the results are rewarding. By the time you are finished, you will be well versed in district policy and procedures, which will probably make you like me, the most hated parent or parent advocate in Syracuse!

Parents, when you become an active participant in your child's education, the response from the school is not always welcoming. Be prepared for push-back if you question the decision made about your child and even more so if you question or disagree with your child's IEP. When you begin to set a no-nonsense tone by becoming familiar with the policies and laws while you advocate for your child, the atmosphere in the school and the school district may begin to change. This is why I am considered the most hated parent!

All that the school district had to do was answer our main questions prior to the release of the discipline data analysis for 2010–11 and 2011–12 to prevent the tension. This tension fueled our quest to have a state or federal agency intervene regarding disparities in suspensions. We wanted answers for the following questions:

1. What is the nature of the 5,460 "other disruptive incidents" reported in the VADIR?
2. How many of them resulted in referral or suspension?
3. Identify the prohibited acts or disruptive conduct, which required referral or disciplinary action as per the code of conduct.

Yes, I took the time to read all the documents and do the math, especially as it related to the other disruptive incidents column. I could not believe that the school district could not/would not provide any information on the 5,460 reportable other disruptive incidents, identified in the VADIR. This is the main reason for the accuracy of the new data being questioned. It did not seem to accurately reflect what our district reported to the State or US Department of Education.

Reporting Violent and Disruptive Acts

"The New York State Department of Education, under the No Child Left Behind legislation, requires all schools to report Violent and Disruptive Incidents for an entire school year in a Summary Report format;" that format is the VADIR.

The VADIR (excel document) was used for my interpretation of the disciplinary data analysis for Syracuse schools from the 2010–11 school year. Statistics were not available at this time for the 2012–13 school year, according to the superintendent, but we know they were available, even though the district indicated they were not. If you are interested in looking up your district's data or data on an individual school in your NYS district, download the spreadsheet titled "The Rest of State Violent and Disruptive Incidents." This is a large document and a labor-intensive task, but I am known for reading everything, and I am the most hated parent or parent advocate in the district when it comes to statistics, data, and policy.

Note to parents: Question everything you don't understand until you get an answer that you do understand! I find myself telling the district all the time, "If you don't want me to ask questions, why do you ask me to read it?" Become known for dissecting misinformation!

Chapter 9

The Second Look at the Disciplinary Data Analysis: Disruptive Conduct and Teacher Removals—the Second Review

On May 7, one of my friends and a colleague joined me at my office to assist in examining the disciplinary data document. I wanted to tell them what I had found, but this needed to be a blind review. Deep down, I think I really wanted them to say, "Twiggy, we don't see anything out of the ordinary." I wanted to believe that my own findings were off; however, I never got the opportunity to utter those words.

As they entered my home office, each looked astonished to see the number of spreadsheets on the walls and on two six-foot-long banquet tables. I also provided printed copies of the district's disciplinary data analysis, the NYS VADIR for our district, the online link to the school calendar's ethnic breakdown, and the code of conduct. I waited to present the UCLA report from 2009 to 2010.

After about an hour had passed, my fears were confirmed. There was an overuse of suspension among African American and Latino students. There was no need to question my findings, and in fact, the more we studied the documents together, the greater the disparity grew.

Once our meeting concluded (some three hours later), I continued to research the numbers against the data provided in the NYS VADIR and the UCLA report.

One of the highest offending schools was Bellevue/Shea, and the district's data needed to be reviewed against the US Department of Education's data on this school. The UCLA report indicated that their data was collected from the data our district had submitted to the US Department of Education. Now I needed to know what data the US Department of Education Office of Civil Rights (OCR) was using. What I found was again unsettling. The summary of the Data Collection Unit of the Office of Civil Rights is also given below. At the middle-school level, four out of seven middle schools had suspension rates above 50%, but Bellevue/Shea, and the Westside Learning Academy had much higher rates.

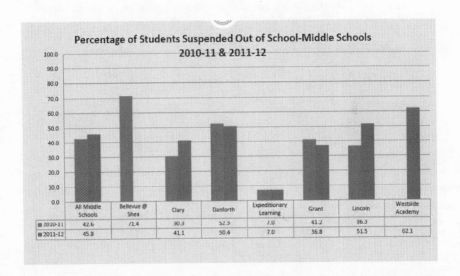

The OCR summary of selected facts also indicated (survey data from 2009) that African American and Latino students were suspended at twice the rate of their white counterparts in this school.

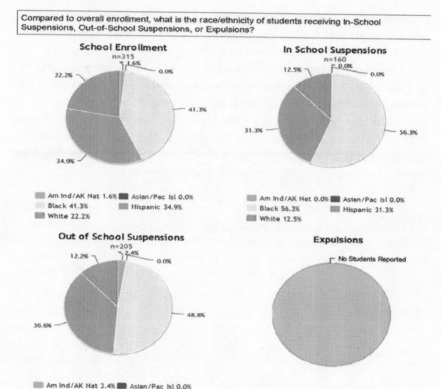

Compared to overall enrollment, what is the race/ethnicity of students receiving In-School Suspensions, Out-of-School Suspensions, or Expulsions?

School Enrollment
n=315

Am Ind/AK Nat 1.6%   Asian/Pac Isl 0.0%
Black 41.3%   Hispanic 34.9%
White 22.2%

In School Suspensions
n=160

Am Ind/AK Nat 0.0%   Asian/Pac Isl 0.0%
Black 56.3%   Hispanic 31.3%
White 12.5%

Out of School Suspensions
n=205

Am Ind/AK Nat 2.4%   Asian/Pac Isl 0.0%
Black 48.8%   Hispanic 36.6%
White 12.2%

Expulsions

No Students Reported

* Section 504 Only discipline data is not available by race/ethnicity. Number of Section 504 Only students disciplined: In-School Suspensions=0, Out of School Suspensions=0, Expulsions=0

The high suspension rates for out-of-school suspension (OSS) and in-school suspension (ISS) are still evident in the new disciplinary report analysis conducted by the school district. However, there was one major difference. Our disciplinary data analysis did not contain disaggregation by school level, race, and disability status data. Our data was disaggregated by gender, grade level, and race for 2010–11 and 2011–12 school years. Teacher removal of a student was not being documented and the student was being sent home. The rate among principals in Syracuse rose in those same two school years and prompted our questions to the superintendent and the school board. Now we knew that the removal lasted for more than one class and that there were parents who could verify the occurrences, but we could not get the district to seriously address the issue. I knew I needed to look at how the policy was written before I presented my findings. I needed numbers for students with disabilities and numbers on teacher removals that resulted in the students being sent home to identify what conduct resulted in the suspensions and if these suspensions were for minor infractions.

This was in essence to make sure that school discipline policy via the code of conduct was being implemented correctly, especially enforcing due process and progressive discipline.

I also wanted to check on the changes made in 2001 regarding SROs. The change in the code was pushed by parents and community civil rights agencies to ensure the district maintained clarity in the overlap between criminal law and the school's discipline code.

In previous years, it had come to our attention that SRO could use excessive force on students for non-criminal matters and "remove a student from the school." Removal from the school is considered suspension and the suspending authority in any school is the principal.

The underlined text is one of the many changes in police conduct in school that we assisted in implementing with the assistance of the US Department of Justice's Conciliation Unit.

2) Enforce all criminal statutes appropriately and fairly. There may be an overlap between the criminal law and the school's discipline code; the SRO is responsible for handling the criminal matter, and the principal is responsible for handling all discipline issues according to the policies approved by the Board of Education.

Absent a potential, immediate or ongoing threat to the safety of an individual or group of individuals at the school, the SRO should not intervene unless requested by the principal.

The SRO should investigate criminal activity committed on or adjacent to school property, or reported to them in their capacity as a police officer. They should remain knowledgeable relative to criminal behavior occurring within the city that might directly or indirectly affect the school and their attendant responsibilities.

(SCSD School Calendar and Handbook, 2012–13 (page 22))

I also reviewed the section on discipline and students with disabilities to see if manifestation determination hearings had been eliminated or the number of days had changed or lessened. They had not.

Discipline and Students with Disabilities

Factors considered when determining any discipline include: student's age; grade in school; prior disciplinary record; the superintendent's belief that other forms of discipline may be more effective; input from parents, teachers, or others; and other extenuating circumstances. A student with a disability may be suspended and scheduled for a Manifestation Determination meeting to determine if there is a connection between the behavioral incident and the student's disability. The Syracuse City School District's Code of Conduct is applicable to all students.

(SCSD School Calendar and Handbook, 2012–13 (page 23))

The number of African American students suspended in our district, with disabilities, in 2009 was staggering. Fifty-five percent (55%) of all African American males in secondary school with disabilities were suspended. We had found out that disabled students were being suspended without manifestation determination meetings and were already working on the issue. I had no idea it was of this magnitude! Didn't the district know the policies and laws covered students with disabilities? How could the UCLA report for 2009–10 contain the data and the district's report not include the information? Was it because the rates were even higher now and for the 2010–11 and 2011–12 school years? Now I wondered, *Were these the reasons we could not get disaggregated data on students with disabilities? Why was this data not included in the disciplinary data analysis?* The IDEA came to mind, so I reviewed that law to see if my interpretation of the policy for suspending a student with disabilities was accurate. Again it was!

At specific times, and for certain violations of the student code of conduct, IDEA's discipline procedures require school systems to conduct what is known as a "manifestation determination review."

The purpose of this review is to determine whether or not the child's behavior that led to the disciplinary infraction is linked to his or her disability. Manifestation determinations were first introduced into IDEA with the 1997 amendments.

The process has been simplified under IDEA 2004, which now:

- limits the requirement to perform a manifestation determination to removals that constitute a change of placement under IDEA's disciplinary procedures; and
- does not require a manifestation determination for removals for less than 10 consecutive/collective school days that do not constitute a change in placement.

The above is taken from the Web site of the National Dissemination Center for Children with Disabilities. The IDEA's discipline procedures require school systems to conduct a manifestation determination review, and that has not been occurring in our school district.

Parents should become familiar with the manifestation determination meeting and discipline procedures if their child has a disability.

I noticed there are a lot of acronyms and definitions that has hidden meanings in the code of conduct, so understanding this document is crucial to the parents and the students.

I began to look at the definitions of discipline authority to see who is authorized to discipline, what methods of discipline are used, and what conduct is considered disruptive.

D. Discipline Authority

Students who are found to have violated the district's code of conduct may be subject to the following penalties, either alone or in combination. The school personnel identified after each penalty are authorized to impose that penalty, consistent with the student's right to due process.

- Oral warning – any member of the district staff.
- Written warning – bus drivers, hall and lunch monitors, coaches, guidance counselors, teaching assistants, teachers, deans of students, administrative interns, vice principals, principal, superintendent.
- Written notification to parent – bus driver, hall and lunch monitors, coaches, guidance counselors, teaching assistants, teachers, deans of students, administrative interns, vice principals, principal, superintendent.
- Detention – teachers, deans of students, administrative interns, vice principals, principal, superintendent.
- Suspension from transportation – director of transportation, deans of students, administrative interns, vice principals, principal, superintendent.
- Suspension from athletic participation – coaches, deans of students, administrative interns, vice principals, principal, superintendent.
- Suspension from social or extracurricular activities – activity director, principal, superintendent.
- Suspension of other privileges – deans of students, administrative interns, vice principals, principal, superintendent.
- In-school suspension – deans of students, administrative interns, vice principals, principal, superintendent.

- Removal from classroom – teachers, deans of students, administrative interns, vice principals, principal, superintendent.
- Short-term (five days or less) suspension from school – principal, superintendent, Board of Education.
- Long-term (more than five days) suspension from school – superintendent, Board of Education.
- Permanent suspension from school – superintendent, Board of Education.

What the code of conduct revealed was alarming, especially for students with disabilities.

A. Student conduct that is disruptive. Examples of disruptive conduct include:
- Failing to comply with the reasonable directions of teachers, school administrators or other school personnel in charge of students.
- Running in hallways.
- Making unreasonable noise.
- Bringing in unauthorized pets.
- Using language or gestures that are profane, lewd, vulgar or abusive.
- Obstructing vehicular or pedestrian traffic.
- Engaging in any willful act which disrupts the normal operation of the school community.
- Trespassing. Students are not permitted in any school building, other than the one they regularly attend, without permission from the administrator in charge of the building.
- Computer/electronic communications misuse, including any unauthorized use of computers software, or internet/intranet accounts; accessing inappropriate websites or any other violation of the district's acceptable use policy as further outlined in SCSD Acceptable Use Policy for All Computer Technology in Section XV – R.
- Unauthorized use of objects (i.e. beepers, cellular phones, boom boxes, walkmans, CD players, etc.) during regular school hours or school events.
- Bringing in unauthorized objects (i.e. laser pointers, obscene materials, etc.)

7

Symptoms that are associated with normal adolescent behavior and/or students' disability are considered disruptive conduct. Now the crisis and the realization of the intent of the systemic intuitional push-out of students of color and students of color with disabilities were painfully clear. This was a double-edged sword for the students of color and/or the disabled students.

Now I wondered just how many students and parents were aware of this.

The one thing I had noticed in all the years I have worked with students and parents on educational issues and policy was that parents were not familiar with school policies. Whether the issue was academic eligibility or the suspension process the appeal processes were virtually unknown to students and parents.

Parents often said, "What appeal process?" There was not one single instance that I could recollect where a student or a parent had requested assistance because their appeal of a student's academic ineligibility or suspension had been denied. In fact, it was because they did not know those two issues could be appealed.

How could a parent or a student invoke due process protections or ensure progressive discipline is being followed if they are unfamiliar with the terms and the policies? How would a parent know if teacher removals are being followed to the letter of the law? Parents, take advantage of school board meetings to ensure your voices are heard if you meet roadblocks at the school. This is your opportunity to speak up for all the voiceless families in your district.

Undocumented teacher removals were resulting in suspensions of students at an alarming rate. Did parents really understand teacher removal? The code of conduct on teacher removal has two distinctive parts: classroom management or student removal and removal of disruptive student. We will go into more detail later on, but for now, let's get some clarity on the policy.

E. Teacher Removal of Disruptive Student
 1. Classroom Management/Student Removal
    A student's behavior can affect a teacher's ability to teach and can make it difficult for other students in the classroom to learn. In most instances the classroom teacher can control a student's behavior and maintain or restore control over the classroom by using good classroom management techniques. These techniques may include practices that involve the teacher directing a student to briefly leave the classroom to give the student an opportunity to regain his or her composure and self-control in an alternative setting. Such practices may include, but are not limited to: (1) short-term "time out" in an elementary classroom or in an administrator's office; (2) sending a student to the principal's office for the remainder of the class time only; or (3) sending a student to a guidance counselor or other district staff member for counseling. Time-honored classroom management techniques such as these do not constitute disciplinary removals for purposes of this code.

This first part spells out "good classroom management techniques and short term." These may include directing the students to leave the class and regain self-control in an alternate setting. It also states something very specific: Time-honored classroom management techniques as the ones listed above do not constitute removal. That statement was odd because the policy above was being followed with one distinction. Students sent to the principal were being sent home with a parent to gain self-control and composure, constituting an undocumented suspension.

The second part was disturbing; I noticed the term *disruptive* kept creeping in.

2. Removal of Disruptive Student
   On occasion, a student's behavior may become disruptive. For purposes of this code of conduct, a disruptive student is a student who is substantially disruptive of the educational process or substantially interferes with the teacher's authority over the classroom. A substantial disruption of the educational process or substantial interference with a teacher's authority occurs when a student demonstrates a persistent unwillingness to comply with the teacher's instructions or repeatedly violates the teacher's classroom behavior rules.

   A classroom teacher may remove a disruptive student from class. **The duration shall be determined by mutual discussion between the principal and teacher, and the removal will not exceed two days (48 hours). If a mutual consensus is not reached, then the student will be removed for one day (24 hours).** The removal from class applies to the class of the removing teacher only.

Look closely at this second part of the policy. It states, "Persistent unwillingness to comply with teacher instruction or repeatedly violates the teacher classroom behavior rules."

I wondered if parents were aware that disruptive conduct and substantially disruptive are codes for being symptomatic of DBD. In fact, did any parent realize this label *disruptive* was the pathway to being medically diagnosed with DBD, CD, or ODD?

Most of the disruptive conducts listed in the code of conduct align with the symptoms that are listed in the medical diagnoses and codes DSM-IV. Dr. Umar Johnson conducted a presentation on this very matter, so I was familiar with how both were being used to push out students of color, especially students of color with disabilities.

I couldn't believe it, even though it was in my face. I really didn't need to know the number of students with disabilities who were suspended. The behaviors identified in the code of conduct under disruptive behavior aligned with symptoms of students' disabilities.

Could this be accurate?

I needed more assistance with this interpretation, so I called on the assistance of Dr. Umar Johnson to help verify what I thought to be true. There was disproportionate suspension of African American and Latino children with and without disabilities occurring in our district. The call to Dr. Umar was the best call we could make. Dr. Umar advised us when he came to Syracuse to assist us. Since his initial visit in 2010, he had conducted three presentations on suspension and students of color with disabilities and the conspiracy to destroy black boys.

I found that parents are not aware that being considered "routinely disruptive" not only leads to suspension but it's also a potential pathway to a medical diagnosis and being put on medication. Knowing how to advocate for your child will be the determining factor if your child receives regular disciplinary action, is removed from class by the teacher, and has a short-term cooling-off period with the principal or the social worker for behavior and disruptions. All the above could lead to a determination that your child needs to be seen medically for ADD or ADHD or even for a psychological consultation instead of testing for a potential learning disability. If your child has a mental disorder, specific learning disability, ADHD, or IEP with a behavioral intervention plan, they may be suspended for exhibiting conduct associated with disability in school. Remember all the symptoms of DBD have prescription counterparts. What do parents really know?

Chapter 10

Findings and Correlation—
What the Data Revealed

Presenting the Findings and Questions for the School Board
I had to put it all together, but how? This was going to create tension, and it was not going to be received well by the board of education or the superintendent of schools. How would I deliver this disparaging news? There was nothing lighthearted about this whole thing; in fact, parents and committee members thought the board was arrogant in its delivery of the data. The newspaper printed it, and the district had not provided one single overview of the document. Now I needed to decide: Would I give a brief outline and overview or produce a summary of findings of the whole review and my entire assertion?

When I looked at the ethnic breakdown versus the actual number of white, Asian, African American, Latino, and Native Indian or Native Alaskan students, I noticed inconsistency with the enrollment data and the percentage of students suspended. Suspensions remained consistently high among the three groups or categories of students; actually all three had higher rates than any other category or group of students, i.e., African American, Latino, and Native Indian or Native Alaskan. Now I knew the presentation would not be brief in any format.

I wondered how Native American or Native Alaskan students made up one percent (1%) of the student population, but they were suspended at a rate far higher than their white counterparts for both school years. That was almost impossible! African American students make up 50% of the student population, and they were suspended at a far higher rate than their white counterparts. Actually, half of the African American student population had been suspended in both school years. Latino students represent 13% of the student population; they were suspended two times more than their white counterparts at 26%, leaving one to wonder how many were in school if twice the population had been suspended?

Now I had to correlate the findings with the recent disciplinary data analysis conducted by the school district and pose some tough questions:

How many suspensions are for disruptive behaviors?

Is this data based on single or multiple suspensions?

How many are three-, four-, or five-day suspensions?

How many are repeat offenders and over what period of time?

How many of the students suspended had a disability?

Why are all the schools with high suspension rates in predominantly African American and Latino neighborhoods?

Why has the middle school suspension rate at Bellevue/Shea, escalated from 60% to 70%?

Why is the rate at Westside Learning Academy at 62% during the 2011–12 school year?

Now the phone call from the African American politicians was running through my mind. They indicated they had two issues: the number of suspensions, which was nearly ten thousand students in both school years, and the number of K-1 grade African American students who were suspended. While these were truly troubling statistics, the hidden implications were staggering for students of color. I was outraged and upset, and I could feel a storm coming.

Anyone can do basic math, and the district should have known we would not just accept the data without questions.

I did the math and was incensed! There are 19,720 K-12 students in our school district. African American students constitute 50% of the overall student population (9,860). There are approximately 2,563.6 Latino students, which represent 13% of the overall student population. The reports did not include pre-K; therefore, it is not included here.

Student Information

- 19,720 K-12 students
- 1,310 prekindergarten children (including Universal, Experimental, and other Pre-K programs)
- Services to students speaking 11 languages
- 10,000 breakfasts and 14,200 lunches served daily
- 10,569 total public school students transported daily
- 1,698 total non-public school students transported daily to 35 non-public schools
- Free/Reduced Lunch   85%
- Special Education   20%
- English as a Second Language (ESL)   14%

Ethnic Breakdown

- Black   50%
- White   26%
- Hispanic   13%
- Asian   7%
- Multiracial   3%
- Native American/Alaskan   1%

If you look at the out-of-school suspension and in-school suspension summary below, it would appear that suspensions outnumber the overall student population of these combined ethnic groups. This aspect is one of the reasons this report was unsettling.

The following has been taken from the district's disciplinary data analysis:

Out-of-school and In-school Suspension Summary

	2010-11	2011-12
Total number of out-of-school suspensions	9,545	9,988
Total number of students suspended out-of-school	4,167	4,210
Total number of in-school suspensions	13,967	12,135
Total number of students suspended in-school	4,539	4,305

(Source: http://test.scsd.us/tfiles/folder514/SCSD%20Student%20Disciplinary %20Data%20Analysis.pdf)

What the African American leaders had indicated was correct, but in the context of the student population numbers, there were major disparities in suspension by race. How could I move forward without the numbers of disabled students?

Then it dawned on me that I could approximate the number of students with disabilities using the UCLA data for students with disabilities and for each subgroup of African American and Latino students for the 2009–10 school year.

During the review, we found the district's discipline analysis showed that 6–7% of kindergartners through second-graders had been suspended. It was hard coming to terms with the fact that five-, six-, and seven-year-old students were being suspended out of school. This was an alarming rate for that group, and the rates were even higher for the number of in-school suspensions. When I looked at secondary schools, it was unbelievable.

How could I get any sense of the numbers for that common practice among teachers and administrators using the policy of teacher removals to send students home for the day or a couple of days to calm down or cool off? How many suspensions included in this data are legal suspensions (with documentation) and how many are left out because they are illegal suspensions (without documentation)? Was this issue even being addressed since the school that was identified as the number one offender had been closed the previous year? Lastly, how many of these suspensions were appealed?

African Americans make up 25.7% of students who are suspended and represent 50% of the student population. Why did these numbers keep replaying in my thoughts? *That's twice the rate of their white counterparts; this cannot be right.*

The UCLA report is comprehensive; it's called out of school and off track. This report provides access to excel spreadsheets with directions on how to interpret the data. This is just what I needed in order to move forward.

Below is what the sidebar on the Web page looks like, containing this information. I used the Secondary Report District by Gradespan and excel document to find the number of students with disabilities for 2009. I used a margin of error of 5% +/- for the 2010–11 and 2011–12 school years. http://civilrightsproject.ucla.edu/resources/projects/center-for-civil-rights-remedies/school-to-prison-folder/federal-reports/out-of-school-and-off-track-the-overuse-of-suspensions-in-american-middle-and-high-schools/Instructions-to-Secondary-Schools-Suspension.pdf

The comprehensive material is located on the Web page of the report under related documents:

- Executive Summary: Out of School and Off Track
- Secondary Report District by Gradespan CRDC 0910 FINAL
- Instructions to Secondary Schools Suspension Spreadsheet
- Spreadsheet: High Suspending Secondary School District Count
- Spreadsheet: Low Suspending Secondary School District Count
- Full Report: Out of School and Off Track

I easily found our school district in the excel file and scrolled over to the total number of secondary school (middle and high school) students with disabilities. The number of secondary students with disabilities was 1,690 students in 2009. The data contains ethnic breakdowns.

Enrollment— Students with disabilities	Enrollment— American-Indian Students with disabilities	Enrollment— Asian Pacific Islander with disabilities	Enrollment— African American with disabilities	Enrollment— Hispanic with disabilities	Enrollment— White with disabilities	Enrollment— Two or more Races with disabilities	Enrollment— ELL with disabilities
1,690	20	5	920	195	540		65

The ethnic breakdowns for male and female secondary students are as follows:

Enrollment—Male—Students with disabilities	Enrollment—Male—American Indian Students with disabilities	Enrollment—Male—Asian Pacific Islander with disabilities	Enrollment—Male—African American with disabilities	Enrollment—Male—Hispanic with disabilities	Enrollment—Male—White with disabilities	Enrollment—Male—Two or More Races with disabilities	Enrollment—Male—ELL with disabilities
1,025	15	0	560	125	325		35

Notice the high disability rates among African American male and female disabled students.

Enrollment—Female—Students with disabilities	Enrollment—Female—American Indian Students with disabilities	Enrollment—Female—Asian Pacific Islander with disabilities	Enrollment—Female—African American with disabilities	Enrollment—Female—Hispanic with disabilities	Enrollment—Female—White with disabilities	Enrollment—Female—Two or More Races with disabilities	Enrollment—Female—ELL with disabilities
665	15	5	360	70	215		30

Remember, this data is from the UCLA Civil Rights Project report in 2009 on the secondary schools in Syracuse.

The total number of secondary students with disabilities is 1,690. Now it is time to look at the total number of secondary students with disabilities who were suspended in 2010. There was absolute outrage when I realized the number of suspension of African American students and other students of color with disabilities. What would happen once I added the elementary school numbers to the secondary school numbers?

Secondary School Data: Suspended Students with disabilities	Suspended Students—American Indian Students with disabilities	Suspended Students—Asian Pacific Islander with disabilities	Suspended Students—African American with disabilities	Suspended Students—Hispanics with disabilities	Suspended Students—Whites with disabilities	Suspended Students—Students with disabilities reporting 2 or more races	Suspended Students—ELLs with disabilities
745	0	0	480	70	155		40

There are 1,690 secondary students with disabilities, and 745 of them were suspended, that is, almost half of the entire secondary population for students with disabilities, especially African American students.

This worried me because these were only the figures for secondary students, not for elementary students. I was afraid to look at the elementary numbers, but my curiosity got the better of me.

Elementary Students Suspended, All Students							
Suspended Students—Total	Suspended Students— American- Indian Students	Suspended Students— Asian Pacific Islander	Suspended Students— African American	Suspended Students— Hispanics	Suspended Students— Whites	Suspended Students— Reporting two or more races	Suspended Students— ELLs
910	5	0	600	75	145		70

I was almost afraid to look at these numbers. Once I did, I felt sick to the stomach; a feeling of uneasiness had come over me—a troubling feeling, a feeling of panic and fear just like when the sky darkens prior to a storm or before a whirlwind hits a town or city.

There were 910 elementary students suspended. Out of that, 600 of the suspensions occurred among the African American student population. More than 66% of all elementary students enrolled were suspended during the 2009–10 school year.

This was a compelling discovery because the rates for the 2010–11 and 2011–12 school years had increased dramatically in some instances by 15–20% at individual schools.

The anxiety, suspense, and even the fear of what was to come challenged my ability to keep calm.

The next data set is only for elementary schools in Syracuse. This is the problem!

Elementary Enrollment—Students with disabilities							
Enrollment— Students with disabilities	Enrollment— American- Indian Students with disabilities	Enrollment— Asian Pacific Islander with disabilities	Enrollment— African American with disabilities	Enrollment— Hispanic with disabilities	Enrollment— White with disabilities	Enrollment— Two or More Races with disabilities	Enrollment— ELL with disabilities
1,485	15	0	770	170	510		115

This shows half of the enrolled population of students with disabilities is African American.

Now I had an approximate number of students with disabilities for secondary and elementary schools within our district based on actual 2009 data.

These are the numbers I used (5% +/- error rate) to assess the disparities within the subgroup African American and other students of color with disabilities in the 2010–11 and 2011–12 school years.

I had the proof I needed to force the school district to conduct a more thorough investigation of the implications. African American male and female elementary students have unbelievable disproportionate suspension rates. I had to review the rest of the UCLA data now. It was really compelling for me to review all the UCLA data before presenting the finding to the politicians, the NAN Education Committee, and the public at large.

Elementary Suspension Risk, Male Students with Disabilities							
Suspension rate among male students with disabilities	Suspension rate—Males—American Indians with disabilities	Suspension rate—Males-Asian Pacific Islanders with disabilities	Suspension rate—Males-African Americans with disabilities	Suspension rate—Males-Hispanics with disabilities	Suspension rate—Males-whites with disabilities	Suspension rate among male students reporting 2 or more races with disabilities	Suspension rate—Males-ELLs with disabilities
25.0%	0.0%		29.5%	12.5%	15.6%		23.5%

Elementary Suspension Risk, Female Students with Disabilities							
Suspension rate among female students with disabilities	Suspension rate—Females—American-Indians with disabilities	Suspension rate—Females-Asian Pacific Islanders with disabilities	Suspension rate—Females-African Americans with disabilities	Suspension rate—Females-Hispanics with disabilities	Suspension rate—Females-whites with disabilities	Suspension rate among female students reporting two or more races with disabilities	Suspension rate—Females—ELLs with disabilities
6.9%	0.0%		8.2%	0.0%	0.0%		0.0%

Look at the rates of suspensions for African American, Latino, and English language learners; I knew the statistics could not be much different for the 2010–11 and 2011–12 school years.

Secondary Suspension Risk, Students with Disabilities							
Suspension rate among students with disabilities	Suspension rate among American Indians with disabilities	Suspension rate among Asian Pacific Islanders with disabilities	Suspension rate among African Americans with disabilities	Suspension rate among Hispanics with disabilities	Suspension rate among whites with disabilities	Suspension rate among students reporting 2 or more races with disabilities	Suspension rate among ELLs with disabilities
44.1%	0.0%	0.0%	52.2%	35.9%	28.7%		61.5%

Now the disconcerting statistics from 2009 made me even sicker to my stomach. I wanted to cry out, but I continued to review the data in disgust.

The thoughts running through my mind were overwhelming. My children, my niece, and so many others have experienced this covert technique to push black students out.

Back then (1994), it was just an attempt because we pushed back. We were armed with the code of conduct and knowledge of laws and policies for the disabled students. We used due process and the appeal procedures to fight the battles and win for all children.

Today (2013) I realized something profound! Am I the only person monitoring the policies and deciphering the data? I had to continue fighting the push-out of African American students, African American students with disabilities, and other students of color with disabilities, according to these numbers.

Now I had to step up my game on paper and in the public eye. NAN, the African American community, and our leaders had to add some tension and publicly hold our elected officials accountable. This was not a game!

The school district was not going to be prepared for this whirlwind as a mighty wind was coming! This is an issue I am determined to make known; the district will not be allowed to ignore me any longer.

Secondary Suspension Risk, Male Students with Disabilities							
Suspension rate among male students with disabilities	Suspension rate—Males—American Indians with disabilities	Suspension rate—Males-Asian Pacific Islanders with disabilities	Suspension rate—Males-African Americans with disabilities	Suspension rate—Males-Hispanics with disabilities	Suspension rate—Males-whites with disabilities	Suspension rate among male students reporting 2 or more races with disabilities	Suspension rate—Males-ELLs with disabilities
47.8%	0.0%		54.5%	43.0%	30.8%		85.7%

There was no need to do the math; the suspension percentages were provided by UCLA's Civil Rights Project. The percentages are provided in the chart above and the chart below. It didn't matter if the student was in elementary or secondary school; I had the answers.

Secondary Suspension Risk, Female Students with Disabilities							
Suspension rate among female students with disabilities	Suspension rate—Females—American Indians with disabilities	Suspension rate—Females-Asian Pacific Islanders with disabilities	Suspension rate—Females-African Americans with disabilities	Suspension rate—Females-Hispanics with disabilities	Suspension rate—Females-whites with disabilities	Suspension rate among female students reporting two or more races with disabilities	Suspension rate—Females-ELLs with disabilities
38.3%	0.0%	0.0%	48.6%	14.3%	25.6%		33.3%

The rates are staggering among African American boy and girl students and other students of color with disabilities, including English language learners with disabilities.

Could this be why there was no public outrage when the media released the data? The data was so cumbersome and time-consuming that no layperson would figure this out.

Once I figured out the combined total number of students with disabilities, I could look at the implications.

Students with Disabilities in 2009
Secondary school students   1,690
Elementary school students   1,485
Total   3,175 students with disabilities
Elementary and Secondary Enrollment (2009)
Students enrolled   Secondary   8,180
             Elementary   7,220
             Total   15,400 students enrolled

If you look at the numbers below for African American students against the total number of elementary students suspended with disabilities, both are far greater than any other subgroup.

The number of African American students with disabilities suspended at the elementary level was 175 students. Take note that the overall number of students suspended with disabilities was 280. If you add Latino students and English language learners as students of color, the numbers skyrocket!

Elementary Students Suspended, Students with Disabilities							
Suspended Students with disabilities	Suspended Students— American– Indian Students with disabilities	Suspended Students— Asian Pacific Islander with disabilities	Suspended Students— African American with disabilities	Suspended Students— Hispanics with disabilities	Suspended Students— Whites with disabilities	Suspended Students— Students with disabilities reporting two or more races	Suspended Students— ELLs with disabilities
280	0	0	175	15	50		20

Again, African American students lead the rate in suspension of students with disabilities at the elementary level.
Secondary students with disabilities suspended (overall)   745
Elementary students with disabilities suspended (overall)   280
Total   1,025 students

Now the total number needed to be put into the context of male and female students of color. I was not ready to admit that was something sinister occurring, but I braced for it to materialize.

The Elementary and Secondary Levels

Elementary Enrollment—Male Students with disabilities							
Enrollment—Male—Students with disabilities	Enrollment—Male—American-Indian Students with disabilities	Enrollment—Male—Asian Pacific Islander with disabilities	Enrollment—Male—African American with disabilities	Enrollment—Male—Hispanic with disabilities	Enrollment—Male—White with disabilities	Enrollment—Male—Two or More Races with disabilities	Enrollment—Male—ELL with disabilities
980	15	0	525	120	320		85

I was actually troubled by the 2009 statistics. Of the overall 980 male students with disabilities enrolled, 525 were African American males.

Elementary Enrollment—Female Students with disabilities							
Enrollment—Female—Students with disabilities	Enrollment—Female—American-Indian Students with disabilities	Enrollment—Female—Asian Pacific Islander with disabilities	Enrollment—Female—African American with disabilities	Enrollment—Female—Hispanic with disabilities	Enrollment—Female—White with disabilities	Enrollment—Female—Two or More Races with disabilities	Enrollment—Female—ELL with disabilities
505	15	0	245	50	190		30

Of the overall 505 African American female students, almost half were suspended during the 2009–10 school year.

I did not want to believe that it was a conspiracy to destroy African American children, especially males. I was fooling myself! I knew there was a conspiracy to destroy black children. All the leading African American scholars on education and special education have conducted in-depth presentations and workshops on the issue. First, I heard it from Dr. Frances Cress-Welsing, an elderly scholar. Dr. Cress-Welsing's theory was powerful, and it made me realize the conspiracy theory against the African American community was true.

In 2011, the subject came up again with Dr. Kunjufu and Dr. Umar Johnson, both visiting Syracuse in June and July. However, the most compelling information on disabled students was from the young and rising scholar Dr. Umar Johnson! This was the reason for calling Dr. Umar to assist with the implications for the disabled students.

Presenting the Findings to the Public and Elected Officials

Now it was time to put the questions and the findings together and send them to the African American leaders who had requested the review. I sent the findings by e-mail to the local NAN president, the two African American politicians, the director of NYCLU, and the local chapter of the NAACP.

Within two-three hours after e-mailing the findings, I was invited to present them to the superintendent of schools and the school board at the upcoming board meeting. NAN held a press conference and special meeting on the findings in conjunction with the NAACP and/or other local leaders. The findings and forty-eight questions were first presented and posed to the superintendent and school board members at a local church on May 8, 2013.

Report of Findings

From the Desk of Twiggy Billue to the National Action Network Syracuse Chapter
FINDINGS & Questions to the School Board—5/8/2013
Presented to the SCSC District on 5/11/2013-48 Questions outlined below

Greetings,
Below are the questions from Saturday's meeting that NAN posed, we would like answers in writing specifically geared to each question below.
Page numbers noted in this document correspond with the page numbers in the district's "Disciplinary Data Analysis 2010–11 and 2011–12.

Questions:

1. How many of these students in this report have disabilities?
2. How many Manifestation Determination Hearings were held for students suspended with disabilities?
3. What percentages of out- of- school & in-school suspensions were students with disabilities?
4. What is the average number of days suspended out-of school and in-school?
5. What percentage is the same student suspended more than twice, more than three times? Out-of-School and In-School.
6. Suspension rates outweigh the number of students enrolled in some areas of the district's report, why?
   Suspension out of school—the rates for 5th—8th grades particularly needs addressing as well as the suspensions of 10th graders.

Out-of-school suspension rates by grade reflects that in-school suspensions have a greater focus on K-4, but out-of-school suspensions have a greater impact and seem to be a recommended plan of action or common practice for grades 5–12 where students are suspended at very high rates (see below).

Page 6—Percentage of Students Suspended Out of School by Grade 2010–11 and 2011–12

2011

K	1	2	3	4	5	6	7	8	9	10	11	12
4.2	5.0	9.6	11.9	14.5	20.9	31.4	39.3	42.7	34.2	28.5	18.9	14.4

2012

3.7	6.9	9.4	16.0	17.9	24.6	33.4	45.5	39.7	32.1	21.7	17.3	12.3

The above rates reflect at least 5%–7% of all K-2nd graders are suspended out of school; these are 5–7- year-old children/students. Students are suspended at much higher rates when they reach grades 6–10 jumping almost 10%–20% for grade 7, 8 and 9.

7. There is no indicator showing how many of these students had disabilities for grades K-2 and 5–12 or average length of suspension. Why?

8. How many K-2 and 5–12 where repeatedly suspended (suspended out more than twice)?

9. How many sent or moved to alternative settings or buildings or suspended for five days?

Page 7—Out-of-school suspension rates by gender has remained unchanged for the past two years—males 25.5% in 2011 and 25.0% in 2012; however, this report shows that male students are suspended in greater numbers than their female counterparts. Females were suspended out of school at 16.4% in 2011 and 14.8% in 2012.

10. How many male students are black, Latino, and white, Native American, or other?

11. How many female students are black, Latino, Native, white, and other?

12. How many male students had disabilities and how many had Manifestation Determination meetings? What were they suspended for?

Page 8
Out-of-school suspension by race/ethnicity indicates that African–American students' rates at 25.7% in 2011 and at 26.3% in 2012 with rates for Latinos following at a close 23.8% in 2011 and 19.9% 2012. What is absolutely astonishing is that African–American and Latino students are suspended almost two times more than their white and multiracial counterparts.

13. What is the average number of days African–American students were suspended? How many five-day suspensions and how many formal hearings held?

14. What is the average number of days Latino students were suspended? How many five-day suspensions and how many formal hearings held prior to being readmitted to school?

15. What is the average number of days white and other ethic students suspended including refugees/immigrants, especially Somalian and from Cosovo? How many five-day suspensions issued to white students and how many formal hearings?

This data leads one to question the data reported on page 7 (out-of-school suspension rate by gender) which indicates that 24.5% of all male students were suspended out of school in 2011 and 25.0% in 2012.

16. How many of these male students are African–American?

17. How many are Latino?

18. How many are white?

19. How many Native Americans/Native Alaskans?

20. What identifiers are used to define the category multiracial?

21. Why is there no number for 2010–2011 multiracial subsets of students?

Page 9

	Asian or Native Hawaiian/Other Pacific Islander	Black or African–American	Hispanic or Latino	American– Indian or Alaska Native	Multiracial	White
2010–11	2.5	25.7	23.8	14.5		13.2
2011–12	3.0	26.3	19.9	13.6	13.5	13.3

While the data stated the percentages varied from school to school, we noticed some alarmingly high suspension rates at the following elementary schools:

Dr. King suspensions rose in 2011–2012 school year by almost 8% from 15.9% to 23.2%, McKinley Brighton suspensions rose from 8.4% in 2010–2011 school year to a *whopping 21.2%* in the 2011–2012 school year—a 12.8% increase.

The only elementary schools that lowered their out-of-school suspension rates in 2011–2012 were Delaware by 4.2%, Seymour by 1.3%, Van Duyn by 2.4%, and Webster dropped from 4.7% in the 2010–2011 school year to 4.3% in 2011–2012 school year (.4%).

22. Why are the highest suspension percentages at schools located in predominately African–American and Latino neighborhoods? At Dr. King, McKinley Brighton, and Seymour, how many of the male students suspended were African–American?

23. At Dr. King, McKinley Brighton, and Seymour, how many male students suspended were Latino?

24. At Dr. King, McKinley Brighton, and Seymour, how many male students suspended were white?

25. The question here is what is going on at Webster, Bellevue, LeMoyne and Van Duyn but especially at Webster which has a 4.7% and 4.3% suspension rate for consecutive years? What corrective measures are in place at each of the schools above that are not at other schools?

Page 10—Percentage of Students Suspended Out of School—K-8 Schools 2010–11 and 2011–12

Blodgett suspended 37.6% of its students during the 2010–2011 school year, which is high, but there is no data for the 2011–2012 school year. What is the reason for this omission? Frazer's suspensions rose from 21.1% in the 2010–2011 school year to 28.1% (a 7% increase in suspensions in one school year).

26. Blodgett—what percentage of that 37.6% are African–American, Latino, white, Native Americans, and multiracial?
27. What percentage is for males and females?
28. What percentage are students with disabilities?
29. What corrective measures are in place to lower the suspensions at Blodgett, Hughes, and HW Smith?

Hughes suspensions also rose from 15.3% in 2010–2011 to 23.3% in 2011–12 (8% increase), and HW Smith also increased suspensions in 2011–2012 to 14.8 from 9.9%—a 4.9% increase.

30. What corrective measures are in place at Hughes and HW Smith? Page 11—Percentage of Students Suspended Out of School—Middle Schools 2010–11 and 2011–12
Most disturbing of all the data is the data on Bellevue @ Shea, which reports a 71.4% suspension rate during 2010–2011 (no data for 2012), Clary increased suspension even with male and female classes divided from 30.3% in 2010–2011 jumping a dramatic 11% during 2011–2012 to 41.1%.

Danforth suspensions were 52.3% in 2010–2011 and 50.4% in 2011–2012 falling slightly but in actuality Danforth suspended at least half of the enrolled student population.

Grant and the Westside Learning Academy also have high rates but Lincoln Middle School increased suspension in one year from 36.3% in 2010–2011 to 51.5% in 2011–2012 (15.2% increase) also suspending half the enrolled population.

31. What percentages of Bellevue/Shea, Clary, Lincoln, Danforth, and Westside Academy are African–American, Latino, white, Native Americans, multiracial, etc.?
32. What percentages are students with disabilities?
33. What is the average number of days students were suspended at Lincoln, Clary, and Danforth?

34. How many have been suspended more than once, twice, three times . . . ?
35. What percentages of suspension are male and female at each school above?
36. What percentages of students suspended at Clary, Bellevue, and Lincoln are students with disabilities?
37. How many Manifestation Determination Hearings were held for students with disabilities?
38. What corrective measures are in place to lower the suspensions at Lincoln, Clary, Bellevue @ Shea, and Danforth?

Page 12—Percentage of Students Suspended Out of School—High Schools 2010–11 and 2011–12
There was a slight decrease; however, Corcoran 27.0% in 2010–2011 and 22.6% are still high rates and equal missed instructional time.

39. How many African–American, white, Native, etc., are from Corcoran, Fowler, Nottingham, and Henninger?
40. What is the average length of days suspended for high school students, African–American, Latino, Native American, white (1, 3, 5 days, etc.)?

Pages 14–16 reflect grade, gender, and color, but particularly concerning are pages 14—16 which indicate in schools, suspension rates are off the chart, there is a lot of missed instructional time and the rates are highest for grades 4, 7, and 8 (all ELA testing grades). How can we expect student to do well on the ELA and other test when they miss so much instructional time to in-school suspensions? In addition we are concerned that these high rates equal missed classroom time.

41. How many total days of missed classroom instructional time do these suspension rates equal (hundred hours, thousand hours, and ten thousand hours) overall?
42. How many lost instructional hours have accumulated due to suspensions at the   elementary, Middle and High School levels?

Page 14—Percentage of Students Suspended In School by Grade 2010–2011

K	1	2	3	4	5	6	7	8	9	10	11	12
6.9	9.0	18.5	19.4	22.7	29.5	35.2	41.3	37.2	26.0	24.1	16.6	12.2

2011–12

K	1	2	3	4	5	6	7	8	9	10	11	12
6.7	14.2	16.8	24.1	27.0	28.0	34.5	39.4	37.3	22.8	15.3	11.8	6.2

Page 15—Suspended by Gender
Males are suspended at a higher rate than any group—27.3% in 2010–2011 and 26.1% in 2011–12, i.e., 9.4% more than their female counterparts.
Page 16—Percentage of Students Suspended In School by Ethnicity
It's disturbing; it reflects that African–American and Latino students are suspended at almost twice the rate of their white counterparts.

We are also surprised that Native Americans or Alaska Natives are suspended at a rate 4% higher than their white counterparts at 18.9% in 2011 and 17.0% in 2012, and they have a very small population attending SCSD. 14.7% of white students were suspended in 2010–11 and 14.6% in 2011–2012.

Page 17—Percentage of students suspended in school— Elementary Schools: Delaware 40.6% in 2010–11, and 39.0% in 2012. Delaware, Elmwood, Seymour all have very high rates compared to the other elementary schools.
Page 18- Percentage of Students Suspended In School—K-8 Schools
Blodgett 47.7% (no data for 2011–12), Hughes, Ed Smith, and Frazer all increased suspension in 2011–2012 but it seems overall.

43. Blodgett consistently suspends almost half the population; what are the missed classroom instruction hours for Blodgett?
44. At Frazer, almost 30% of the student population was suspended, what are the missed instructional hours for Frazer? How many fourth- and eighth-grade students were serving suspension during the ELA testing periods?
Page 19- Bellevue, Lincoln, Clary, Grant have high in-school suspension rates, however in 2010–11 Clary's in-school suspension rate was 59.2%, Bellevue @ Shea sent 46.3% (no data 2011–12) to in-school suspension, Grant sent 41.3% in 2010–11.

However, Lincoln Middle School and Westside Learning Academy's In-school suspension rates are absolutely outrageous! Lincoln increased from 48.4% in 2010–11 to 56.9% in 2011–12 and Westside Learning Academy 56.0% in 2011–12 is disgraceful!

45. How much instructional time did students sent to ISS miss at Bellevue, Lincoln, and Westside Academy?
46. How many are male and how many female? How many are students with disabilities?
47. Why are Lincoln's rates so high?
48. What corrective measures are in place at Lincoln, Bellevue and Westside Academy?

Why didn't the Board communicate the results of the 2009–2010 UCLA report to parents?

Respectfully submitted by

Twiggy Billue

The findings had been presented, and they were not received well. In fact, it was the whirlwind of deciphered data that overwhelmed and panicked the school board and the superintendent of schools.

The board indicated they did realize the implications and had some answers but would get back to us with answers. The superintendent acknowledged the issue with the teacher removals that it was a "common practice among administrators to send the student home." The superintendent admitted that she had "looked into the complaint on the undocumented suspension" and it was occurring.

Attempting to mask what she had found, she added that parents were not appealing the suspension. It was not mentioned in the context of it being an illegal practice or that the practice was in violation of State Education Law. It was just that the district's legal staff was providing in-services on proper and legal suspensions for administrative staff due to our concerns.

This was a small victory, but it was a victory nonetheless. Now it was time for accountability and transparency. We had to publicly state the elephant in the room at this meeting, no matter who was offended. The "lack of transparency!" We needed answers, so we had to turn up the heat. This meeting was attended by the press, elected officials, parents, civil rights agencies, and the school district. I publicly acknowledged that the district "should be ashamed of itself!" We had to call our own meeting; if not, the district would not have volunteered answers to the information.

These questions would not have been asked and this disproportionate practice of suspending students of color would remain the same. "You (the district) published a twenty-page document, distributed it to the media and the public, and provided no explanation on the data it contained."

"We want transparency; we want the disproportionate suspension among students of color investigated!" They knew our allegations of discriminatory practices had standing. We wanted the district to rectify the matter, but what was the remedy for students suspended without due process? The district couldn't take back the days when a student was suspended unfairly or without due process, and they never identified any potential corrective measures being implemented.

Two months passed, and the school board did not respond to the findings and questions posed. They ignored us even after they were presented the forty-eight questions again at the school board meeting and entered into the district's official record. Since then I did receive a letter, thanking me for the concern and notifying me that UCLA's Civil Rights Project was retained to do the follow-up and answer the questions.

It's almost like a double-edged sword, waiting for answers and attempting to work with our superintendent and school board. The district put the data out because we asked for it, to prove transparency, but we exposed the disparities and disproportion. We didn't blame the parents or the students solely for the alleged conduct; we blamed the district for failing to teach and using suspension to push out our children. Now I am viewed as the opposition instead as a partner. It is what it is!

Syracuse history has proven that African American citizens have no say! In this city, the teachers' union, administrators, and board members have more control and power over the school district than the common council, the mayor, and the taxpayer. Historically, Syracuse School District has a reputation for being unwilling and taking an adversarial tone when a parent attempts to resolve a dispute. Parents know that dealing with the school district will go one of the two ways when they attempt to resolve problems or issues—"It's their way or the highway."

In our district, no matter how little or how big the issues are, "it's either going to get worse and remain unresolved" or "it's only going to get better with a fight." Sadly, the fight mentality is usually the only recourse the parents have. In this city, no matter who is in the office, the school district's superintendent and board often come across as uncaring. The school district has a "we'll show them" mentality; it's never "a let's work together" mentality to save the schools unless it's for increased funding. Sadly, we did not expect it to be any different this time even with a multiracial female superintendent due to the history of the institution.

The Fallout—Angry White Parents: I attended the next school board meeting a few days after the initial presentation to enter the forty-eight questions into the official board record with the board clerk.

The fallout was greater than anticipated. There was a divide, a great divide, in the room, especially from white parents. The room was segregated, and it was evident at this meeting.

The school board's conference room was packed; there was standing room only, and people were locked out due to seating capacity, but the tension in the room could be cut with a knife.

The room was segregated: African American and Latino parents on one side of the room and white parents on the other side of the room.

The outrage was not over the disciplinary data analysis; it was something much more. White teachers and parents had called for resignation or firing of the newly hired superintendent on social media and were holding secret meetings with the principals. The outrage was at the district failing to implement more stringent discipline tactics. Even with the high suspension rates, white parents insisted that enough was not being done to control "these kids." Most of the white parents either on social media or in the room viewed African American students as "unruly and wild." They stated that "these students" made "teachers feel unsafe." I was incensed at the accusation. "They all are in need of more serious discipline measures at home and at school."

The dynamics had changed instead of outrage over disproportionate suspension. African American and Latino parents found themselves condemning the comments of the white parents. Talina Jones took the podium; she quietly stood there, looking across the room at the white parents and stated, "We (African American and Latino parents) noticed the room is segregated, and it's OK." She further stated that it "sends a strong message and symbolizes that Jim Crow tactics are OK if they are used on black children in this district." This was painful for people in the room to hear, but it was true.

Talina went on to state that she "is a proud parent of a disabled African American student." Then she indicated how that was a double sentence for a male student of color.

After that distinction, African American and Latino retired principals, teachers, and community leaders led their assault on the school board over the suspension data. Parents commended the superintendent for being "bold" enough to bring the real issues to the table and protest the routine suspension of students of color.

Of course, my message was a little different. It was directed only at the board members: "We know who is in control. It's the board. It's the board that sets the policy. The superintendent only implements policies of the board, NYS Education Department, and US Department of Education, so the real problem rests with you!"

I told them very sternly, "All of you should give back the money you earned last year as you really didn't earn it! Especially if you didn't realize problems with suspension existed prior to this report because UCLA published a similar report in 2009. Shame on all of you!"

The board didn't know how to take me, especially the new members. I remembered the look on their faces when I announced a new slate running for school board. It was at the community meeting in May when we presented the findings. I indicated this slate was picked secretly to unseat the currently sitting board members; my name was announced first on the list.

Silence descended on the room while I paused for a few seconds and announced the full slate of candidates. Now the elected officials were staring at me as I looked into the crowd without any expression on my face. The elected officials began to turn their heads to see if the other potential candidates were in the room. I wanted to laugh as I could tell that the statement and the list of candidates really agitated them. Then I stated, "I am just kidding for now," and left the podium.

Our district is a failing district; all the schools are focus schools or schools in review. Therefore, if half of the students of any ethnic student population are under suspension, how can they be expected to perform well or be prepared for the ELA test?

Bottom line:

"You can't teach them if they are not in the classroom!"

The *CNY Vision Newspaper* conducted an interview with me after that racially segregated meeting. This is an excerpt of my comments:

> "At the meeting the other night (school board meeting), you had a group of white parents saying they wanted her out and us (black parents) saying thank you for making the hard decisions but you can't keep letting them suspend our kids like that."
>
> "We don't want to direct this to you (Superintendent Contreras) but to the board, because y'all set policies, she only implements policy."
>
> "You have a policy you're not following, which is the code of conduct; you're following the code of conduct it says students receive progressive discipline."
>
> "There's no provision or measure in the code of conduct that recommends being suspended for three days, every week or every other week."
>
> "That's not progressive."

Now that we see that suspension is clearly used to push out students of color, we also learn what happens when a student's conduct is labeled disruptive or your child is labeled a substantial disruption. It doesn't matter if they are a regular student and if they are a student of color or a disabled student of color, especially male. They will be labeled at-risk for being suspended. Teachers and administrators will use the terms to push out your child. Be ready to *push back!*

Chapter 11

Labels and Suspensions

Parents must also learn and understand the labels, course of actions, myths, and stereotypes that may also be associated with your child. It is all due to your socioeconomic status, your neighborhood, and yes, their disability. It doesn't matter whether the disability is a specific learning disability or a physical disability. If doesn't matter if your child does not have a disability and if his or her conduct is symptomatic of disruptive conduct disorder or ADHD; they may be on the path to suspension and/or a diagnosis and eventually medication.

Suspension for minor infraction is common, but the labels associated with disruptive conduct and insubordinate conduct can stigmatize a student. According to Gibson, there are "stigmas and labels hidden in coded messages that can predetermine your children's path to success in school and even graduation." These coded messages could "be the path to your student dropping out of school" or even being medicated (Gibson, 2008).

In general, you must familiarize yourself and your child with the definitions of disruptive conduct and the prohibited behaviors associated with the term, especially for the disabled students. For example, our school district's code of conduct describes the following three types of disruptive conduct:

1. Failing to comply with the reasonable directions of teachers, school administrators, or other school personnel in charge of students

2. Making unreasonable noise
3. Engaging in any willful act that disrupts the normal operation of the school community

Syracuse City School District, *Handbook of Student Responsibilities and Code of Conduct*, Revised July 2011: However, what a parent may not be aware of is that disruptive conduct consists of the behaviors that are defined medical conditions or mental disorders. They are the symptoms of DBD. This also includes ODD, CD, anti-social personality disorder, ADHD, etc. I found that there is also a DSM-IV for academic problems.

Parents, please pay close attention to the labels associated with our children, regular education, and special education as defined in the school district's code of conduct. Parents must arm themselves with the information and knowledge to ensure that they understand the behavioral labels attached to children of color. These labels are the hidden codes used to push out our children. Children of color are being warehoused in in-school suspension classrooms and pushed out of the educational system by the zero-tolerance practice of suspensions and expulsions.

You must stay the course to ensure that the very teaching staff who is supposed to assist your child in overcoming hurdles associated with learning or physical disabilities does not stigmatize or label your child. Being attentive, reading the code of conduct, and communicating concerns with school and teaching staff could make the difference. The IEP could be the difference in your child receiving proper support services (including the IEP being properly implemented), obtaining an IEP diploma versus a Regents Diploma, or staying in school.

I learned quickly that a teacher could interpret a designation in two ways: abnormal behavior and stereotypical behavior. Then they proceed to treat the child accordingly with implicit bias. The school district also found out early on that stereotypical treatment of my children and others (including the disabled) would not be tolerated! The fight ensued in 1998 and continued now in 2013.

Realizing that educators, resource teachers, and occupational and physical therapists often associate a stigma with black children with disabilities was disconcerting. Learning that the stigma exists could stifle your child's learning environment. That can be overwhelming, but that is when the fight in you shows up!

I recalled hearing a student state in 1994 that "once a teacher labels you, you are always labeled!" That statement touched me; it was profound, coming from a fourth-grade student. From that point forward, it is a real uphill climb for your child, so be ready to get your climbing gear ready as well, Parents. You are their safety line!

Our school district provided the disciplinary data analysis that led to outrage among parents, but they did not provide answers to our questions. What was even more disturbing was that they could not provide data for suspensions of students with disabilities. There was not one single piece of data that covered suspensions of disabled students.

I knew this question had hit a nerve among school board members. There are specific guidelines concerning the process for suspending a child with a disability. The entire district knew by now that "I am well versed in those guidelines."

It was due to our own family's experience and public advocacy efforts on education that caused our intimacy with the guidelines. We learned about the process for suspending students with disabilities when my child had a suspension incident in 2006. However, without any data on disabled students, the district did not anticipate the accuracy of my findings, but they did not question the findings.

Now the accuracy of the statistics contained in the disciplinary data analysis became the question. How accurate is the report? How do you exclude this information from a comprehensive report on suspensions? Why does UCLA have the data in their 2009–10 report and the district doesn't?

If your child is learning or physically disabled with other mitigating factors such as ADHD or disruptive conduct disorder or even identified as routinely disruptive, they may be on a collision course with the school's code of conduct—and could be pushed out the door via suspension.

Dr. Umar Johnson pointed out to me that a lot of disruptive conducts identified in our district's code of conduct are conducive to the symptoms identified in DBD or the pathway to medication.

I have a favorite saying: "Sometimes you have to recall the past to fully understand the implications of the present!" Looking at this report, in the months after, I have said that phrase over a thousand times.

Prior to this report becoming public in the 2010–11 school year, I was the president of a PTO. Our five-year-old nephew had come to live with us. I had volunteered at every school my children attended, so it would be the same in his case. I was at his school quite a bit and almost every day because he was considered a routine disruption with disruptive conduct by the second week of school. This was kindergarten, so I was puzzled. So again I relied on my own investigation to see what was going on. This was his first school setting; he was five years old and just starting kindergarten.

He was not given any time to acclimatize to this new structured setting by his teachers. In fact, his teacher suggested that he be tested for ADHD and auditory problems, so his mother called me for assistance. The teacher didn't call us his legal guardians but his mother, who was not his legal guardian. I had volunteered in the classroom from 9:00 a.m. to 1:00 p.m. on that day, but at approximately 2:00 p.m., the teacher phoned his mother for a meeting.

We arrived at the school early the next morning, and this was when a parent asked me for assistance. This parent indicated that she was picking up her child, a five-year-old student, every day and missing work. The student had a physical disability and was on medication for ADHD, so I knew the student had an IEP. I noticed she hadn't received any documentation for the brief out-of-school suspension. I assisted her by requesting documentation of the suspension from the principal. I told her in front of the principal that it was illegal to send a child home without documentation. The principal quickly ushered her into the office and "unsuspended the student." The student was to remain in school since the disruption was minor but in an alternate setting until the principal could speak with the teacher.

When the parent came out of the meeting, she hugged me and said, "Thank you, you saved my job!" The principal didn't know what to say, but he knew I was correct. The interpretation of a teacher removal was not just intended to send a student home without documentation. NAN was looking into complaints of undocumented suspensions, but we didn't realize there was a suspension epidemic in our district until that day. Just take the child home and bring him or her back when they calm down; this was not all right. I witnessed three more parents, while we waited, taking their children home due to a misinterpretation of teacher removal of a disruptive child. While I didn't know if any of the three had a disability, I knew the practice was occurring at a rapid pace. So now that you have the context, the question is: "How many students with disabilities were illegally suspended?"

This question was not taken lightly by the superintendent or school board, but it was a good question. In fact, it ignited her response. They acknowledged there was a problem and that they were fixing it. The district didn't identify a timeline or the corrective measures on how to remedy the illegal suspension. They didn't have any data on the number of documented student suspensions of students with disabilities. To date, that information still has not been provided.

Once this report appeared in the news in 2013, my phone started to ring and ring. Parent after parent were requesting assistance with appealing the suspension of a "routinely suspended" student with a disability. I began to question the parents about their understanding of rights for students with disabilities and requested that together we should review the IEP, behavioral plan, etc., prior to any advocacy intervention. From May 3, 2013 to August 31, 2013, I had reviewed fifty-three IEPs with parents and students.

What I learned was alarming: Parents were not able to interpret all the IEPs and were not familiar with the code of conduct or the laws and rights of their disabled children.

I knew the district had the resources to provide guidance on the documents and even held code of conduct meetings. I knew the IEP was difficult to decipher, but why did I know this? It was hard for us to decipher when our children received their IEP in 1995. While looking for a document, I came across my own child's IEPs, beginning in 1994 to 2007 along with several other documents from the school district. The 1995 IEP was marked up and had highlights on terms. These are terms I was not familiar with, so I dissected the document. This is how I knew about the difficulty of parents in understanding the IEP.

I had to make my own outline, starting with the IEP for my children in 1994, and I used it until they graduated. This was the only way I could ensure I understood the document was being implemented correctly. It was mailed without explanation, and it was not a self-explanatory document. Also, that search for past school documents led to the documents governing suspensions of students with disabilities, which we will cover in the next chapter.

Chapter 12

Suspension—Students with Disabilities: Manifestation Determination Meeting

Any suspension is a serious matter. Suspension of a student with disabilities is a more serious matter. There are policies and laws regarding the disabled students. At least, that is what is told and what I believe.

There was no data concerning suspension of disabled students in the disciplinary data analysis provided by our district, only in the 2009 UCLA report that indicated racial disparities in suspension, especially among disabled students of color. How long had this practice of suspension been instituted? I was really bothered by the rates. It reminded me of past experiences with this school district attempting to warehouse disabled students via in-school suspension. Now it has become an institutional practice to suspend the disabled student out of school, even when the "behavior is a manifestation of the disability."

Sometimes you have to recall the past to fully understand the implications of the present.

Past experiences, personal experiences, and recollections started to flood my mind. Why are the manifestation meetings being ignored? I knew the policy regarding the manifestation determination meeting was still valid. I knew the law had not changed, but I could not figure why the director of special education was ignoring our concerns and the policy. I searched through old school district documentation regarding suspension of students with disabilities. I was trying to lay my hands on the process or policies governing the issue. I was surprised and dismayed at what I found and what I remembered.

I came across paperwork of an incident in February 2006, and that is why I constantly state,
"You have to recall past experiences to fully understand the implications of the present and the future!"

I came across the copies of the annual IEP and the annual review that occurred on January 17, 2006. I saved the document to preserve the copy of the NYS Education Department Procedural Safeguards Notice, titled "Disciplinary Procedures," which was included in the mailed packet.

I read the old document and wondered what had changed. Upon review of a current version of this document, I found that not much had changed. What we didn't know was that we would be faced with using this document and the IDEA the next month regarding a proposed suspension of a disabled student—my child.

In February 2006, the district attempted to suspend our younger son because of "a serious disciplinary issue"—fighting with another student in the class. Our son had never been suspended out of school or in school. In fact, our children had very little or no experience or encounters with in-school suspensions . . . attempted suspension—but no actual suspensions were ever imposed. We knew he didn't fight; he was quick with his tongue, and that was his weapon. The bottom line was that neither of our children had gotten into fisticuffs in school or in the neighborhood prior to this encounter.

The proposed five-day suspension was a surprise. It was a first offense for both children, and the proposed five-day suspension during their senior year seemed quite severe. It was described by the teacher as a violent disruption that put her safety and that of other students at risk. However, that was not the story of the resource teacher or most of the students in the class.

It started out as the dozens game with several football players and track team members in the class. Somehow, it turned into something much more. All indicated it escalated when the teacher began to laugh instead of intervening.

The odd thing was the resource teacher and the students seemed to think the teacher had egged them on and enjoyed the personal attack.

They indicated that she did not ask the students to stop until after the first punch—not when either left their seats, but only after the first punch was thrown. Neither child had behavior issues prior to this incident. Neither had been suspended out of school prior to this incident. Both were aspiring athletes on the path to graduation and to college, and the penalty seemed too severe for a first infraction. The suspension was for five days with a formal hearing prior to returning back to school for both children.

We could not figure out what was going on until a black male high school administrator explained it to us. "Being a young black student labeled disabled is a double sentence!" Both students had disabilities. It didn't matter that we raised and instructed our children not to fight in school. It didn't matter that we told them that they were not slow, stupid, or retarded. It didn't matter because we didn't live what they lived! We as parents didn't experience what they experienced.

Now I needed to appeal the suspension. The number of days was not fitting for either of them, but we could not identify a clear process for an appeal. As we began to inquire about the process, we received a letter from the local committee on special education. The letter informed us of a meeting scheduled on February 15, 2006, regarding the fighting incident. A manifestation determination meeting was being conducted to determine if our child's misconduct was related to the disability and to recommend the most appropriate educational program for our child.

The letter was accompanied by a booklet. The *NYS Educational Safeguard Notice; Rights for Parents of Children with disabilities, Ages 3–21* contained the answer. We had a child with special needs, and now we needed to be more familiar with the document.

I wondered if this booklet was still given and reviewed with parents in 2013. I was amazed to learn from this 2006 document that specific data and procedure must be followed when suspending a child with a disability. The lack of manifestation determination meetings occurring in past school years brought into question if the policy was being followed correctly. Remember, our experience with harsh suspension was in 2006, and in 2013, the appeal process was still not clearly outlined.

After obtaining an updated version of the document, I found the suspension policy was not being followed for disabled students during the 2009–10 school year, the 2010–11 school year, the 2011–12 school year, and it remained the same at the beginning of the 2013–14 school year.

What Every Parent and Disabled Student Should Know?

The *NYS Educational Safeguard Notice; Rights for Parents of Children with disabilities, Ages 3–21*: This booklet contains rights for parents of children with disabilities aged three to twenty-one years. It gives you, the parent, a sense of legal rights under federal and state laws. It ensures your child receives a free appropriate public education (FAPE). Most importantly, it also covers disciplinary procedures for a child with disabilities.

With the questions still lingering about the 2009–10 UCLA report and the 2010–11 and 2011–12 disciplinary data analysis, I needed to give parents a heads-up on how to appeal suspensions of disabled students.

We had answers for the 2009–10 school year from the UCLA report, but none from our district.

The school district didn't answer any of our questions, so with that in mind, I still wondered and had the following questions:

1. How many of the students in the disciplinary data analysis had disabilities?
2. How many manifestation determination hearings were held for students suspended with disabilities?
3. What percentages of out-of-school and in-school suspensions were students with disabilities?
4. What is the average number of days suspended out of school and in school?
5. What percentage is the scenario where the same student was suspended more than twice or more than three times, out of school and in school?
6. How do we get the word out to parents?

I wondered how many parents today in 2013 knew their child's rights under the law. The number of phone calls I received for assistance seemed to be the indicator. Not many parents are aware of the process and the law.

A parent must become familiar with the laws asserting their child's rights, especially if the child is disabled. I have found that the policies governing the rights of disabled students are just as easily ignored as the rights of the regular students. This is why it is imperative for the parents to become familiar with the laws. The laws and policies covering suspensions of the disabled student and manifestation determination meetings are unique and must be followed.

Below are a couple of those rights:

1. For your child not to be suspended or removed for behaviors that are determined to be related to your child's disability, except for suspensions or removals for ten school days or less in a school year and for removals to interim alternative settings.
2. To a "CSE meeting to determine whether the child's behavior which led to disciplinary action is related to his or her disability (manifestation determination) when suspension or removal results in your child being suspended or removed for more than ten school days in a school year (disciplinary change in placement)."

Until 2006, our family never had to deal with the outlined disciplinary procedures. Prior to that incident, none of our children had behavioral issues, only specific learning disabilities. It was this very experience that currently enables me to effectively advocate for students with disabilities and teach parents how to do so! I was only familiar with some of the laws and policies prior to this incident. Now it was evident that I would have to become intimate with them and matters relating to suspensions. Effective communication is a key factor for a parent to successfully advocate for their child's rights. Being able to effectively communicate your rights and your understanding of the laws and policies that govern your child is a valuable asset. It starts with knowledge of the laws. Parents, it may be devastating to have your child suspended, but not knowing your child's rights can be just as devastating.

The Present:

During the 2008–09 school year, I began receiving increased requests for assistance from parents of students with disabilities who had been suspended. That morphed into community action on the issue in 2013 with the UCLA and our district's disciplinary analyses. What was surprising was that the parents who contacted me that school year had students with IEPs, and the parents did not:

1. Know their child's rights in school
2. Understand progressive discipline
3. Know how to appeal a suspension

4. Have a copy of the students' rights and responsibilities and code of conduct
5. Have a copy of the rights for parents of children with disabilities, aged three to twenty-one years old, their legal rights under federal and state laws to be involved, and make sure that their child received a FAPE.

So as a concerned parent, I set out to provide parents with this information.

Throughout the years, I have worked on many educational issues including declining graduation rates, police conduct in schools, disparities in suspensions, undocumented teacher removals, and any matter concerning the denial of due process protections for students with disabilities.

Even with the UCLA 2009 report confirming racial disparities, our school district officials just pushed us aside and indicated, "It was not occurring." That was the unofficial official comment until May 2013.

Parents, prior to proceeding with this book or advocacy efforts for your child, it is important to start becoming familiar with the documents listed below.

The code of conduct for the upcoming school year should be the first. If your child's school has a parent or student handbook, this should be the second document. If your child has a disability and you reside in NY State, the next set of documents is the Holy Grail. Become intimately familiar with the NYS Education Department Procedural Safeguards Notice— Rights for Parents and Children with Disabilities, the Individuals with Disabilities Act (IDEA), and Section 504 of the Rehabilitation Act of 1973, more commonly known as Section 504.

IDEA and Section 504 will be covered later.

NYS Educational Safeguard Notice—Rights for Parents of Children with Disabilities, Ages 3–21, ensures that your disabled child receives a FAPE, and it also covers disciplinary procedures for a child with disabilities.

IDEA ensures services to children with disabilities in the USA and oversees how states and public agencies provide early intervention, special education, and related services. http://idea.ed.gov/

Section 504 is enforced by the portion of US Department of Education that prohibits "discrimination against individuals in programs or activities that receive federal financial assistance" such as schools. http://www2. ed.gov/about/offices/list/ocr/docs/edlite-FAPE504.html

New York State Safe Schools Against Violence in Education (SAVE), the VADIR, the school report card, the No Child Left Behind Act (NCLB), and the Family Education Rights and Privacy Act (FERPA) are others interrelated to each other and govern your child's education. These documents, laws, and policies are a valuable source of information, and parents must have access to all of them.

If your child has a disability, your district may consciously or unconsciously count suspension incidents instead of the days suspended, so you must know the law. As a parent, you may have to understand the difference between both—the incidents and the days suspended. Some school districts may purposely count instances of suspension (suspended nine times) to avoid holding a manifestation determination meeting. If your child is disabled, this law and policy must be interpreted and applied correctly. The only way for a parent to know if it is done correctly is to learn the law.

If your school district counts suspension incidents (instances of suspension) rather than the total number of days a student is suspended in a school year, they are in violation of federal and state disability laws.

For example, let's say your child was suspended out of school eight times this school year for two to four days each time. That would equal approximately twenty-two suspended days in a school year. On the tenth day of consecutive or cumulative suspensions and/or on the twentieth day of consecutive or cumulative suspensions, a manifestation determination meeting must be held. If no manifestation determination meeting is held, the district is in violation of disability law.

Would you know if your child was entitled to but denied a meeting to determine if the conduct resulting in suspension was a manifestation of the disability? In short, was the student's behavior linked to the disability?

New York State Education Department's policy states, "Ten consecutive days OR ten cumulative days can constitute a change in placement" and "require manifestation hearing." More on this will be covered in the upcoming chapters.

Chapter 13

Appealing Suspensions

After revealing the racial disparities (May 3, 2013) in the school district's 2010–11 and 2011–12 data, it hit the news and newspapers. The phone continued to ring with calls from parents with requests for assistance in appealing suspensions. Remember, as indicated previously, appealing a suspension is not a clear process or clearly outlined in the code of conduct.

This was puzzling because no one was outraged by the 2009 UCLA report indicating racial disparities, which was released in April 2013. It became frighteningly clear that parents were not protesting against the suspension of regular education or disabled students because they didn't know they could! This is a huge issue in the SCSD.

My encounters with lack of clarity in the code of conduct for the regular student began during the 1994–95 school year. During the 2005–06 school year, we experienced a lack of clarity in the code of conduct for discipline of disabled students, and in 2013, the problem had still not been addressed by the school district. Parents were still not aware they could appeal their children's suspension. Call after call kept coming from parents regarding a suspended student. Not a single parent knew that they could appeal a suspension and that there are appeal processes for short-term (less than five days) and long-term suspensions (five days or more). They could appeal the decision rendered, if they were not satisfied with the decision.

It was seven years later and still there was not a clear path for a parent to follow to file an appeal of a suspension. Our children's suspension experience occurred in 2006, and in 2013, the appeal process was still not clarified or made easier for parents. This is why I decided to develop a letter any parent could use.

On or about 20 May (during the ELA Review period), I was called by a parent of a child with a disability, who had been suspended for two days. It was the sixth or seventh time her child had been suspended that school year. Each time, the student was suspended for two to three days. The parent was not aware of her right to appeal the suspension.

During the phone interview and assessment with this parent, I inquired if the child had an IEP. The parent indicated yes. At that point, I encouraged the parent to appeal the suspension in writing immediately and hand-deliver or e-mail the letter, appealing the suspension directly to the building principal. The parent indicated that the building principal never called her back, was condescending, and always assigned a vice principal. I instructed her to copy the letter to me and that she would get immediate assistance.

Very hesitantly, the parent agreed. We drafted the letter and e-mailed it to the principal. Within an hour, the principal called her at home. A time was set for a meeting with the principal the next day and the child was to return to school. The appeal letter was developed in response to the overwhelming number of parents who did not know they could appeal a suspension.

Another parent called; she was the parent of a first grader. The parent was clearly upset due to undocumented teacher removals. This first-grade student with a disability was constantly sent home or suspended for two to three days. This was truly an egregious act. This was a six-year-old student. Why was this student missing so much valuable classroom instruction?

Yet another parent called. This time it was a well-known community activist. This parent was clearly in distress and upset. The parent indicated that her child had been suspended for three days for a disruption. The student was suspended in disregard of her disability and her behavioral intervention plan. Somehow, the principal and the vice principal did not communicate to one another—the student was off medication and waiting for a new doctor's order.

Parents, note that teachers can remove a disruptive student or a student causing a substantial disruption. This means sending the student to an alternate location or to in-school suspension, not sending the child home.

The suspending authority is the building administrator or his or her designee, no one else. I also learned that a manifestation determination meeting had not been conducted, even though this disabled student had been suspended a total of twenty-two cumulative days during the school year.

Ten consecutive or cumulative days suspended during a school year may constitute a "change in educational placement" as per the NYSED. This student's record of suspensions would have required a manifestation determination meeting. Why didn't the parent know she could appeal or that she was denied due process?

This student had a behavioral intervention plan and was constantly and consistently being sent home or suspended at least twice every month. For some reason, the behavioral plan was not enacted when the student was in crisis. This time, like many other times, the student was suspended; however, the severity of the discipline implemented did not fit the infraction. This student's behavior or conduct was a direct manifestation of the disability. The behaviors as mentioned previously are symptoms of the student's medical diagnoses and her disability classification.

After the parent and the principal described the number of suspensions this child had accumulated over the course of the school year, a few questions came to mind (in lieu of the disciplinary data analysis):

1. Why was there misinterpretation of the law?
2. Did we need to meet with the director of special education and identify the systemic issues through manifestation determination meetings that did not occur?
3. Is this why there is no data for students with disabilities in the district's report?
4. How many manifestation determination meetings were held in 2009 for disabled students?

Again, we sent the newly drafted appeal letter, and again within an hour, a meeting was set with the principal, the director of special education, the NYCLU, and the parent. I could not attend due to prior commitments.

The meeting concluded with the suspension period for the student being reduced. This was to minimize the loss of valuable classroom instruction. During this meeting, the NYCLU's director won a significant victory by getting the district to recognize and acknowledge that "sending this student home" must be counted as one day of out-of-school suspension and documented. Now everyone was aware that we had revealed to the public the illegal yet common practice of misapplying teacher removals by "sending the student home for a couple of days to calm down" (undocumented suspension). We knew this was a district-wide problem, but getting the district to admit the practice was really occurring was almost impossible. In fact, I believe the superintendent tried to suppress our efforts and keep us quiet about the matter until the district had its own legal team investigate our interpretation of the law.

In a system-wide review of suspensions of students with disabilities, the NYCLU and NAN found that the school district, whether consciously or unconsciously, counts suspension incidents instead of days suspended, which is an illegal practice.

They did not correctly apply suspended days to the suspension record on incidents of suspension.

Understanding Suspension Incidents:

First Incident   In-school suspension for three days for being routinely disruptive (documentation)

Second Incident   Suspended for four days out of school for being disruptive (documentation)

Third Incident   Your child is sent home for a day (no documentation)

Fourth Incident   Your child is sent to in-school suspension for two days

The district counts ten suspension incidents rather than the number of days a student is actually suspended in a school year, which is incorrect. The New York State Education Department's policy states that "ten consecutive days OR ten cumulative days can constitute a change in placement and require manifestation hearing."

This student had been suspended out of school eight times this school year. No manifestation determination meeting was ever held, and the district stated it was not aware of the law. Was this the twilight zone? Could it be possible the director of special education was not familiar with the laws governing his department and his own disability? Could it be possible? Hell, no! It's not possible, not with the big buck he earns!

Misinterpretation definitely! It was confirmed at the board meeting where he confidently stated, "The number of suspension incidents did not require a manifestation determination meeting." I could not believe what I had just heard.

Immediately, the director of NYCLU pointed out, "Each of the eight suspension incidents lasted for two to three days," and she did the math for him:

$$8 \times 2 = 16 \text{ and } 8 \times 3 = 24$$

"That's more than ten days in a school year, constituting a change in placement."

Neither of us are experts in NYS Education Law or Regulations nor do we pretend to have expert knowledge in the matter. Both of us have participated in several joint efforts on education matters and education law relating to SRO in schools, code of conduct changes, and suspensions of students with disabilities.

Parents, use caution if you know the law better than the experts, which means something is very wrong. We noticed that the director of special education was not well versed in the policy given below; make sure you are.

NYS Regulations of the Commissioner of Education,
Part 201.2—Definitions

Disciplinary change in placement means a suspension or removal from a student's current educational placement that is either:

"(1) for more than 10 consecutive school days; or
(2) for a period of 10 consecutive days or less if the student is subjected to a series of suspensions or removals that constitute a pattern because they cumulate to more than ten school days in a school year; because the student's behavior is substantially similar to the student's behavior in previous incidents that resulted in the series of removals; and because of such additional factors as the length of each suspension or removal, the total amount of time the student has been removed and the proximity of the suspensions or removals to one another. The school district determines on a case-by-case basis whether a pattern of removals

constitutes a change of placement. This determination is subject to review through   due process and judicial proceedings."

Below are the questions posed by the director of NYCLU during our debriefing:

"Manifestation determination—how could they have missed this?"

"How could the director of special education not be well versed or aware of the process?"

"How was it they were only paying attention to the first part of the definition?"

It is our collective understanding that "a manifestation determination meeting is required when there is a change in placement due to discipline."

Again, I'm no expert in education law, disability law, or statues. I have a gift; I have been blessed with the ability to read, do research, and ask questions. I have had the privilege and experience of interning for several local lawyers and legal agencies, which enabled me to understand and interpret certain laws. The starting point is understanding the definition section of any law, policy, or statute for wording you do not understand.

The NYCLU also discovered that the district created and implemented a new tool, a "manifestation checklist." This checklist was created as an addendum for students with IEPs below the ten-suspension incident threshold. However, after our discussions, the form is being revised to reflect the changes indicated by the NYCLU. Now the form will include notes and/or explanations of actions taken, actions not taken, and space to include a history of past instances.

Due to this student's situation and that of other disabled students in a similar situation now, several more questions needed to be publicly addressed by the director of special education, the school board, and the superintendent of schools.

These questions are stated below:

Why was there no mechanism on this district-wide form to measure the following:

1. Was the intervention plan being followed?
2. Is the incident related to student's disability?
3. Are there unique circumstances which led to this behavior?

4. Is there a pattern of removal for the behavior?
5. How many number of days was the student suspended?

Using terms such as *illegal suspension* sets the school district in an adversarial mode. Changing the language and becoming just as familiar with the policy as they are will get you the desired results. Remember, winning small victories is just as important as winning the big ones.

After the June 2013 school board meeting, an impromptu meeting occurred. The director of the NYCLY, the director of special education, a parent, and I were present. The director of special education acknowledged that they were "fixing" the suspension incident versus suspended day's interpretation. He acknowledged, "As a result of your insistence, the district is now counting a day of out-of-school suspension (OSS) any time a principal makes a decision to 'send a student home' after an incident." This was our huge victory!

Did this student receive progressive discipline as stated in our code of conduct? Did this student and her parent receive due process? Would the district acknowledge any of this? We needed the district to make it public, but would they? Of course not! If this issue or any of the issues indicated were addressed with the community as allies, *I would have no reason to write this book.*

I mentioned in previous chapters the common practice in our school district of incorrectly applying the policy on teacher removals. The undocumented suspension is that practice where a teacher removes the student from the class for disruption and the principal sends the student home for a day or two to calm down or regain composure. It is a double sentence for the disabled student; it is an illegal suspension.

Now it was finally being admitted that "many schools weren't counting that practice as an out-of-school suspension (OSS)." The district was not willing to make a public acknowledgment of the finding. This was not a change in policy. We just made sure the policy was and is being implemented correctly. The victory was in the fact that the district openly admitted it was guilty of the practice. What it had denied to parents and the community for so long was truly occurring.

The other victory, the change, was a "direct result of the collective push and intervention by our groups and agencies." That shake-up and system-wide review of special education process and procedures were a whirlwind that hit like a tornado! The winds of assertive activism caused the investigation. Now it was the aftermath of the storm and now the winds had shifted, causing the district to implement the policy to the letter. The watchdog is out!

Really, it was the parents who were using the appeal process! I needed to make this process a clear process and find a way to get it in the hand of the parents and students requesting my assistance. Each time we used the letter to appeal a suspension, the child was returned to school, and it has not to date proceeded to the next step—the actual suspension.

Suspension Process (NYS): Let's Go over It Again

Parents, you can use the letter included in this book to request an informal meeting or conference with the principal or his or her designee and to appeal the suspension.

After the informal meeting or conference, the following should take place:

1. The principal must advise you (the parents or guardians) immediately in writing of his or her decision.
2. If you are not satisfied with the decision and wish to pursue the matter, you must file a written appeal to the superintendent within five business days of the informal meeting or conference unless you can show "extraordinary circumstances" prevented you from being able to do so.
3. The superintendent shall issue a written decision regarding the appeal within ten business days of receiving the appeal.
4. If the parents or guardians are not satisfied with the superintendent's decision, they must file a written appeal to the board of education with the district clerk within ten business days of the date of the superintendent's decision unless they can show extraordinary circumstances precluded them from doing so.
5. Only final decisions of the board may be appealed to the commissioner within thirty days of the decision.

It is imperative for parents to engage community leaders. It is important to speak up and speak out at school board meetings. If you don't speak up on issues concerning the push-out of students of color or students of color with disabilities, the schoolyard will become a direct path to the prison yard or the graveyard.

This particular practice with manifestation determination meetings and the appeal process had to be exposed to show the parents that zero-tolerance tactics and practices are still being implemented and used to push out students of color in our district. Until June 2012, our district did what it wanted to do instead of following the actual policies that govern education.

So, parents, take heed and stay vigilant!

You must be intentional when advocating for your child. That means intentionally becoming familiar with any polices regarding suspension. You must understand what is meant by progressive discipline in your district's code of conduct.

What happens to the normal student without learning disabilities or the highly intelligent student? Well, that is our next advocacy story, the story of a gifted female student.

Chapter 14

Teacher Bias: Young, Gifted, Black, Labeled Disruptive and Targeted for Suspension (2010–11)

Unconscious beliefs and attitudes have been found to be
associated with language and certain behaviors such as eye
contact, blinking rates and smiles.
—*Teaching Tolerance*
http://www.tolerance.org/supplement/
test-yourself-hidden-bias

What happens when the suspension is for a regular student with a high intelligence level?

Why would an honor student be routinely suspended?

In our school district, every program for the intellectually gifted has been eliminated. The Center for Inquiry's program was reportedly discontinued because of a lack of funding at the end of the 1997–98 school year. This was the only program in our school district for the intellectually gifted. The program was touted by the district until the flood of high-preforming students of color was referred to the program. These were students of color who performed at a higher level than their peers in any one of the five categories: general intellectual ability, specific academic aptitude, creative or productive thinking, leadership ability, or visual or performing arts as defined by US Education Law and the Javtis Act.

After the end of services in our school district, elementary school students of color, especially those with IQ above 145, are made to sit in classes that do not gauge their intellectual intelligence or allow them to share their gifts. High school students have the ability to participate in the International Baccalaureate Program (2004), but that is often not a program for the gifted student of color. It is a program that is only offered to ninth- to twelfth-grade students, so measuring intelligence in earlier grades often leads to referral to this program.

In our district, gifted and talented students of color are often judged by the socioeconomic factors of their neighbors instead by intellectual intelligence. Cultural bias plays a role, but teacher bias may play a larger role than anyone is willing to admit publicly. Gifted and talented students of color are often considered unruly, hyperactive, disruptive and are removed by the teacher from the classroom, warehoused in in-school suspension, or routinely suspended out of school.

The more egregious consideration for the intellectually gifted student of color is the recommendation for testing for behavioral issues (ADHD or ODD) and/or a specific learning disability instead of nurturing the gift or talent as you would water and care for a newly planted tree.

How do you identify an intellectually gifted student? There are many tests a district can use to measure if a child is gifted. However, if the district does not have a gifted program to address the unique needs of intellectually gifted students, no testing occurs.

Remember, I am not an expert in education policy or law nor do I pretend to be! The only expertise I have is the expertise of being a parent! That parental expertise coupled with years of community organizing and advocacy experiences ignited my passion to assist and teach parents to advocate for their child. It is important to understand the hidden language and labels governing the education system in Onondaga County and the State of New York.

Advocacy for others actually began as a result of the win-win situations and relationships gained, negotiating and advocating for my own children's rights. Gifted and talented students of color have unique needs as we have seen with the International Baccalaureate Program in Syracuse. Students and parents complain that the program segregates students, especially students of color. If your child is performing at a higher level of academic achievement than his or her counterparts or is an honor roll student who has been routinely removed or suspended by the teacher, you need to act fast.

These students', in fact any student's, first line of protection and/or defense is the parent! Many times, I have realized that only the persistent or annoying parent can effectively communicate concerns and policy to ensure their child is adequately challenged in the classroom.

This is not an easy task, but you cannot be silent. You must attend school meetings and meetings of the school district. Becoming that challenging, annoyingly persistent parent played a major role in developing my community advocacy or action. Teaching parents to successfully advocate for students is invaluable information and knowledge that had to be shared! No question was a dumb or stupid question, and I put that old saying to work for me and every parent and student I have advocated for.

As you begin to read the documents such as the code of conduct, questions will arise, so you must be ready to inquire about any information you don't understand. Write your questions down and ask them publicly at school- and district-level meetings. I am not saying that you will get an immediate response or that you will get your question answered with clarity. What I am saying is the level of persistence you display, especially if you continually ask for clarity, will get your questions answered. The school and the district will find the answer and the clarity if for nothing more than to get you off their backs.

Many parents work and cannot attend meetings regarding their child during the day. If you are unable to attend school or district meetings, make sure the building principal schedules meetings with regard to your child for a time that is not in conflict with your work schedule. Early morning meetings worked best for us; however, there have been a few years when we took advantage of the options to schedule telephone conferences and had the meetings scheduled during non-working hours.

The policies set by the school board versus a teacher's, social worker's, or principal's actions can be totally different. The differences and blatant disregard of policy can cause a parent to wonder what is going on. Parents, your answer is always in the code of conduct.

Some schools have individual parent or school handbooks, so pay close attention to the student behavior code sections to make sure it aligns with the code of conduct. Also, Parents, see if the school's parents' handbook has additional rules that apply to your child. If the school's rules are different from the district policies, every parent should ask publicly, "Why doesn't the school district's polices align with the rules of my child's school building?"

You will find that once you acknowledge publicly that policies are not being followed, enforced, or interpreted the same district-wide, you will get immediate response and action from district officials. Lots of parents want to give up homeschool or transfer the student to a charter school when they feel their child is being pushed out or is receiving unfair treatment. The main goals during my intervention or advocacy are to get the issues resolved and meet the needs of the student, the teacher, and the parent. Once this is accomplished (every case) and everyone's needs are met, transfer to another school is off the table. Together all the parties begin to work to implement the changes in the academic setting, in turn ensuring educational success for the student and the teacher.

The next story is a story that is close to my heart and fires me up. It wasn't until after the meeting with the school staff that I was reminded of our own experiences.

What happens if your child is gifted or a regular student or even a disabled student with a visible difference in appearance? It is one thing to be teased, insulted, or embarrassed by fellow students, but it is an entirely different matter when it is generated by a teacher. Now some may not want to discuss this topic or believe it could be true as it is a tough subject to discuss. Nonetheless, I have found teacher bias to exist in two main forms in this school district: white female teachers' implicit bias and snobbish African American administrator bias. The former will be discussed in more detail in an upcoming chapter. For now, I will define snobbish African American administrator bias as a black female school administrator demeaning their own children and using culture differences in the context of "I am up here and you are down there." This snobbish attitude is what African Americans call bourgeoisie (booshie), living a white middle class lifestyle to forget their upbringing and their roots.

The biased white female teacher and the biased white male teacher are dangerous, particularly for inherently intelligent students of color, disabled students of color, and their parents. I remember working at the local IB High School in 2009, conducting violence prevention and conflict resolution services for students and teachers. On this day, I was called to the dean of students' office located in the ninth grade wing or hallway because my niece had been assaulted.

Mrs. K was the administrator, and her office was located next to Coach P's classroom. Out of nowhere, we heard a young voice (stress in his voice) ask for help. "Someone please help me. Help me before this man." I immediately left the office and went out into the hallway. There was one very tall African American male with tears in his eyes. He recognized me and started to proceed in my direction.

Suddenly, Coach P stormed out of the classroom with his fist raised, shouting, "Come on, little nigger. You want some of this?" I was floored! I think I transformed into Mother Lioness, not a person at work but a lioness ready to defend her cub at any cost and by any means necessary!

I jumped in between Coach P and the student, putting the young man behind me and pushing him back further just in case the coach threw a punch. I yelled at Ms. K to take the student to her office and call for assistance. The coach kept coming nearer, so I put up my fists and very loudly yelled, "Come on, Coach, what do you want to do?" Then I told my niece to call Chief Fowler from my cell phone and then to call my husband. I weigh less than hundred pounds, but I command power and I do not fear man or woman! Silence fell in the hallway.

I told the coach loudly again to *back off and that I was not joking!* Ms. K didn't take the student away, but she did call for assistance. Police and hall monitors arrived, and we were still toe-to-toe. I knew this man; he had coached my child and family members, but I couldn't figure this out or let it slide.

I knew without a doubt (because of my husband) this would not have occurred if he was addressing my child, even if the behavior on the part of the student was the same. Coach P now became animated as backup came, but to his surprise, they bypassed us and attempted to calm him down.

However, one hall monitor had witnessed it, and as the coach began to progress toward the young man again, I guess her mother's instinct came to the fore. This largely built woman pushed Coach P in his chest, backing him up, and stated, "Coach P, stop it! He is a child. What are you doing?" And she used her body to stop his progression. It seemed like his lightbulb came on and then he realized how it all looked to the onlookers. I was livid, still standing there with my fist clutched, but something told me to turn around. It was dismissal and a group of African American male students now stood behind me, providing a barrier between us and the clearly agitated Coach P. Most were athletes, but all of them knew me as Aunt Twiggy or Mrs. Billue from the neighborhood; however, they were now concerned about the coach's progression and his intentions as they related to me.

I had to make sure that every teacher, administrator, and student of color knew "Coach P is not going to get away with this." At least that's what I thought, so I guess now is a good time to inform the reader that the good old boys network still works for white men, especially biased white male teachers. This was not going to be played down. I took my concern to the building principal, and a meeting was set for the next morning.

What he wasn't prepared for was whom I was bringing to the meeting. To make a long story short, this teacher is no longer in the classroom. He still is employed by the district but maintains an office position. This man was rewarded, instead of disciplined, with the position of dean of students. It was a tough spot because I knew this man's daughter married an African American man and they had children. Maybe this was the best sentence for this man better than anything we could do to point out his conscious or unconscious bias. Of course, we shared his comments with the public. My current boss at AFSC made sure of it, especially the intervention of the white female hall monitor. I admire that woman to this day! That was an overt insertion of bias, but what about the subtle and covert bias that is played out in sacrificing your child's education without justification other than implicit bias?

My first experience with teacher bias or implicit bias or any sort occurred at the beginning of the 1991–92 school year prior to the designation of services. My son and my niece (intellectually gifted) often complained of what I now consider teacher bias, so I had to investigate. This was during second grade, but it was this experience that let us know you cannot just write it off or look the other way.

Could you imagine a child describing an incident where his teacher told him to lie down on a mat and then picked him up by his legs (in front of the classroom), stating, "Look at my mop" referring to his hair-locks.

What would you do? Would you believe it actually happened or would you push it aside? What would you do if other children in the classroom confirmed it happened? Well, the reader will have to wait for that story. At this point, the reader should be told that my husband is infamous in Syracuse for standing up to the institution and discriminatory practices. Even worse, he is the protector, which has caused parents to nickname him as Mufasa as his voice sounds as deep and tremendous as the voice of James Earl Jones in the role of the Lion King. He doesn't play around when it comes to his children or his wife. My husband always listens to school matters due to his own experiences. It was important; no matter what the issue was, he listened and investigated. During that time, the entire family had dreadlocks, so the bias based on stereotypical assumption and prejudice was inflicted on our child. That was not OK, and that was the last incident of that type at Dr. King School or with the school district. Our written description and request to "retrain or remove the culturally insensitive teacher was addressed and honored."

This next story and incident reminded me of my own experience with my niece. This motivated me to become a watchdog to ensure implicit bias was being addressed and to relate the issue to the suspension data.

I was reminded of a painful time for my family, and the story, about this one child in particular, caused me to realize that race and poverty do play a part in miseducating the African American students. I wondered why the "Bridges Out of Poverty" method was still being used in our district. I remembered something from the book and workshop that stuck with me. "Work and schools operate on middle-class norms." It means implicit bias is normal for the white upper and middle-class teacher. I had seen it firsthand during the 1996–97 school year but did not think I would see it again, but I was very wrong.

This child was a very smart child, from a loving two-parent home located about two blocks west of the school in an affluent neighborhood. This student was very well mannered, highly intelligent, and intellectual. The child was in the fifth grade and never had difficulty with behavior or focus or being disrespectful prior to this school year. This student could be considered an overachiever with a straight A average, who excelled in all subject areas and had a natural inclination to music and art until now. The student was now having difficulty with focus and behavior.

The student was being sent out of the classroom and to the social worker's office routinely for disruptive behavior. In turn, there was the potential for in-school suspension or an out-of-school suspension if the behavior was not addressed. Remember, there were no more gifted and talented programs in our school district, only a program for high-achieving high school students. This child was an honor student, whose parents believed she was intellectually gifted; it was evident. I am sure her IQ would have exceeded the 145-genius measure if administered.

On this occasion, her parents had received a letter in the mail, requesting a meeting "due to the student's disruptive and potentially violent behavior and a possible suspension." The cause for concern was the terms *violent* and *disruptive*. This letter was the first indication that there was a problem of any sort with their child. The letter was not sent from the principal; it was sent from the school social worker, and the classroom teacher was copied. No one called the parent for assistance prior to the letter being composed and mailed.

This surprised me, but it shouldn't have. After the parents answered a few of my questions, I had one condition prior to agreeing to accompany them to the meeting. The building principal had to be present for the meeting. The parents agreed and called the school social worker to confirm the meeting. When they told her about their request for the building principal to be included, the response was "The principal's involvement was not necessary." The social worker stated that the meeting was an informal one to discuss the issues before the principal became involved. The call ended, and they did not get their needs met. In fact, now they were confused even more. The parents became agitated, wondering why they couldn't meet with the principal, the classroom teacher, and the school social worker. I encouraged them to take that energy and use it to contact the principal directly, and they followed through.

Note: Parents, when you invite the principal to attend a meeting regarding a student, they are compelled to conduct a short investigation, if for nothing more than to see the nature of the issue and, if not already familiar, to become familiar with the issue and/or with the student and the behavior. There have been many occasions when the building principal was aware of an issue and many occasions when the principal was not aware of an issue. It's your child's plight, and the ensuing investigation must be fair and independent. Parents, ensuring that the due process occurs is what is important.

This student was a very mild-mannered straight A student, at times appearing to be shy but not afraid to speak up if asked. From the first to fifth grades, this student never achieved a mark lower than an A minus if at all. Now the parents wondered how could their straight A student, a motivated student and a quick learner, now struggle with behavior issues. None of the issues was identified as academic matters, so this was concerning.

At this point, I will share something about this student rather than wait until the end of the story. The miseducation and misunderstanding were becoming clear. It is why I founded Project Hotep Resource Center, a venue for advocacy and resources for students of color and their parents.

Realizing early on that a child has unique potential can be misinterpreted due to hidden bias propelled by stereotypes and economic status, but do we really want to believe it exists? The next day, we contacted the principal; within a few hours, she called back to schedule the meeting. The principal indicated that she needed time to conduct her own investigation into the matter and encouraged the parents to call her with any issues until then. She also encouraged the parents to visit the classroom and indicated that she would inform the teacher of the invitation. The parents told the principal that they would like to come in the next few days to observe their child. The principal encouraged the visit, notified the teacher, and proceeded to conduct a brief investigation into the concerns. The meeting was scheduled for the following week, but the next day, the mother took off work and visited the classroom. I think the principal assumed that if the mother observed the behavior it would put more perspective on the behavior. That would only occur if students of color acted out when a parent was present. That was often not the case in the African American household with single parent or married parents. Children, especially students of color, are on their best behavior when a parent is around. No one wants to be popped by their parent at school for anything, especially behavior.

Normally, a phone call from the school to an African American parent about disruptive behavior would lead to discipline at home. Not many students of color dare this feat. So my first suspicions arose upon learning the open-door visit; the classroom policy was not received or wanted by the teacher.

Parents and teachers must work together to create a positive learning environment for the student, and this visit was not taken that way by the teacher.

I wondered why parent participation wasn't being encouraged. Why wouldn't the teacher want the parent to become involved if the child was disruptive and potentially violent? Could it be possible the teacher already had it in her mind's eye that due to community, race, and economic status this parent could not be of assistance? Could it be this teacher had turned her back on this child, and if so, for what reasons?

The keywords that stuck with the parent from the conversation were that the teacher kept mentioning poverty and speaking in formal register. Now the terms *formal register* made us wonder if assumptions were being made based on race, class, or socioeconomic factors instead of the talent of the student.

The teacher indicated that she was surprised the child could speak and write using formal register. As most students of color used only a casual register, these terms confused the parent. When the parents informed me of the context of the conversation, I grew more concerned. Why was the teacher using these terms? The parent called me after the encounter and indicated she felt as if her presence was unwanted and she felt "spoken down to." She indicated that the teacher "was surprised that her student could write and speak formal register" and inquired about the meanings of those terms.

The parent asked if I knew the meaning of formal register and what did it imply if a child could write and speak in formal register. I was silent and thrown off a little, but now I really wondered in what context the phrase had been used. I was familiar with the terms and the hidden meanings and began to explain my understanding to the parent. The parent described the conversation, and then she stated something to the effect of "low-income students normally use casual register." How would the parent be aware of that if she was not familiar with the terms? Neither parent was familiar with the terms or knew the association with "dealing with the poor." I had to believe the reference came directly from the teacher during the visit. I didn't like what I was hearing.

Where had I heard this before, "dealing with the language and the story" of the poor? It was a workshop I had taken, called Bridges Out of Poverty (I needed to find that book). The workshop facilitator mentioned "middle-class hidden norms" and "hidden cues in dealing with the poor in school and in business."

That evening, I searched for and found the book, and to my surprise, some of the phrases were highlighted. I had placed notes around the key words and terms that were uncomfortable for me as a professional African American woman who works with people who have low incomes. I remember the conference and the dismay of most of my African American colleagues. We had discussed walking out of the conference during the morning break. I was raised in the face of racism to treat all people equal. Even more compelling, I was accustomed to treating everyone as equal. No one is better than anyone else! In a different place or situation, no one is better than anyone else.

"Bridges Out of Poverty" methods and approaches challenged that thinking when the middle class addresses or assists the poor. I realized that the book and the workshop were actually for the middle-class and the upper middle-class workforce that primarily worked with low-income people, i.e., welfare agencies and schools. This teacher had formed her opinion of this student and of the parents on learning from this systemic institutionalized approach.

In essence, for this teacher, this student lived in a very low-income community with parents fighting the reoccurrence of drug addictions. The teacher incorrectly assumed that this student's parents never attended a college or held a degree. Because of conflicts with work, they missed school meetings or open house events and were perceived as "poor people who didn't care" by this teacher.

No matter how bright or intelligent this student was, it was overshadowed by the stigma of her assumed poverty. How this white female teacher and white society at large deem black youth is evident from the high suspension rates in our school district. I didn't know the magnitude prior to this time period, but now I could see a pattern within the rising suspension rates for the 2009–10, 2010–11, and 2011–12 school years.

To devalue any life is inhumane, especially if they are not valued due to stereotypes and poverty. This is what I began to think, and it was disturbing—a classic "Bridges Out of Poverty" methodology, but why was it being used to define behavior and discipline?

After speaking with the parent and the child, I was eager for the child to tell her side of the story. It was a story that no one was ready to hear, especially not the parent. The teacher or even the principal was not prepared for this account. The student wrote out what had happened. I was impressed that she had a journal with all the dates, times, and details of every incident that would be mentioned and much more. This was definitely a gifted and talented student. She had produced a well-put-together factual version of what was occurring. Remember, this was a very smart child, well, a highly intelligent child who only wanted to learn.

On the day the meeting took place, the parents were nervous. I am sure they thought in the back of their minds, "What if she is acting out?" The meeting took place in the principal's office, and the teacher and the social worker were the first to speak. The teacher spoke for nearly twenty minutes, indicating that the social worker was brought in because she could not get the student to "follow instruction or follow reasonable request."

The teacher indicated that the student had routinely "tuned her out," flat out "ignored her request," and often "lost focus, wandering off into space." Then the teacher described the "tantrums." She indicated these were "violent episodes." "The student flung herself onto the floor and became unruly and loud when she was not able to do what she wanted."

The social worker indicated that the student's behavior, especially the tantrums, was the reason the student was repeatedly sent to her office. The meeting was called because the teacher requested for intervention. Thus, the social worker requested a meeting between the parent and the teacher. The social worker indicated both believed (the teacher and the social worker) there may be a need to test for behavioral disorders and learning disabilities.

The parents seemed dismayed, and the last part of the statement must have gone over their heads. They wanted to know why this was the first time they were hearing these concerns, behaviors, and actions if they were recurrent.

Both the teacher and the social worker attempted to justify why they didn't call home, but the principal interrupted. The principal indicated from this point forward there would be a new approach. The teacher was instructed to call the parent as soon as the behavior surfaced or the teacher should send the student directly to her office and they would call the parent together.

I interrupted, asking the parents if I could speak, and they indicated yes. The principal and I knew each other, and she also indicated she would like to hear my comments.

First question: What is the predisposition for this child to be considered having a behavior problem? I handed each person a packet, containing copies of the student's report card and the elementary interim report the parents had given me at a prior meeting.

I explained that the elementary report card was not only an indicator of academic achievement but also a measure for personal development, work habits, and organization. There were sections that inferred that the student followed directions and obeyed rules. One question asked if "the student completes and returns class work or homework on time." This section of the report card used the same "progress key" for marking academic progress to assess the categories. This was a straight A student, and every category was assessed by this same teacher as "(4) Demonstrates consistently" for every marking period (MP). I asserted that the report card contradicted the behavior the teacher alleged was occurring.

I insinuated that something else must be going on that only the two of them knew about. This made the whole room uncomfortable. Now the student entered the meeting. I wanted to know (since this report card was distributed less than three days back) how the behavior could be considered routinely disruptive. I continued to review the documents, starting with explanations of the highlighted sections, the progress key, and the responsibilities of the learner (see below).

The progress key below reflects the scale used to assess the responsibilities of the learner table:

Progress Key
4 Demonstrates Consistently
3 Practicing
2 Beginning
1 Skill Not Yet Demonstrated
*Modified Program In Place

Responsibilities of the Learner:

Personal Development	MP1	MP2	MP3
Treats others with respect	4	4	4
Accepts responsibility	4	4	4
Organizes and takes care of materials	4	4	4
Demonstrates self-control	4	4	4
Follows school rules	4	4	4
Work habits	4	4	4
Listens and responds appropriately	4	4	4
Follows directions	4	4	4

Participates in discussions	4	4	4
Seeks help when needed	4	4	4
Works independently	4	4	4
Completes and returns	4	4	4
Classwork on time	4	4	4
Homework on time	4	4	4

In the above categories, this student was marked consistently, every marking period having the highest marks for the section. For this school year (reflected above), all areas indicated "(4) Demonstrating consistently." The packet contained reports from prior years that the parents had meticulously kept. The teacher, the social worker, and the principal looked in awe at the documentation and the recently distributed interim report.

I indicated that both documents contradicted the alleged behavior and it even contradicted the teacher's assessment of the student's behavior. During the three previous marking periods (MP) in the personal development section, all areas indicated "(4) Demonstrating consistently." Now less than two weeks later, the child was routinely disruptive.

Now attention was called to the document titled the "Elementary Interim Report." The contradictions grew with the teacher's report dated May 17, 2011. It was for this school year (2010–11) written by this very teacher. The statements of the teacher would make anyone believe that this student was routinely disruptive; however, the teacher's own documentation suggested otherwise.

The documentation contradicted the teacher's current view of the student's behavior. There were no concerns prior to the request for a meeting. Disruptive behavior was not an issue, nor was the behavior indicated in the interim report. The report was dated April 15, 2011, and the date we were meeting was April 19, 2011. This report indicated that the student was "meeting expectations" in reading and mathematics and in the section titled "Behavior, attitude and effort:"

Behavior, Attitude, and Effort

_____ Poor attendance in class	__X__ Prompt and attentive
_____ Lack of preparation	__X__ Shows effort in and out of class
_____ Lack of effort	__X__ Understands basic concepts
_____ Poor study habits	__X__ Consistent study habits

_____ Needs to understand basic concepts	__X__ Works beyond requirements
_____ Inconsiderate toward others	__X___ Considerate of others
_____ Uncooperative and disruptive	__X___Respectful and cooperative

I asked two questions:

1. Could anyone explain why the documentation seemed to contradict the teacher's assessment of the student behavior?
2. Why did every school-generated report indicate exemplary behavior while now the teacher indicated the behavior as disruptive?

The principal intervened and attempted to take control of the meeting, but I indicated this was a process. This was when I invited the student to speak. I asked her if she understood what was going on, and she indicated yes. The principal asked the student if she wanted to tell us anything about the disruptive behavior, the tantrums, and the ignoring. The student indicated yes, and the principal told her to begin any time and that this was a friendly place to find solutions and resolutions. The student pulled out her journal and began her statements.

This student described situations according to date, time, and the subject area studied in great detail. The points focused on the why. The why is, why did the incident happen? Why is not based on a perception but on the facts. The why of it was the cause of and the solution to the problem; it was the reason for the subsequent frustrations. The real question was, would the teacher, social worker, or the principal be open to hearing the student's opinion and feelings? What if she was lying? As you will see, and is even more disturbing, what if she was telling the truth?

The student indicated that she was "ahead of most of the class but was often told not to proceed to the next topic or chapter until the rest of the class had caught up." According to the student, "this stuff with the teacher" started occurring during the second marking period, when the class was assigned independent study during completion of the chapter review questions in preparation for the weekly chapter test in all the subject areas.

Apparently, this student had the ability to read, interpret, and finish the chapter work and test in half the time of the other students. Instead of waiting for the other students to catch up and/or finish the chapter review, she had already begun or finished the next two chapters and was awaiting the chapter test. The student explained that she always passed with an A+ or an A. She again indicated that she had maintained an A average during her entire school history. Now she indicated using dates, times, and subject areas that if she "moved on to the next chapter or moved on to a chapter in another subject while the rest of the class was catching up, it was a problem for the teacher."

The student continued using her journal to identify dates, times, the subject she was working on, and the harsh verbal treatment she received from the teacher in front of the entire classroom. She indicated by description the use of hand gestures, including "pointing her finger in my face" and the inappropriate tone used while addressing her. The student indicated that for each date and passage, it always concluded with "yelling." "Yelling at me only causes me to clam up and not speak." Then she held up the journal and pointed to several random dates, all containing the phrase "yelling at me only causes me to clam up and not speak." The parents did not know the journal contained this information; all they knew was she liked to write. They thought it was a diary, and since she wasn't having a behavior problem, they thought nothing about its contents—until today! The student expressed again, using dates and times and subject area, "that the teacher's reaction caused her to feel frightened and to shut down."

The daydreaming, the student explained, was not done to ignore the teacher; it was her way to occupy her time while she waited for the rest of the class to catch up. The journal again was referenced; she read her statement out loud, "On March—, once again, the teacher told me very loudly to stop daydreaming. I pulled out my math book, and she yelled louder, 'WE ARE NOT studying math. We are not studying math and put that book up!" This journal entry was in capital letters. The student indicated in the journal that the teacher knew she had finished the subject at hand. Math was the next subject, but she knew if she proceeded with anything or sat quietly, she would be assaulted.

Now the room was all ears, and the look on everyone's face was blank, but all the school staff were uncomfortable. They began to twist and turn in their seats, so I knew they all had heard her say "assaulted."

Now I was amazed that no one interrupted or attempted to stop her from going further, but they just sat there in a daze. Then she described, using the journal, the alleged tantrums, indicating this was a much different situation. Her eyes filled with tears as she explained. Yes, she did have a tantrum; it was caused by the teacher "denying me the ability to use the restroom." Her voice was now cracking; I put my hand on her shoulder and told her it was OK to tell what happened.

"I have a documented medical condition from birth. I have taken medicine that increases my water intake and my need to use the bathroom."

The student paused for a second, turned, and looked at everyone, and then she asked, "What part is not true, Ms. _____?"

The student continued to tell the principal that she believed the teacher treated black students differently from the white students. When the student questioned the teacher about it, the teacher called her disrespectful and again sent her to the social worker's office. "Isn't this true, too, Ms. __?"

The student proceeded to acknowledge that she noticed "if a white student finishes early they are encouraged to move on. Ms. ____ tells them, 'It's OK to do so,' but it's not OK for me to do the same! Is it, Ms. _____?"

The look on the face of the teacher, the social worker, and the principal was one of absolute horror as if they all had just seen ghosts. The room remained quiet until the teacher began to cry. The social worker just sat there, looking at the parents. "Is this true?" I asked. The room was silent, with the exception of the student and the principal who indicated to the student, "That question was not for you. It was for us."

The next thing that happened totally knocked me for a loop. I was truly taken aback when the teacher in a tearful voice stated, "Yes, it is true," but she said it was "her first time teaching inner-city children." The look on the principal's face showed she was utterly astonished!

The parents totally missed the boat; they didn't even think a teacher would admit to doing these things to any child. Their child had indicated it was occurring, but it was easier to question their child's behavior rather than to question the teacher. Calling for outside assistance as these parents did indicates you "chose to believe and defend your child!" This student journaled everything because it was easier to document the occurrences than risk not being believed when they were revealed. In fact, in some cases, we punish our child for the teacher's hidden and implicit bias.

The parents asked, "Where did that come from? Are you saying you can only teach white students?" The parents indicated they wanted the child's classroom changed for the remainder of the fourth marking period. The mother now angry stated, "The cultural differences are why you mistreated my child," and she rose up from her seat. Her husband quickly grabbed her, and she sat down. Then standing behind his wife with his hand on her shoulders, he stated, "Now I know what's wrong with my child. It's your biased attitude toward our child."

Just as the principal began to intervene, the parents asked, "Just what did you mean when you said that most poor students don't speak or write with formal register?" The principal's head spun around like the girl's head in the movie *The Exorcist*. The hidden bias was on the table, revealed and painful to acknowledge, but nonetheless the bias was exposed and acknowledged!

The principal had to interject and take control of the meeting. She suggested this meeting should end and a series of subsequent meetings be set (convenient for the parents) to discuss the situation further. Our time was now getting over—one and a half hours—and she had another meeting. The principal indicated that she would be visiting the classroom over the next few days, but the student would be moved to an alternate setting during her continued investigation. If the student had any needs, the principal would address them. The parents agreed, and the principal set the next meeting for the following Monday.

Addressing the hidden bias means acknowledging the stereotypes and prejudices that lead to implicit bias. The "Bridges Out of Poverty" methods should be removed from the classroom and the school system also needs to be addressed. This teacher could not control her feelings and was intimidated by the number of students of color; in turn, she favored those from her cultural background instead of seeing all students as valuable.

It was Tuesday, so the principal had three days to investigate further what she had learned from the teacher and the student. The principal now needed to follow up on the statements of the students. That had to happen immediately, especially since the teacher acknowledged they were truthful statements. When I attend school meetings with parents, it is in the capacity of the director of the Hotep Resource Center. Most building principals and district administrators know my business is affiliated with over twenty civil rights groups and agencies. Everyone knows I am not afraid to call on that assistance if issues are being ignored.

I believe we all were astonished that the teacher admitted that the student's statements and accounts were accurate and truthful. Moreover, I was more astonished that the teacher admitted race and economic status played a factor in educating our children in 2010. With all the accomplishments African Americans have made, some implicit bias makes these accomplishments nonexistent. I did not want to think this teacher or any teacher would have this type of bias, but coupled with our own experiences, sadly some do, and it affects how children of color are treated and educated.

The parents questioned the letter sent from the social worker. It bothered them so much that their child was described as "routinely disruptive" that it made them call in outside help. This was the first time the school or the teacher had attempted to discuss the matter with the parents. So picking up the phone should always be the first attempt in reaching out to a parent.

Don't be afraid to ask for assistance. If there are no watchdog groups to ensure the right to free and appropriate education for students of color, create one.

According to the principal at the final meeting, the prevailing issue was that the parents needed outside assistance to gauge her involvement and she was not aware of the matter until we requested intervention. That request led to an investigation, which pinpointed the issues and the misidentified behaviors.

Always make it a point to ask the student "what happened?" They are the ones directly involved and can give a firsthand account; take it into consideration.

After the student allowed me to read the journal entries, I felt the student's story needed to be explained. Truly, she could write and speak very well. Her sentence structure and use of descriptive words were incredible. Her writings should have been entered into competitions, but her ability to naturally write in formal register was due to the parenting skills of the parents and grandparents. All were college educated and earned upper middle-class wages, but because of the neighborhood they lived in, it went against the grain of what this educator was taught about poor African Americans, especially children.

"Bridges Out of Poverty" asserts bias and hidden cues in speech and writing. It infers that "formal register in language is the standard sentence syntax and word choice of work and school." Payne suggests that "minority students and poor students do not have access to formal register at home and it is further complicated by the fact these individuals don't have the vocabulary or knowledge of proper sentence structure to use formal register" (Bridges Out of Poverty, Payne).

This was truly what it states in *Bridges Out of Poverty*. Now I knew this mind-set lived in our school district, hidden in the bias of a lot of white teachers.

Don't be afraid to call it what it is! "Most tests and education curriculum are based on formal register," so the above statement leaves one to conclude that it is hopeless teaching the minority and the poor student (Bridges Out of Poverty, 2004).

This type of thinking in 2012 was unbelievable, but in lieu of the suspension rate, I could see this eventually leading the student down the road to suspension.

This exceptional student, although described as quiet, was very respectful, showed good manners, and not once during her statement did her tone become loud or aggressive. The student was confident in what she had put in the journal and in her statements. Everyone with the exception of the student was astonished by the teacher's acknowledgments. The student had maintained the entire time "the teacher treats me differently because I am smart and the teacher is nicer to the white students than the black students."

The adults around her had a hard time dealing with the statements, so most wrote it off as excuses or expressed disbelief but they were true statements. This is why she had journaled everything.

Parents, schools, and businesses operate from middle-class norms that use hidden rules and cues. The white middle-class teacher of course has a deeper connection with her white students. These are students who can relate to her, and she empathetically relates to their cultural norms. She distances herself from the African American student, having minimal contact because of preconceived stereotypes and prejudices. Was she even aware that hidden bias was guiding her treatment of this student? Implicit bias caused her to care nothing about their cultural norms other than stereotypes and "Bridges Out of Poverty" strategies. This time the bias was identified, and it would definitely be addressed and dealt with building-wide by the principal.

My question is, "Is the teacher bias going on here indicative of other incidents and instances reported by parents' district-wide, which was ignored?"

Is the topic ignored because the conversation was too intense a topic to discuss? How could anyone who was afraid to speak on the topic determine if this teacher's implicit bias was guiding her treatment of this child? I knew this would be an important aspect of the high suspension rates, but it was not an easy topic to bring up, especially connecting the bias to the rise in teacher removal of students of color and students of color with disabilities by white teachers. It was evident in the suspension data released by UCLA for the 2009–10 school year and by the district for the 2010–11 and 2011–12 school years.

Dispelling of the "Bridges Out of Poverty" method needs to be addressed by the school board and the superintendent as they directly provide the needed stereotypes and myths about the minority students that cause conscious and unconscious bias in teachers and school staff. Often this bias results in fear of black boys, frustration due to a lack of understanding cultural differences, and the lack of culturally enriched curriculums.

Moreover, a look at teacher demographics in your district can tell a particularly frightening tale about the teachers in the school district. Parents of color have stated for a long time that the diversity of teachers in our school district does not reflect the diversity of the students; now it is out in the open but not being addressed in any meaningful way except to blame the parent and the child. It couldn't possibly be the teacher, could it?

This encounter brought concerns to the forefront regarding the implicit bias, but now it is being totally ignored.

Find out about your child's teacher. It is your right. Once this teacher was transferred to a different setting, I learned the teacher had over ten years' teaching experience, but nine of them were in a rural white school district in Oyster Bay, NY. This was fine, but her fear of minority students and her hidden bias overwhelmed her and her ability to teach all students. Last year, this teacher was mentored by a master teacher and the building principal.

The teacher also stated that she was raised in a rural farming town from elementary to high school. She had little to no contact with minority students, especially African American students. She didn't have any minority interaction until she attended college. However, she was placed in a failing inner-city school with stereotypical feelings toward the majority of the students.

Parents must be attentive to the learning environment and the hidden norms and cues. It may be an indicator that outside assistance is needed in advocating for fair and equal education for your child. Until this family moved out of state in 2013, I continued to monitor this student's progress by providing the following:

1. Weekly and/or monthly visits to the school to sit in on classes
2. Attending open house and any meeting the parents could not attend but at their request (normally award ceremonies)

Why was this so important to me? Why did this agitate me to act the way I did? You will see in the next chapter!

Teacher bias does exist, and it can result in the push-out of your child if you are not willing to question anything that doesn't seem right! We all think, *Nah, it couldn't be happening. What did my child do?*

It may well be the student was wrong; however, it could well be the teacher's implicit or hidden bias.

Chapter 15

Teacher Bias: Young, Gifted, Black, Labeled Disruptive and Targeted for Suspension (1996)

Identified in the fifth grade as disruptive by the very teacher that taught her in the gifted program, later this student became one of the smartest achieving seventh graders in NYS and graduated high school with honors.

Once the teacher bias is uncovered, your parent radar goes into effect. Sadly, it's to make sure bias isn't rearing its ugly head again with your child. You must be ready and able to visit the school regularly, meet with the teacher(s) monthly, volunteer to chaperone, sit in on classes, provide your child with the ability to advocate for self, and be the watchdog or school monitoring system for your child.

No one wants to talk about biases or accuse anyone of bias. We even say it doesn't exist in our educational system. I am not talking about racism but bias!

Teacher bias is not something that is comfortable to talk about or address. We would rather find something wrong with a student who points out that the teacher could actually have hidden bias. The story in the previous chapter occurred in 2010; however, my passion to follow up on this student until graduation comes from a place deep inside my heart during the 1996–97 school year.

When the student brought up the subject of teacher bias to her parents and the social worker, both found something wrong with the child's behavior (even if the child had not misbehaved) instead of asking the teacher their underlying question, and this disturbed me. It was like déjà vu. Could this still be occurring today as it was in 1996–97 with my own niece? If you say, "It's bias," you are called a racist or being prejudiced, and to avoid that designation, many parents will not challenge the bias. Students, however, are in a difficult place if they are experiencing bias because they cannot effectively learn in a biased environment.

In the acknowledgment section, you can see special acknowledgment has been made to a host of former and retired principals and teachers. These are the people who dealt with bias head-on and found creative ways to ensure that teacher bias was combated with cultural understanding of your children. Thank you all!

Once you understand you have a hidden bias, you can counter it. Teaching tolerance is a project of the Southern Poverty Law Center. This is the Web site I often refer to when an educator questions my intent or the parents' intent, when we say a teacher is biased. It is much easier to call a parent racist or a student's opinion absurd or brush it under the rug because admitting bias is uncomfortable. Most of us refuse to acknowledge that we have bias, including hidden bias.

But the case of teacher bias with regard to a gifted and smart regular student in 2010 caused me to again rely on the expertise of my own experiences.

"Sometimes you have to recall the past to fully understand the implications of the present:"

When your intent for teacher bias is perceived as racism or prejudiced intentions, refer the teacher or the school administrator to the Southern Poverty Law Center's Web site on teaching tolerance. There is a professional development tool called test your hidden bias. This is a resource schools can take advantage of. They are truly committed to addressing the issue of teacher bias. You will not have to explain anything further as the person will look up the Web site and see for himself or herself the betterment of the student, the teacher, and the district by taking advantage of this powerful tool. We are not asking for public admissions of bias but for teachers and administrators to take this test.

Visit Project Implicit's Web site and deal with the results in private or as a whole, but deal with the bias instead of ignoring it! Teacher bias is directly affecting the fair education of minority students, especially African American students.

It was on this site I found something that took me back to 1997 and our experience with teacher bias. Teaching tolerance asserted that "studies have found that teachers telegraph prejudices, so much that some believe black and white children in the same classroom receive different education." This I found to be true on many occasions. However, getting the teacher, the principal, and the superintendent to acknowledge that bias exists will not be an easy task.

It is easier to accuse or blame the student for wrongdoing than it is to address bias. Parents, if you have experienced something similar to the story in the previous chapter or like the next few experiences, you will see why you must be diligent and vigilant. It will begin to show you why I am steadfast and not afraid to speak truth to powers!

Sometimes you have to remember the past to fully understand the implications of the present.

At some point during the 1996–97 school year, my son and his teacher Mrs. T called me at work to ask if I could stop by the school and that something was wrong with my niece. The call seemed strange as my son was the caller, and he then handed the phone to his teacher, and she was not my niece's classroom teacher. My niece and my son are of the same age and attended the same school, but they were in different classrooms; the nature of the visit was still unknown.

Once I arrived at the school, I signed in at the office and proceeded to Mrs. T's classroom, passing my niece's classroom on the way. As I walked in the classroom, Mrs. T told the assistant teacher to take over. She and I went off to another corner of the classroom. As she began telling me about the reason she had called me, we began to hear loud noises coming from the classroom across the hallway, and then she told me that was the teacher and my niece.

I was confused. Why was my niece sounding like that? Why? I attempted to leave, but this older African American teacher told me to wait and listen. "This is why we called you." Mrs. T explained that she was concerned about the well-being of my niece. My niece had a medical condition and a prescription (on file at the school). It indicated that she could "excuse herself" at any time she needed to do so. This time the teacher refused or just flat out ignored the doctor's order. And my niece had had an accident. Mrs. T indicated that Mrs. Moose had loudly demanded her to leave the class to "tie her sweater around her bottom," and now the other students were making fun of her. I was confused and angry. My niece had the medical diagnosis written into her school record in the second grade, in part to verify the condition and in part to remove any thought she was using her condition as a way to leave the classroom repeatedly.

I had no words and was just speechless! I just left Mrs. T's classroom to get my niece and call her mother. Once I walked into her classroom, everything changed. The teacher was in my niece's face, pointing her finger at her and yelling at her to "get out the classroom and go to the social worker's office!" I wanted to explode and lay my hands on this woman, but this was a classroom filled with young minds. So I cleared my throat loudly and stated, "Why are you speaking to my child like that? Back off her!" When the teacher looked up and saw me standing inside the classroom, she froze. I had that look that my family and others around me describe as the look of a dragon. Now it was coupled with a feeling of utter disgust and discontent. Mrs. Moose moved back quickly, and as I proceeded forward, she backed off behind her desk. The tone of her voice softened, and she asked if she could help me with something. The children in the classroom were silent. Everyone seemed in awe that I had actually walked in during the rant. Now I had to use all my violence prevention, conflict resolution, or community-organizing skills to defend my niece, but also I would later learn I had to use these skills to protect all the black children in this classroom. Everyone knows I don't play games when it concerns any child (especially my own children). One student who lived on our street stated, "That's Mrs. Billue, uh-oh!"

My niece stated with tears in her little eyes and her voice cracking, "That's my aunt. Now you're in trouble!"

Indeed, she was in trouble! I put my arms around my niece and wiped the tears away from her face. I told her it was going to be OK. "Auntie is here now," and I looked at Mrs. Moose and stated, "This is far from being over!" So many questions were running through my mind; I was overwhelmed! First, I needed to know why my niece was standing here in wet clothing. Why was the teacher yelling at her that way? What had occurred that made the teacher so mad at her?

The teacher looked at me, and indeed, she knew she was in trouble; she knew my reputation! Our family knew this teacher. She had taught both my son and my niece at the Center for Inquiry for over two years, and we had been excited she would be her fifth-grade teacher.

What we did not know was that the very thing that I had mentioned at the beginning of the chapter was a factor. In fact, we didn't even consider that teacher bias was the issue even when it was expressed. It was this single incident that was a proof that bias exists in the educational system, particularly teacher bias toward a black student.

I told the teacher I was taking her home to change, but I wanted a meeting with the principal about my concerns before returning my niece to the classroom. I took her home to change and met up with my sister, and we all proceeded back to the school.

We requested to speak with the principal, and the secretary told us to be seated.

The principal looked surprised to see us, especially seeing our faces and the look on the face of my niece. Mrs. W asked, "Is everything OK?"

I stated, "Not at all." She motioned us to follow her into the office. We briefly told her about the incident that day and that we wanted to schedule a meeting with the teacher. The principal agreed to have the meeting, but she said she needed to speak with the teacher and investigate the situation.

At that point, my sister interrupted us, stating that her daughter would not return to school until the meeting happened or unless a classroom change occurred. My sister handed me a letter she had received in the mail that afternoon. It was from the social worker, with the teacher copied. It was titled "Request for a Behavioral Intervention." My sister proceeded to tell the principal she was puzzled. "Why send a letter instead of placing a phone call?"

I scanned the letter quickly, and I was also surprised. There were no prior indications of behavioral issues, and this puzzled me, coupled with our experience in the classroom. My sister stated that she and I had never received any phone call regarding my niece this school year for any reason.

I was concerned because she was a very smart student and intellectually gifted! This child only got *A*'s in class work and homework, was never in trouble, and was a very quiet, well-behaved student, but now she was being accused of acting out in school. It was strange to me that now all of a sudden she was being considered and labeled to be having a behavior issue. *How could this be?* I thought. The letter described tantrums, refusing reasonable requests, and daydreaming. I wondered and asked the principal, "Are we sure this letter is talking about the same child or student?"

The meeting was set for the next day, but none of us was prepared for the meeting. None of us was prepared to hear from my niece what was in her journal. The principal began the meeting by stating that she had conducted a preliminary investigation. As a result of that investigation, she wanted the parent and the teacher to address the issues of behavior with the child.

I interrupted, "Absolutely *not*! That method infers that my niece did something wrong and I am not convinced of that yet! What are the results of your investigation?"

Now remember, I was called to the school that day by my son's teacher. I had also walked into the classroom and seen firsthand that my niece was being singled out and intimidated. If the principal's investigation did not contain a statement from Mrs. T, it was just that—preliminary. I told the principal just that and indicated, "Now is the time for answers." This was not a meeting to address issues we didn't know existed; this meeting was requested for the incident that had occurred yesterday in the classroom and in the hallway! I was not in the mood to be stroked or for my niece to be made the perpetrator instead of the victim. I told the principal, "This is the time to either disclose the results of your investigation about the incident yesterday or for Mrs. Moose to explain what occurred in the classroom to all of us!"

The classroom incident was going to be addressed one way or another! We could address the teacher's allegations once we found out what had occurred and why. Standing firm was the only method of defense I could use. I needed to show my niece, my children, and other students that this was not going to go unchecked! Once the incident was resolved, we could address the allegations of failing to respond to reasonable requests, daydreaming, and the tantrums, but not before then.

Then I asked the principal if she was aware that Mrs. T (my son's teacher) was the person that called me and witnessed the incident. The mere fact that the principal did not know this was evident in her answer. The principal was not aware that this incident had taken place in the classroom and in the hallway. She was not aware that another teacher (Mrs. T) had intervened and then at the insistence of my son called me. In fact, the principal indicated that she thought "my niece or Mrs. Moose had called me," but she was incorrect in that assumption.

I still had the same questions:

Why was my niece in wet clothing, with a sweater tied around her waist?

Why was the teacher yelling at her that way?

What had occurred that made the teacher so mad?

Why didn't the teacher call my sister or me if she was being disruptive?

I was not leaving without the answers! I was ready to call the press, the NAACP, and child protective services if the matter wasn't addressed. The principal indicated that she needed to continue her investigation. The principal indicated she only had Mrs. Moose's version of the incident, and her description alone led the principal to state that "she wanted the parents and the teacher to address the issues with the child."

Now was the real test. I turned directly to the teacher and asked the questions above, and she began to answer. The teacher indicated that she could not get my niece to "follow instruction or follow reasonable request" unless she raised her voice or yelled. She thought it was a cultural thing (so you already know I wanted to smack the culture into or out of this woman) because when she raised her voice, the student would "act submissive."

Yes, she used these terms. Mrs. Moose indicated, "At times your niece will lose focus and her mind wanders off into space, often when she can't have her way." She finished by adding, "Your niece thinks she is smarter than the teacher. While she may be ahead of her peers, she is not smarter than I am."

I rose up from my chair and looked at the principal, my sister, and the teacher, saying, "You must be out of your mind!"

"How dare you!"

I looked at the principal and said, "Did you hear that?" This teacher had really just stated my niece was submissive when she raised her voice, as if this was a plantation. Now she was associating yelling with our culture. I was heated, but I sat down and let Mrs. Moose finish the rest of her statement. However, the principal didn't want Mrs. Moose to say another word, and she attempted to take control of the meeting—"attempted."

Okay, by now, the reader should be able to see the hidden messages and hear the coded references. You can deny they exist if you want to, but our children are subjected to this bias on a daily basis while attempting to get a fair and equal education.

Mrs. Moose finished by stating, "The tantrums are a new behavior. They only occur when your niece can't do what she wants to do, like going to the bathroom when she wants to."

I was floored. What did she just say? I asked my sister (now holding my knees still) and stated again, "What did she just say?" My sister was literally holding my chair, telling me to stay seated.

The principal jumped in, acknowledging the medical condition and verifying the physician's statement in her student record. Mrs. W stated that it should not have been and never should be an issue concerning this student! This was when the rubber met the road; now I was really angry.

I use anger differently on most people. When I am angry, I see clearly. I can act cool, calm, and calculating. I am literal and exact in my thought process and my actions. I am really dangerous when I am angry and policies and laws are my weapons. Due process meant that we could address the allegations of the accuser in the presence of the accuser.

The predisposed conditioning of this teacher was to ignore the medical diagnosis and statement and deny the student to use the bathroom because of her bias and cultural assumptions.

The teacher noted that defiance was seen frequently as skipping steps in problem-solving and using unexpected strategies in math and science, resulting in correct answers, but defiance was refusing to follow the given instructions. The teacher explained, "I felt your niece would do this just to frustrate me." The teacher also stated, "Your niece showed pleasure in posing difficult questions from chapters not yet reviewed, which I view as being difficult."

Silence fell over the room as the principal stated very firmly, "From this point on, all matters concerning this student should be referred to me!"

My questions had not been answered, but after hearing the teacher's assertions, they were answered. I had a discussion with my niece that evening, and I knew that my niece's version of the incident was documented and very different from the teacher's account. For some unknown reason, the principal never interviewed my niece about what took place, but after today, she would have to!

Now everyone would hear what they didn't want to hear or acknowledge. What happened in the classroom was real for my niece. This teacher assaulted her young mind, and the scars and pain were true for her!

Remember, this was a gifted student who learned more rapidly than her classmates. While she was ready to move on, the rest of the class was not. She had exceptional written and verbal skills, which I put to use that evening prior to our meeting. My niece journaled everything, writing down everything in her diary or journal (a composition book), including poetry related to her feelings. On the evening of the incident (prior to the meeting), she handed me her journal. She wanted me to read the whole journal because it contained her description of the clothing incident and other incidents. Once I read it, I knew she had to tell her own story at the meeting, so once the teacher finished, I gave her the opportunity.

When my husband, my sister, and I spoke with my niece that evening, she indicated she had begun to cry and fell to the floor because the teacher "denied me the ability to use the restroom," and it resulted in the accident. Then she indicated, "Mrs. Moose laughed and said, 'You don't have a medical problem, and it is a mental problem.'" This was not the first time I had heard the accusation regarding Mrs. Moose, but I missed it prior to now. When I thought about how long my niece may have endured this treatment, I was sickened. Now I had to pay attention to her, other adults, and her classmates. My niece had continually stated to my sister, "Ms. Moose treats black students differently from white students." On this night, she elaborated further, "It's OK for white students to skip steps or to finish assignments early, but it's not OK for me to do the same." Mrs. Moose would always say "you people" to black students and would "lessen our accomplishments to praise the accomplishments of white students and never praises the black students." My niece indicated during the first marking period she was accused of cheating when she had perfect scores in a test and was made to sit in a corner chair for speaking up.

The principal looked at the teacher, and when she asked for clarity, Mrs. Moose was silent. My niece continued to state that even though she was ahead of most of the class, she was often told not to proceed until the class caught up. If she proceeded, she explained that the teacher would begin to yell. If she got up to use the restroom (as indicated by doctor's orders), she was told loudly to stop faking and to sit down. She indicated that Mrs. Moose used a tone loud enough for the entire classroom to hear. This day, after being denied access to the restroom, my niece indicated she returned to her seat, put her head down, and tried not to think about it. This caused Mrs. Moose to become angry, so she approached her desk and began to yell at her. According to my niece, this was what happened when the accident occurred. "Mrs. Moose ordered me to leave the classroom, but it was too late. All the students began to laugh, and I dropped to the ground and cried out for my aunt and my mother." My niece further indicated, "That was when Mrs. T intervened. Then Mrs. Moose told me to wrap my sweater around me and stop crying, but I could not. I just wanted to die."

Everyone was in tears now, but she continued to explain, "Ms. Moose always uses a rough, loud tone with me. Mrs. Moose would be in my face (up close), yell, and point her finger at my face in front of the class. It embarrasses me and causes me to shut down, and yesterday it actually frightened me!" The daydreaming was not to ignore the teacher; it was done to take up time while the rest of the class caught up.

Before she could finish the statement, the teacher interrupted and stated, "I am so sorry. I am very sorry," and she sobbed! All the recollections were true. The room was silent, and I think we all were in awe! The teacher continued to state that she was guilty of the behavior, but she was not aware that she caused my niece to feel frightened, embarrassed, and unsafe and apologized again. Then she stated this was her first time teaching inner-city children in an inner-city school and the cultural differences were frightening. Although she had taught both my son and my niece at the Center for Inquiry, it was located in a white—predominately Irish—neighborhood in Syracuse. CFI was in a much different community—much different from the crime and poverty in the neighborhood.

The principal needed to end this meeting quickly if for nothing more than to shut the teacher up. I knew this teacher had to be removed from the classroom! I made up my mind it was going to happen.

The principal needed to complete her investigation and speak to Mrs. T about what she had witnessed, but my mind was made up. This teacher had to *go!* I am sure she wanted to speak to the teacher in private since she admitted my niece was telling the truth and apologized, but it was out in the open. No one wanted to think that a teacher could be biased, but this was a firsthand account.

Now you can see why the case in the previous chapter stood out to me; it was my niece's experience during the 1996–97 school year in the same district at the same school.

There are many students who share my niece's story as was the case in the previous chapter, but now you can see the reason why the student's story in 2010 agitated me! My niece's circumstance in 1997 made me do something uncomfortable back then and call out bias now! It also made me listen to the child and acknowledge it may not be always be the child; it just might be the teacher!

I will not leave you hanging; of course, this led to a series of meetings to identify what was really going on since a review of the report cards and interim reports all indicated that she had exceptional social skills, work skills, and behavior as indicated below:

*Progress Report Grades 2–6 *

SOCIAL AND WORK SKILLS
Social and work skills are evaluated using the Effort Scale.

EFFORT

Evaluation is based on listening, following directions, and completing assignments, including homework, and participating in class.

O - OUTSTANDING
V - VERY GOOD
S - SATISFACTORY
I - IMPROVEMENT NEEDED
U - UNSATISFACTORY

	First	Second	Third	Fourth
Respects Others				
Assumes Responsibility For Own Behavior				
Works Well In A Large Group				
Works Well In A Small Group				
Works Well Independently				
Chooses Appropriate Activity When Assigned Tasks Are Done				
Solves Problems Appropriately				
Completes Homework				

*My niece's report in 1996–97 reads the same as the report in 2010–11; however, here it indicates that her social skills and work skills are outstanding.

Parents, you are the first line of defense for your child. If you fail to investigate situations (regardless of the end result), you fail your child. Parents must keep copies of report cards, interim reports, and weekly and monthly progress reports. These documents could be the visible factor in determining if your child is being singled out or is actually in need of behavioral intervention.

I had to question the letter from the social worker as no prior behavior problems were ever recorded regarding my niece. There were no prior calls; no meetings had been held or scheduled with her mother or me prior to the incident that led to this meeting. The principal indicated that she needed challenges that matched her skills, pace of mastery, and her level of learning. Actually, she needed a teacher who was unbiased and one who wanted to nurture this intellectually gifted student. Instead, she was uncomfortable and felt harassed by my niece. The principal concluded that in order to properly develop and challenge this student to reach her full potential, the following would be addressed:

1. An assessment of "mastery of material" to avoid wasting time on what is already known
2. IQ assessment from CFI and evaluations from teaching staff to encourage independent exploration on subject matter and assess mastery of concepts and steps
3. To be able to go to the bathroom without teacher permission, following the instruction of the physician

In the seventh grade, my niece was recognized along with 122 students from across New York State as one of "the smartest achieving seventh and eighth students in NYS" for two consecutive years at a middle school deemed to be failing with hard to educate students, but again she prevailed.

In 2004, she was a member of Jenna's Kids and HOBY, the Hugh O'Brian Youth Leadership Program. HOBY empowers exceptionally gifted students to embrace their unique attributes. My niece excelled throughout high school, being chosen for the highly touted International Baccalaureate Program (IB Program) at Corcoran high school. She graduated fifth in her class in 2006 and attended Buffalo State University. She is currently married and a mother of three children.

Note: From 1992 to 1995, my children attended Dr. King School. In 1996–97, my niece and my children attended Elmwood Elementary School. They each attended Shea Middle school and the same high school. All attended and graduated from Corcoran Senior High School. In the nineties, Dr. King, Shea, and Elmwood schools were known as the worst elementary and middle schools in Syracuse.

This is important when you look at past results and the current data on test scores and suspensions. Shea Middle was joined with another school and was renamed, while Elmwood Elementary School was closed at the end of the 2010–11 school year. Both stories occurred at Elmwood Elementary School.

"Bridges Out of Poverty" or Jim Crow tactics are still being used to attack and assault students of color. This was an effort to crush the spirit of a truly gifted child—an attempt to push her out of the classroom under the disguise of disruptive behavior and eventually to be suspended. I was directed to the Southern Poverty Law Center by the Washington Lawyers Association for Civil Rights regarding this very matter. What I learned and uncovered is still being used today (2014) to address implicit and hidden bias whenever it rears its ugly head!

Teaching Tolerance asserts, "African–American teenagers are aware they are stigmatized as being intellectually inferior and that they go to school, bearing an overwhelming burden of suspicion that affects their attitudes and their ability to achieve."

If crime, poverty, and inferiority are all some white people/teachers have ever been taught (from childhood) about African Americans, how can they provide a fair and equal education to African American children?

What would you do if this was your child? Would you dismiss the child and believe the teacher? Would you investigate on your own? Would you reprimand your child on the teacher's word?

My son and my niece have a unique relationship. Both are intellectually gifted and strong academically (if in the proper environment), but being academically strong, analytically astute, extremely observant, or charismatic can be diminished if the white teacher has a fear of black people or children.

They understand each other and are very protective of each other. What I didn't realize until later was how justice oriented my son was about his cousin. This incident caused him pain, and it was his insistence that caused his teacher's involvement and her subsequent call to me. This incident troubled my son, and from that point forward, he always checked in on his cousin. No matter what, he spoke up for her, and he had her back. They understand each other because they share unreal, horrible experiences for a child to experience. They both were fighters because I raised them to stand up for themselves and point out injustice. My son did just that to defend his cousin.

According to Mrs. T, my son was so persistent that it was at his insistence she called me. At one point, he asked to go to the office, and when questioned why, he stated, "I need to call my mother. My cousin is in danger." Mrs. T indicated it was also the look on his face—the way he ran to her aid in the hallway and stood between the teacher and my niece as the teacher yelled at her. "I was watching this child push his cousin behind him so he could take the brunt of the yelling."

It was his determination, concern, and anxiety that something was really wrong that surprised Mrs. T. It was the way he pleaded for someone to call me with tears in his eyes that caused her to intervene. I can't imagine what they went through that day, and I cringe every time I recollect or share this story in public. My son understood the wrath of white teacher bias, but now that his cousin was the victim, he felt the need to act. It was time for this district to feel the wrath of the whirlwind of his parents, especially his mother. Mrs. Moose was reassigned at the end of the school year. I spent three days a week in my niece's classroom, making Mrs. Moose very uncomfortable until the end of the school year. My husband, my sister, or I would have lunch at the school every day from that point forward. I became the most hated parent by many teachers and the most adored by others! I no longer stayed silent about anything concerning my children, especially these two children! I proudly wear the label "Most hated parent!" I filed a teacher grievance and kept filing them weekly until the district listened to the building principal. If the principal recommends teacher removal, the district should support them, especially if they don't want a lawsuit from a parent. This was disturbing back then, as is now. I realized in 2010 the potential these incidents based on bias had of scarring or even destroying the psyche of innocent students because of implicit bias. Are you aware that teachers can misunderstand the attributes of a gifted child as a learning disability? Do you know how to file a grievance about a teacher or school staff? Do you understand how progressive discipline is applied?

I refuse to let it slide by anymore! I was able to see a clear pattern of attempted push-out and actual push-out of children of color using disruptive behavior to suspend the student. Our experiences are included to show that from 1994 to 2013, a systemic pattern of institutional discrimination occurred. Suspension rates have soared for children of color compared with their white counterparts, especially those with disabilities. The UCLA 2009–10 report indicates that English language learners (mainly the immigrant and refugee populations) are also suspended at a higher rate than their white counterparts, but our district does not include this population in its demographic and student ethnic data. Parents must protect the integrity and confidentiality.

African American males, gifted students, and disabled students of color are all suspended at higher rates than their white and Latino counterparts. I have found that in many instances, Latino students are often not included in the phrase "students of color." So be careful when you speak about African American and Latino students. You may have to ensure they are included when the term is referred to.

Recollections from the past have fully helped us to understand the push-out of the schoolyard, but do parents really understand what is going on—the life sentence?

If not, please continue to read on!

Chapter 16

What Every Parent Should Know about Their Child's Rights While Receiving an Education

FAPE   Free Appropriate Public Education for Students with Disabilities
        US Department of Education Requirements under Section 504
        of the Rehabilitation Act of 1973
VESID   Office of Vocational and Educational Services for Individuals
        with Disabilities
        Statewide Coordinator for Special Education, Room 1624, One
        Commerce Plaza
        Albany, NY 12234
        Telephone (518) 402-3353
        Fax: (518) 473-5769
        www.nysed.gov

Documents Every Parent Should Have and Read:
Every parent should have and read the following:

1. School district's and/or the school's code of conduct and handbook of student rights and responsibilities
   a. Progressive discipline
   b. Prohibited acts and disruptive behavior
   c. Disciplinary procedures and disciplinary actions, i.e., interventions and consequences

    d. The suspension process
    e. Appeal processes for academic ineligibility
    f. Hearing and grievance processes
      i. Students
      ii. Parents

Disabled Students—Documents Every Parent Must Have and Read
If you think your child may have, or if your child has, an undiagnosed disability, or if the school treats your child as if he or she has an undiagnosed disability, you should have and read the following:

1. Code of conduct and handbook of student rights and responsibilities
    a. Any section on students with disabilities
2. New York State Education Department—Procedural Safeguards Notice
    a. Rights for parents of children with disabilities, aged 3–21
3. Individualized Education Program (IEP)
4. The Individuals with Disabilities Education Act (IDEA)
    a. Part B three to twenty one years old
    b. Part C birth to two years old
    c. http://idea.ed.gov
5. Early Intervention Programs (county and school district specific)
    a. Pre-kindergarten to five years old
6. Section 504 and the Education of Children with Disabilities
    a. US Department of Education Office of Civil Rights
    b. http://www2.ed.gov/about/offices/list/ocr/504faq.html
7. No Child Left Behind
    a. Zero tolerance and teacher removal of routinely disruptive students

Every parent that has a student with a disability must know how to read and interpret his or her child's IEP:

1. (See Chapter 22 Learning the Language of Special Education: How to Understand the IEP)

In New York State, *every parent* should be familiar with the following:

1. NYS VADIR for your school district
2. Common core standards and ELA test results

Every parent needs to know the following:

1. If your child has been routinely suspended ISS or OSS for disruptive behavior
2. If your child has an IEP
3. If your child receives 504 services
4. If your child has a hidden physical or learning disability

Every parent of a regular or disabled student prior to the beginning of a new school year and at least twice during the school year should do the following:

Step One: Prior to or at the beginning of the school year, call or schedule a meeting with the teacher (if known), the school guidance counselor, and the school social worker. These are the two people who are there to ensure your child is successful. They will listen to your concerns and may even adjust the student's schedule, providing a rigorous but less stressful use of time.

Meetings: Attend every meeting concerning your child. If you don't understand the purpose of the meeting or the language of the letter you receive, informing you of the meeting, seek the assistance of the school, a friend, or a community group specializing in education advocacy to assist you in understanding.

Step Two: Familiarize yourself and your child with the code of conduct. Find out what are considered nonviolent disruptive behaviors. The schools may have its own code of conduct and school rules, so make sure you inquire about and retain a copy of both the district's and the school's code of conduct.

Step Three: Once school begins, attend PTO, 504 Committee, Committee on Special Education, school board, and any other school-related meetings where you can learn your rights and your child's rights. Volunteer in the school or in the classroom to identify the school climate (suspension). Schedule biweekly phone conferences, weekly progress reports (written or e-mail), and quarterly meetings with the teacher or phone conferences on report cards distribution to stay on top of any potential issues. Parents, your presence is a key factor in how successful your child will be. If the teacher does not fit the student, request a meeting, file a grievance, or request a teaching change.

Step Four (if needed):

Suspensions Keep all referral or suspension paperwork; if you do not receive any within twenty-four hours of the incident, request it from the building principal.

Become familiar with the referral and suspension polices and the appeal process for academic ineligibility, referral, suspension, and expulsion.

Suspensions if your child has a disability:

Keep a record of the number of days your child is suspended ISS and OSS, especially if your child has a disability or is considered routinely disruptive.

Education laws state, "Ten days suspended in a school year may constitute a change in placement," and a determination meeting must be held to determine if the behavior was the result of the disability. You may wonder if it is your responsibility to keep track of the days . . . in our district you have to!

The following are medical terminology and definitions associated with disruptive conduct in schools:

1. Conduct disorder (CD)
2. Oppositional defiant disorder (ODD)
3. Attention deficit (hyperactivity) disorder (ADHD)
4. Disruptive behavior disorder (DBD)

Sample
Suspension Appeal Letter

Date
Principal's name
Name of school
Address

Re:
To Whom It May Concern:

On _____ my child _____ was suspended out of school for ___days
for the alleged charges of _____. On _____ less than 24
hours after _____ was suspended, we met with and/or spoke to the
Principal or his/her designee Mr. /Mrs. _____at
_____school about the matter.

I am requesting an informal hearing to appeal the suspension.

I do not agree with the suspension and the allegations charged, and I have
not received any information regarding the results of a formal investigation
into the matter.

I am not satisfied with the decision to suspend my child for _____ days
as he/she is missing valuable instructional time. This letter serves as a
formal request to appeal the suspension of my child _____.

Thank you,

Parent's name
Telephone #

CC
Superintendent
Local ACLU Rep.
Local NAACP or NAN Rep.

Chapter 17

The Code of Conduct: Do You Understand the Code of Conduct?

What is a student behavior code of conduct? What is progressive discipline? What is prohibited conduct? What is the definition of disruptive conduct?

The following has been taken from the SCSD's *student behavior code of conduct* and *district's philosophy of discipline*

> Disciplinary action, when necessary, will be firm, fair, and consistent so as to be the most effective in changing student behavior. In determining the appropriate disciplinary action, school personnel authorized to impose disciplinary penalties will consider the following:
>
> - The student's age.
> - The nature of the offense and the circumstances which led to the offense.
> - The student's prior disciplinary record.
> - The effectiveness of other forms of discipline.
> - Information from parents, teachers, and/or others, as appropriate.
> - Other extenuating circumstances.

"As a general rule, discipline will be progressive. This means that a student's first violation will usually merit a lighter penalty than subsequent violations."

Disability-related clause within this statement is given below:

> If the conduct of a student is related to a disability or suspected disability, the student shall be referred to the Committee on Special Education. Discipline, if warranted, shall be administered consistent with the separate requirements of this code of conduct for disciplining students with a disability or presumed to have a disability. A student identified as having a disability shall not be disciplined for behavior related to his or her disability.

If your district uses a policy of progressive discipline, you may want to explore what this really means. I have found in many instances what is written in the policy above is often not the policy followed.

The sentence above states that disciplinary action when necessary will be firm, fair, and consistent. However, it does not mention that firm and consistent don't always mean fair and progressive; it usually means suspending students of color and students of color with disabilities for every infraction whether ISS or OSS.

First offenses are often suspensions in our district and considered disruptive; therefore, they are reportable incidents on VADIR. These consist of in-school suspensions, out-of-school suspensions, and undocumented teacher removals which are very rarely positive interventions and used unless the parent is insistent! Routine suspensions are very consistent among African American and Latino students including the number of days per instance and among children of color with disabilities.

What is Progressive Discipline?

Below is the progressive discipline model for our school district. However, based on the data contained in the UCLA Civil Rights Project 2009–10 report and in the 2010–11 and 2011–12 disciplinary data analysis, anyone can determine that suspension is the number one model used in implementing progressive discipline; whether in-school or out-of-school, it is the more common and reoccurring option, not progressive discipline.

Understanding what progressive discipline means is imperative if your school district implements this policy and if your child is repeatedly suspended or removed by a teacher for being identified as routinely disruptive.

The following has been taken from the SCSD's student behavior code of conduct implemented in 2011:

Progressive Discipline Model for Infraction in Classroom and on Buses

- Student warned and parent/guardian notified.
- Parent/guardian conference with school personnel to review behavior.
- Suspended from the bus (up to three days), with parent/guardian notified.
- Suspended in school (up to three days), with parent/guardian notified.
- Suspended out of school (up to three days) with parent/guardian notified.
- Other consequences as determined by the school.
- Suspended from the bus until transportation class is attended. (Parent/guardian notified that both child and parent must attend safety class. Call Safety Office 435-4260.)
- Permanently denied bus privilege. (Parent/guardian notified in writing by school.)

Now that you are aware of what it means you will be better equipped to make sure the model is being followed.

Once you learn what it means you will be able to determine if it's being followed or applied as written in the policy.

It is important that parents see the patterns and correlation with suspension. If progressive discipline is the model used for infractions of the behavior code, you must be able to see the correlation with suspension. The patterns associated with suspension will be easy to uncover because once you know what progressive discipline means, you will be able to assess if the school personnel authorized to impose disciplinary penalties applied the appropriate disciplinary action, taking into consideration the following items:

1. The student's age
2. The nature of the offense and the circumstances which led to the offense
3. The student's prior disciplinary record
4. The effectiveness of other forms of discipline
5. Information from parents, teachers, and/or others, as appropriate
6. Other extenuating circumstances

Progressive discipline should mean the student's first violations will merit a lighter penalty than subsequent violations; however, all the above factors must be taken into consideration. Understanding due process is essential in education and, in your school district.. Due process is a protection you have under law. Simply put, regarding education, it means you and/or your child can appeal any decision made regarding your child's education if you disagree.

You have the right to appeal.

A student, a parent, and/or a guardian has the right to appeal any student's ineligibility status.

Parents and/or guardians have a right to appeal decisions of the CSE if they disagree.

In our district, the appeal process is vague and does not outline a real process. The process for appealing academic ineligibility states that appeals must be made within three school days after being notified of ineligibility (written notice) and should be submitted to the principal or his or her designee. This is where it can get tricky. Always demand written notice of any decision regarding your child whether it's regarding a transfer, busing, or academic issues. If you don't get it in writing, demand it in writing! It's the school district, for Pete's sake; they should always provide written and oral verification and notice to all parents, especially if the progressive discipline model is used.

Note: Student conduct that is considered disruptive is also considered a prohibited act as per our code of conduct. So nine times out of ten in the SCSD, if your child is considered routinely disruptive, you can bet money he or she will be routinely suspended. If the parent does not push back, the student will be tested for ADHD, CD, and/or ODD and eventually pushed out of the education system onto the streets.

Now what happens when the prohibited act or the conduct that is disruptive is a symptom of a student's disability? If your child has a diagnosis of ADHD, ODD, CD, autism, etc., in the SCSD, your child will be suspended regardless of his or her medical diagnosis, even if he or she has an IEP or a behavioral plan and if the behaviors are a manifestation of the disability.

Let's take a look at student conduct that is disruptive or the list of disruptive behaviors identified in our district's code of conduct. Disruptive conduct is not considered a violent incident, but it is student conduct that is reportable on the VADIR. The following has been taken from the SCSD's code of conduct (revised 2011):

Students may be subject to disciplinary action, up to and including suspension from school, for the following:

A. **Student conduct that is disruptive.** Examples of disruptive conduct include:
* Failing to comply with the reasonable directions of teachers, school administrators or other school personnel in charge of students.
* Running in hallways.
* Making unreasonable noise.
* Bringing in unauthorized pets.
* Using language or gestures that are profane, lewd, vulgar or abusive.
* Obstructing vehicular or pedestrian traffic.
* Engaging in any willful act which disrupts the normal operation of the school community.
* Trespassing. Students are not permitted in any school building, other than the one they regularly attend, without permission from the administrator in charge of the building.
* Computer/electronic communications misuse, including any unauthorized use of computers software, or internet/intranet accounts; accessing inappropriate websites or any other violation of the district's acceptable use policy as further outlined in SCSD Acceptable Use Policy for All Computer Technology in Section XV – R.
* Unauthorized use of objects (i.e. beepers, cellular phones, boom boxes, walkmans, CD players, etc.) during regular school hours or school events.
* Bringing in unauthorized objects (i.e. laser pointers, obscene materials, etc.)

7

Often the outlined infractions above do not cover the intensive list of student conduct that is not identified in the above text. Our district does not list the infractions using the summary form categories, so clarity will be needed. This is one of the main reasons for becoming familiar with the code of conduct and the VADIR.

In Chapter 8, we focused on providing clarity on the NYS VADIR's other disruptive incidents (columns j–o).

20. **Other Disruptive Incidents**: Other incidents involving disruption of the educational process and that rise to the level of a consequence listed in the Summary of Violent and Disruptive Incidents Form (columns j–o). Reportable incidents are limited to those resulting in disciplinary action or referral.

Disruptive or prohibited conduct leads to disciplinary actions, suspendable consequences, and very rarely progressive discipline.

Most often, parents are not familiar with the documents, the terms, or the definitions for disruptive incidents, disruptive conduct, disciplinary action, or referral action.

NYSED VADIR's glossary of terms defines disciplinary or referral action as follows:

Disciplinary or Referral Action: For purposes of reporting, a disciplinary or referral action includes a referral to: Counseling or Treatment Programs, Teacher Removal, Suspension from Class or Activities, Out-of-School Suspension, Involuntary Transfer to Alternative Education Program or Law Enforcement/Juvenile Justice (refer to definitions below).

Simply put, it means "student conduct that is disruptive." That is, failing to comply with the reasonable direction of school staff results in the consequences listed above in j–o, making the pattern and correlation with suspension very clear. Progressive discipline will not be the model implemented if a hidden consequence for the disruptive conduct is referral to counseling or treatment programs, teacher removal, suspension from class or activities, transfer to alternative education program, or referral to law enforcement or juvenile justice.

Parents, are you aware that failing to comply with the reasonable direction of teachers, etc., is not only a violation of the code of conduct (under disruptive conduct) but also a symptom of ODD, CD, ADHD, autism, and DBD?

Parents, are you aware that failing to comply with the reasonable request of school staff is considered a disruption to the educational process?

Parents, are you aware that the following are the consequences for failing to comply with reasonable direction or the reasonable requests of school staff?

1. Referral to counseling or treatment programs
2. Teacher removal
3. Suspension from class or activities
4. Transfer to alternative education program
5. Referral to law enforcement or juvenile justice

Yes, it is serious enough to lead to one or more of the consequences listed above.

Parents, are you aware these incidents are in violation of the district code of conduct and are also kryptonite to the disabled student?

The Code of Conduct and its Medical Connection—A Life
Sentence for the Disabled Student
Where are all the groups that fight for people with disabilities when black children with disabilities are being discriminated against?

—My husband

There are no groups, even established groups, for the disabled American who fights for disabled African American students. Beaten and tasered by police in school, suspended unfairly, and blatantly discriminated against in education standards, there is no group in Syracuse that continuously stands up for the disabled African American students until now!

My husband used the quote above, so many times I had to pay attention to the facts. Earlier in 2013, a white disabled person was dragged off a bus and tasered. The entire disabled community and organizations for the disabled were in uproar. The disabled person's organizations, groups, and supporters were out in full force, screaming about discrimination and injustices, but when the suspension report indicated that disabled students of colors were discriminated against, when suspended, you could hear a pin drop.

When it comes to the African Americans, the only groups outraged or incensed at the data were the NAN, the NAACP, and the NYCLU. Not one white group, organization, or supporter representing persons with disabilities stood with us in May 2013. Now several groups and organizations are on board, but it only occurred because of agitation, disability facts and research, and communities organizing and filing complaints with US Department of Education's Office of Civil Rights and the NYS attorney general's office.

I learned with the UCLA report that the American Academy of Pediatricians took a stand against suspension, but it was Dr. Umar Johnson and the Web site of the AACAP that really guided me in understanding this tactic.

According to the American Academy of Child and Adolescent Psychiatry, "all children are oppositional; they argue, talk back, disobey, and defy parents and teachers." The very same conduct that is treated by a psychologist, with medicine and counseling listed on the student's IEP, is seen as openly uncooperative. There is zero tolerance for the conduct even when it is a medical condition and it violates the code of conduct. This zero-tolerance discipline methodology will negatively affect your child's academic life if you don't step in!

Parents must be familiar with "student conduct that is disruptive and insubordinate," especially failing to comply with reasonable requests or directions, questioning rules, skipping school, talking back or cursing, or any incident that is considered to "disrupt the educational process."

The American Academy of Child and Adolescent Psychiatry states the following symptoms of ODD:

1. Excessive arguing with adults
2. Often questioning rules
3. Active defiance and refusal to comply with adult requests and rules
4. Deliberate attempts to annoy or upset people
5. Blaming others for his or her mistakes or misbehavior
6. Often being touchy or easily annoyed by others
7. Frequent anger and resentment
8. Mean and hateful talking when upset
9. Spiteful attitude and revenge seeking

Children with ODD, "Facts for Families," Publication No. 72 (3/11) The American Academy of Child and Adolescent Psychiatry (AACAP) 2012
http://www.aacap.org/App_Themes/AACAP/docs/facts_for_families/72_children_with_oppositional_defiant_disorder.pdf

All the symptoms given above are considered disruptive or insubordinate conduct in our district's code of conduct, even though ODD is a medical condition or mental disorder.

Parents, this alone should raise your level of concern. It applies to regular students and disabled students.

According to Losen, the suspension report from UCLA's Civil Rights Project indicated that African American males with disabilities are at a higher risk of suspension than any subgroup.

Figure 1: Risk for Suspension at the Elementary and Secondary Levels by Selected Subgroups

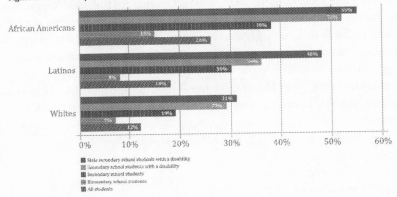

Looking at the chart above, we can understand African American secondary male students with disabilities are suspended at a much higher rate than any other group in our school district.

My concern also peaked when I really took a closer look at the term *routinely disruptive* related to the recent push to label children of color as ADHD, warehouse them in in-school suspension, or push them out using out-of-school suspensions.

The pattern was not hard to uncover as I was familiar with these tactics. They were used on my own children in 1994. As mentioned previously in recent years (2010–13), most parents whom I assisted with a school-related issue were the parents of a child with ADHD, the parents of a child who had an IEP or a behavioral plan, or the parents of a child who needed 504 services or testing for mitigating circumstances.

I noticed that most of the students with ADHD were medicated and a lot of other students had IEPs, but most noticeably, all had behavioral intervention plans (BIPs) in place. However, I would soon realize that instead of being used for intervention or to calm or curb the frustration in learning, it was being used against the student. The symptoms of the disability and/or the frustration in learning were now directly leading to ISS or OSS as was attempted from 1994 to 2004 with my son and my niece.

Gifted and learning disabled students from 2010 to 2013 were systematically being pushed out or suspended, using their inquisitive intellectual nature as defiance or the manifestation of their disability to institute inappropriate discipline or suspension. The progressive discipline model for all students and the IDEA requirements for the disabled students were being blatantly ignored. Federal and state laws require specific guidelines for discipline and disabled students, especially "if the behavior is a manifestation of the disability" and if it is being ignored.

Our district's code of conduct has sections that outline infractions, interventions, and consequences for attendance and behavior. However, there are four sets of conditions relating to behavior rules that parents and students must consider and become familiar with:

1. Prohibited acts
2. Student conduct that is disruptive
3. Student conduct that is insubordinate
4. Student conduct that endangers the safety, morals, health, or welfare of others (violent behavior is not a category that is included for our purposes).

Remember, disruptive and insubordinate conducts are also written (whether consciously or unconsciously) to correlate with the symptoms of potential behavioral conditions such as ODD, CD, and ADHD.

The bottom line is they all relate to suspension! Parents, do you really understand the procedures for enacting penalties and suspension from school? Note: The SCSD implemented an Interim Code of Conduct during the 2013-2014 school year in order to comply with the law. The passage below is taken from the Code of Conduct last revised in 2011 it was distributed to parents throughout the 2012-2013 school year. Our code stated the following:

B. **Procedures for Enacting Penalties**

In all cases, regardless of the penalty imposed, the school personnel authorized to impose the penalty must inform the student of the alleged misconduct and must investigate, to the extent necessary, the facts surrounding the alleged misconduct. All students will have an opportunity to present their version of the fact to the school personnel imposing the disciplinary penalty in connection with the imposition of the penalty.

Students who are to be given penalties other than an oral warning, written warning or written notification to their parents are entitled to additional rights before the penalty is imposed. These additional rights are explained below.

1. Detention
    Teachers, principals and the superintendent may use after school detention as a penalty for student misconduct in situations where removal from the classroom or suspension would be inappropriate.

14

Detention will be imposed as a penalty only after the student's parent/guardian has been notified to confirm that there is no parental objection to the penalty and the student has appropriate transportation home following detention.

15

The above passage is very important in understanding your rights and due process. The process may not be outlined in a manner that is easy to follow or understand, so don't be afraid to ask questions or for assistance.

Parents, do you understand suspension from school and in-school suspension?

Suspension may be imposed only upon students who are insubordinate, disorderly, violent, or disruptive or whose conduct otherwise endangers the safety, moral character, physical or mental health, or welfare of others. Now remember those medical classifications that are pushing out African American students. Do parents really know what this means? Let's look at conduct that is insubordinate:

> **Student conduct that is insubordinate.** Examples of insubordinate conduct include:
>
> - Failing to comply with the reasonable directions of teachers, school administrators or other school employees in charge of students or otherwise demonstrating disrespect.
> - Lateness for, missing or leaving school without permission.
> - Skipping detention *(Taken from the SCSD's Code of Conduct)*

Examples include failing to comply with reasonable directions. Next, look at student conduct that endangers:

Student conduct that endangers the safety, morals, health, or welfare of others.

Examples of such conduct include:

- Lying to school personnel.
- Selling, using, or possessing obscene material.
- Using vulgar or abusive language, cursing or swearing.
- Smoking a cigarette, cigar, pipe or using chewing or smokeless tobacco.
- Gambling.
- Indecent exposure, that is, exposure to sight of the private parts of the body in a lewd or indecent manner.

(Taken from the SCSD's code of conduct)

And now if you look at the section "Suspension from School," you can see the link to mental health as well as how the manifestation of a disability can lead to suspension.

Suspension from school

3. **Suspension from school**

Suspension from school is a severe penalty, which may be imposed only upon students who are insubordinate, disorderly, violent or disruptive, or whose conduct otherwise endangers the safety, moral character, physical or mental health, or welfare of others.

The board retains its authority to suspend students, but places primary responsibility for the suspension of students with the superintendent and the principals.

Any staff member may recommend to the superintendent or the principal that a student be suspended. All staff members must immediately report and refer a violent student to the principal or the superintendent for a violation of the code of conduct. All recommendations and referrals shall be made in writing unless the conditions underlying the recommendation or referral warrant immediate attention. In such cases, a written report is to be prepared as soon as possible by the staff member recommending the suspension.

The superintendent or principal, upon receiving a recommendation or referral for suspension or when processing a case for suspension, shall gather the facts relevant to the matter and record them for subsequent presentation, if necessary.

Your child **could also be suspended for Prohibited Conduct:**
No person, either alone or with others shall:

- Intentionally injure any person or threaten to do so.
- Intentionally damage or destroy school district property or the personal property of a teacher,
- Disrupt the orderly conduct of classes, school programs or other school activities.
- Distribute or wear material on school grounds or at school function that are obscene, advocate illegal action, appear libelous, obstruct the rights of others, *or are disruptive to the school program.*
- Intimidate, harass or discriminate against any person on the basis of race, color, creed, national origin, religion, age, gender, sexual orientation or disability
- Entering any portion of the school premises without authorization or remain in any building or facility after it is normally closed.
- Obstructing the free movement of any person in any place to which this code applies.
- Violating the traffic laws, parking regulations or other restrictions on vehicles.
- Possessing, consuming, sell, distribute or exchange of alcoholic beverages, controlled substances, or be under the influence of either on school property or at a school function.
- Possess or use weapons in or on school property or at a school function, except in the case of law enforcement officers or except as specifically authorized by the school district.
- Loiter on or about school property.
- Gamble on school property or at school functions.
- Refuse to comply with any reasonable order of identifiable school district officials performing their duties.
- Willfully incite others to commit any of the acts prohibited by this code.
- Violate any federal or state statute, local ordinance or board policy while on school property or while at a school function.

(Taken from the SCSD's Code of Conduct)

This is when my real concern started to grow. I realized after reading the code of conduct that there are sections related to conduct and behavior all over the place. I made copies and put my own version of the code of conduct together in order to see all the sections that covered prohibited conduct, disruptive conduct, and insubordinate conduct together to get a clear picture of the conduct that is used to issue suspension.

Then I began to look at the UCLA report and the 2010–11 and 2011–12 disciplinary data analysis and realized that students of color with a disability or diagnosed with ADHD, Autism, ODD, CD, or DBD are destined to be suspended.

It was not the white student counterpart with the same disability, displaying the same conduct, but strictly the African American, Latino/Hispanic, African immigrant, or refugee subgroups only! I was directed to Dr. Umar Johnson's book *The Pyscho-Academic Holocaust: The Special Education and ADHD Wars against Black Boys.*

Dr. Johnson acknowledged, "One of the best kept secrets is that having a disruptive behavior disorder diagnosis is not an automatic qualifier for special education services." In fact, I have come to realize in my experiences assisting parents that most African American parents of children with ADHD are not receiving services and are not aware of Section 504 Accommodation Plans. Dr. Johnson asserts, "Many educators and parents are not clear about their civil right which is asserted in the 504 Plan and educational rights as asserted in the IEP i.e. functionality (504 Plan) and the ability to learn (IEP)."

I learned that *CD* is also known as DBD, but you must realize that there is a scheme being implemented to push out African American students, especially male students with disabilities.

Our district is unique in that the rate of suspension of female students of color is the highest, and it's even higher if they have disabilities as indicated below in the 2009–10 report by UCLA's Civil Rights Project.

Figure 2: Percentage of Enrolled Subgroup Suspended at Least Once by Race and English Learner Status (ELS) with Gender by School Level

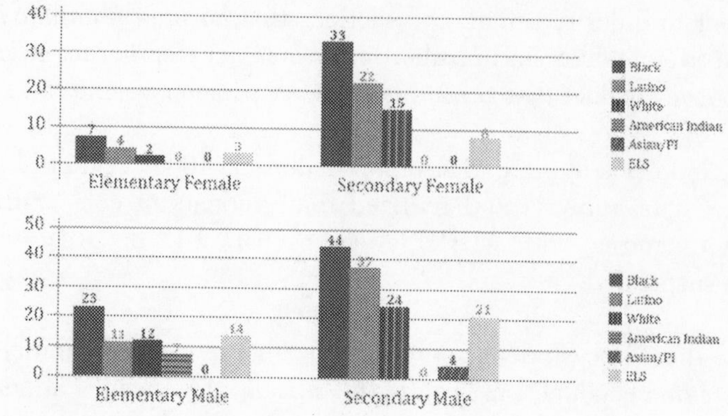

Note: All numbers rounded to the nearest whole number.

The graph shows a steep rise in the risk for suspension at the secondary level in the Syracuse City School District that is especially large for Black male students and Latino male students. Most notable is that 44% of Black secondary school males were suspended at least once. Second, Black females at the secondary level were suspended at a higher rate than most other male subgroups.

This collusion is occurring in the open and without mercy. Diagnosis of a behavioral disorder is consistent with the language of the code of conduct. The conducts that are considered disruptive or insubordinate and that endanger the safety, morals, and welfare of others are all consistent behaviors and symptoms of behavioral disorders.

Looking at the suspension reports and data from 2009 to 2012, it is easy to see that male and female students of color are labeled routinely disruptive and subsequently labeled as having a behavior problem.

Dr. Johnson acknowledges that inner-city children do not receive quality education. In fact, he asserts that black children receive inferior education from ineffective, uncaring, lethargic teachers. He poses a question (pg. 117–119): "How could any school psychologist in good conscience make a psycho-educational evaluation referral for a special education determination when so many receive a substandard education?" So prohibited conduct is a section of the code of conduct a parent and a student must understand and know how to interpret.

This is all quite a bit to take in, but understanding the policies that surround your child's conduct is imperative since suspension is a tool that is most used to push out African American and Latino and even African immigrants and refugees.

Now you are somewhat familiar with the disruptive and insubordinate conducts that lead to interventions and consequences (listed below).

Interventions and Consequences – for infractions of the Code of Conduct relating to disruptive behavior. Notice the first step is to notify parents, but again in our district, that is often not the step taken. It is here the parent will learn if the discipline was fair and consistent and if due process was followed when disciplinary action or referral results in suspension, especially if the administrator followed the code of conduct:

Interventions

1. Parent notification
2. Meet with administrator, parent, teacher, and student
3. Meet with concerned adult with influence in community (clergy, coach, probation officer, etc.)
4. Student court
5. Peer mediation
6. Meet with SIRP Officer
7. Anger management support
8. Meet with social worker/guidance counselor/psychologist to discuss reason and suggest group intervention; i.e. anger management
9. Meet with ADA-PEP counselor
10. Behavior contract with administrator, teacher, parent, student
11. Provide missed assignments with timeline for completion
12. Behavior plan
13. Meet with guidance to discuss course or reason for schedule or program change
14. SBIT referral
15. Functional behavior assessment
16. PST referral
17. Referral to CSE for program change or initial referral
18. Referral to mental health agency (CCSI, pastoral counseling, case management, alliance, etc.)
19. PINS referral by parent
20. Meet with outside agency(ies) and school team
21. Police notification
22. Youth court

Consequences

1. Parent notification
2. Teacher telephone call to parents
3. Written communication from teacher to parent; Re: Incident(s) request return telephone call
4. Meet with teacher or team and parent
5. Meet with teacher, student, and administrator
6. Letter of apology or personal apology
7. Conference with administrator to determine reason and cause
8. Conference with administrator to determine next consequence
9. Denial of privilege(s)—school function (dance, athletic event)
10. Restitution
11. Written description of the behavior and possible solution
12. School or community service that relates to behavior
13. Detention
14. Referral to attendance office/new attendance program
15. Saturday School
16. ISS 1, 2 days
17. OSS 1, 2, 3, 4, 5 days
18. Superintendent's Hearing/possible assignment to alternate program
19. Assigned to alternate to suspension site
20. Police involvement *(Taken from the SCSD's Code of Conduct Implementing Project SAVE Revised 2011 Interventions and Consequences)*

It is the hidden language in prohibited conduct and disruptive conduct contained within certain paragraphs and sections of the code of conduct that will confuse you. Some of these terms will not be familiar to you, so you must ask questions or for assistance in understanding the language contained in the code of conduct.

Parents, it will be difficult to know if due process and progressive discipline are being enforced if you do not understand the terms and definitions used. Become familiar with the document; it is a valuable resource. Take it from a parent who uses this document to assist and teach parents to advocate on behalf of their children, including my own;

it is a valuable resource. It may be time-consuming to read, but it's really beneficial to read the entire document and review it with your child.

Now I knew I needed stronger outside assistance to prove the findings and implement the right policies and procedures to deter the number of disparate suspensions within our district. So I called upon Dr. Umar Abdullah Johnson, nationally recognized school psychologist, to help process our experiences from the past (1993–2004), to know what was going on now (2010–13) with my eight-year-old great-nephew, and to help with our growing suspension rate, especially related to African American children with disabilities.

Since 2011, Dr. Umar has visited Syracuse three times, conducting workshops and presentations, advising parents, and reviewing IEPs. We are thankful to Dr. Johnson for his interest in assisting us in Syracuse in understanding better the dynamics of white teacher and black male student and African American administrators and teachers with snobbish attitudes, especially those making victims of their own race via education.

I sent letters to the Department of Justice, State attorney general's office, and the NYS Education Department's Office of Civil Rights, asking for an investigation of disparate suspensions of African American students and African American students with disabilities (see letters in the appendix).
Checklist of what every parent should know:

1. How to appeal a suspension
2. Rights students have in school
3. SROs
4. District report card—Is your school district a failing district?
5. The code of conduct
6. Rights for students with disabilities
7. Telephone numbers for the local chapters of the NY ACLU, NAACP, and NAN
8. How to handle the parent–teacher conference?
9. How to request services?
10. How to appeal denial of services?
11. How to read VADIR?
12. Medical symptoms related to the code of conduct for ADHD, ODD, and DBD.

Every parent should know that the following situations exist, and every parent should know what to do in these situations:

1. Dealing with black female teachers and administrators—snobbish behavior toward black parents and children
2. The white teacher—white women and men who fear black men and boys
3. The code of conduct and police in Syracuse schools: schoolyard to prison yard—a tool to push out black students

Chapter 18

Snobbish Black Female Teachers and Administrators or Principals: The Female House Negro

It is merely the ancient idea of calling upon the inferior to carry out the orders of the superior.
— Dr. Carter G. Woodson

The above quote answered my question: Why do so many African American female teachers and/or administrators view so many African American children and parents as useless to society and potential criminals?

I used to be a proponent of "black teacher for black children" until I came to Syracuse. I am not saying there are no good black teachers in Syracuse because there are some excellent, dedicated teachers and administrators in our school district. However, one bad apple tends to spoil the whole bunch in Syracuse!

This chapter and the next chapter mainly address the types of teacher attitudes, stereotypes, and prejudices that may be resulting in unfair treatment, bullying, routine referrals, or disciplinary actions, which may result in in-school suspension or out-of-school suspension (OSS). It is also to make the parent aware that it is not in your mind and that it does exist!

Parents, if you feel you are going through something similar or are living this and need assistance, e-mail me at twiggybillue@gmail.com or contact us at Hotep Resource Center (315) 395-2644.

I wanted to cut and paste the entire acknowledgment section of this book here, but it was too large. It contains the names of the finest African American teachers and principals and even district staff in Syracuse from 1992 to 2013. These are just some of the dedicated and committed African American teachers in Syracuse; this list is an ongoing list with additions occurring each year.

This chapter is not about the teachers and administrators mentioned above. This chapter is about a very different type of African American teacher or administrator. This teacher or administrator has been an ally and a buffer in the effort to push out students of color and in assisting to carry out a conspiracy to destroy black children, especially African American boys. The counteragent or the snobbish African American is committed to the miseducation of African American students and looks down on and snubs her nose at the African American parents. These are African American females that reduce their own race to stereotypes and the same prejudices that their parents once experienced.

This attitude is mainly the attitude of many African American female teachers and principals in our district. It is alarming to even consider that most of these females are either single or married parents of an African American child. The other half may not be parents, but they are intimately related by race to family member's children. So the thought of treating some better than others should not even cross your mind. It is hard to believe that because of circumstances that are out of a child's hand, anyone would miseducate or encourage substandard education for an African American child. However, due to failed personal relationships, single parenting, and absence of the father, some of these African American females project their hatred for black men on black students, in particular African American males, while others believe they are above those they teach and the student's parent(s).

I have found that these African American female teachers lost their way during that climb to the top (achievement). Somehow, they forgot where they came from. They forgot what our ancestors had to go through for them to become educated, hold well-paying jobs, and own a home. They forget the sacrifices their grandparents had to make for their parents to survive the racist years. Now that they are successful, they are "too good" to live in the community they were raised, and they despise it.

Maybe these African American females were not raised in the inner city. Maybe their parents gave them a suburban life, but they forgot where their parents had to climb up from. Those African American teachers and administrators whose ancestors and family resided in the 15th Ward have forgotten the destruction of the community. These female teachers feel that they are not a part of the overall black community and are unconcerned about the plight of the African American youth, student, or family.

These teachers and administrators are more concerned about putting other African Americans down, and they promote in telling parents how to parent instead of becoming a better teacher and/or administrator. These African American female teachers do not allow their own child to attend the inner-city schools they work at; instead, they attend charter, predominately white private or suburban schools in the greater Syracuse area.

Thank you, Dr. Umar Johnson, for your direction, wisdom, and knowledge and for being unafraid to state what others are afraid to! Dr. Kunjufu, thank you for coming to Syracuse and addressing our brothers, and I thank both of you for the insight provided in your books and lectures.

Before any person or person of color says this attitude doesn't exist, you should read the following:

1. Zoe Cornwall's *Human Rights in Syracuse: Two Memorable Decades a Selected History from 1963 to 1983*
2. Dr. Carter G. Woodson's *The Miseducation of the Negro*
3. Jawanza Kunjufu's *Countering the Conspiracy to Destroy Black Boys Vol. 2*
   a. *Countering the Conspiracy to Destroy Black Boys*
4. Dr. Umar Johnson's *Psycho-Academic Holocaust: the Special Education and ADHD Wars against Black Boys*
5. *Bridges Out of Poverty: Strategies for Professional and Communities Ruby K. Payne, Ph.D and Philip E. DeVol*
6. Dr. Frances Cress Welsing's *The Isis Papers*

Before any person or person of color says this attitude doesn't promote the unfair suspension of a student, especially students with a disability or ADHD, you should read or view the following DVDs:

1. Dr. Amos Wilson, *Blueprint for Black Power*, Chapter 9, pg. 192
2. *Waiting for Superman*, Paramount Home Entertainment, 2011 (DVD)
3. Dr. Umar Johnson, *Special Education to Special Medication Learning Disabilities and ADHD*
4. Dr. Umar Johnson, *The Psycho-Academic War on Black Boys Exposed Pt. 2 Special*

Our district is failing and schools here are at the bottom with regard to ELA test scores. You may be willing to work with the school, the district board, and the administration; however, they may be reluctant. I am sure of one thing: "Education is supposed to be fair and equal." If parental support and participation is not encouraged (by the teacher, the school, and the district) to keep your child on track, beware!

Don't be afraid to challenge decisions, be persistent, or to request for outside assistance from outside entities such as the local National Action Network Chapter, the local American Civil Liberties Union (ACLU), US Department of Education, the attorney general (in your state), and the State Department of Education (in your state). You will get the assistance you need if you stay persistent.

But what do you do when the harm is being caused by the booshie African American teacher or administrator?

My husband has experienced situations during his own education in Syracuse. These experiences have historical significance in what is occurring in Syracuse schools today. The demolition and the restructuring of the 15th Ward have provided some significant insight into the history of African American students and unfair and substandard education in Syracuse. This is important to mention as we begin to discuss this topic because we have seen a trend in the type of teachers now responsible for educating our children. When my husband attended school in Syracuse, it was during desegregation efforts in the Syracuse School District.

We noticed that most of my husband's teachers were African American teachers who lived in the Syracuse Community and were committed to providing quality education for all children, not miseducating our children—African American children. This is important to note when looking at the discipline or the climate of the school because understanding the culture of the students makes a difference in your teaching. It does not mean you have to be a black teacher to teach black children, but it does mean you have to understand the culture their experiences are based on. When the 15th Ward was demolished and eighty-one was being constructed, our businesses, schools, and homes were demolished. This pushed out African American families and those with little to no means into unreceptive neighborhoods and schools. Those African Americans who desired to follow the white flight from the city fled to the suburbs in search of better homes, schools, and safety. This flight is still occurring today.

In 2013, this piece of history shed light on that segregated school board meeting in May. It also shed light on white and African American flight from the city. Since the early eighties, "black flight" to white suburban neighborhoods has increased rampantly. Moreover, it shed light on the miseducation of the African American students and how that miseducation could lead to suspension.

Some great educators we continue to encounter are Ms. Ranieri, Mrs. Turner, Mrs. Speight, Mr. Dowdell, Mr. Betsey, Mrs. D. Williams, Ms. Debbie Cooke, Mrs. Shield, Mrs. Messina-Yauchzy, Mrs. Schoening, Mrs. Masingale, Grandma, Mrs. Brown, Mrs. Hunter, Mrs. Ellis, Mrs. Caldwell-Gerald, Mrs. Morgan, Mrs. Brooks, Mr. Bacon, Ms. Nelson, Mr. Gangemi, Mrs. Wilson, Mr. Jones, etc. They have set a standard we expect from all educators.

In 1963, the 15th Ward was demolished, and now in 2013, most professional African Americans and whites have moved outside the city.

These were old school teachers; it didn't matter who the child's family was or where the child lived. They lived in the community that was a part of the grapevine. They would chastise the student in a manner that produced the needed results and would not belittle or degrade a child—never a black child publicly or a parent publicly or privately. This is not the case now.

It was bad enough; implicit bias was at play, but now we were experiencing bias from black teachers. Any type of bias is really dangerous when used to attack the psyche of the young black male and female students. What happens when the African American female teacher doesn't like black men because of hurt and past reminders? What happens to the black male students when that attitude is applied to his education? What happens when African American teachers view themselves as different from the African American students they teach and their parents? It is a fact every African American parent must think about. I didn't make this up nor I am writing about it to stir things up, but this story must be told.

In the late 1999, the trend was to move out of the city but work in the city for African Americans wanting to escape the violent and declining city. This was also when my husband began to bring my attention to the attitude of African American female teachers and administrators, especially when dealing with male students of color and male parents of color.

From 1997 to 1999, we encountered two African American teachers who caused us to realize this was real. Even when the teacher's diversity matches the diversity of the children, it may not be a good thing. We thought these aspiring African American teachers (now administrators) would be good influences and role models for our children. They were not!

Both teachers were well known in the community and had attended public schools, but we didn't know they were not liked by other African American parents, especially parents who lived where we use to live—in SHA's Brickcity. There was a visible difference in their attitude and in the way they addressed African American parents versus white parents, especially the way they addressed the parents who lived across the street in the housing projects. They spoke down to parents, looked them up and down, and whispered about a person's clothing or living conditions.

Then there were the Billues and several other parents like us whom people didn't know how to deal with. I, on the other hand, have always learned to assert my privilege. I was raised that way and have never looked back. I have the same privileges as anyone else, but I have learned that in Syracuse you had to assert them or you would be walked over and unheard. We were equal to any white or black well-educated person, working good full-time jobs. The only difference was I didn't have to work, but I wanted to work.

My husband had a very good job at the local housing authority, and all I had to do was raise our children, while he provided everything else. We wanted to buy a house. We lived in Brickcity and were in the process of purchasing a house in the third district, and that was almost unheard of in Syracuse. I never knew how they had attempted to treat my husband until he mentioned an incident at the school. One snobbish African American teacher attempted to dismiss him, my son, and his comments. This African American teacher turned up her nose, then her back on him, and attempted to walk away, telling him to put his concerns in writing.

Often when he picked up our children, the attitude displayed was "I got mine. Now you are beneath me." This did not go over well with my husband. I remember my husband being approached after another encounter with a new black administrator. Two African American male teachers indicated, "This black women shows dislike and disregard toward men and black male students." The fact was they shared a lot with my husband about several so-called educated but snobbish black teachers. Some comments were that they "hated black men" for some personal reason or "baby daddy" issues. I knew it was true, but something you didn't think would be played out on your son or husband, but sometimes it would.

I remember being warned about these teachers when we volunteered for Picture Day at Dr. King School as members of the PTO. We never had any encounter with these teachers, but several friends and family members had negative encounters, especially with one teacher in particular. This senior African American teacher displayed a superior attitude and contempt for students and parents that were not on her level.

I knew this was true when she made the following comment to an African American student. This young man didn't want his picture taken for some reason, and she replied, "You better take this picture. It might be the last picture you take without numbers across your chest," and she laughed out loud. The PTO president and her husband looked astonished, but of course, my rebuttal challenged the other parents present to demand she apologize to the student.

This teacher looked surprised that I had challenged her statement and her authority, but she quickly recanted the statement and left the area. Our problems with this teacher did not surface again until after the principal and the vice principal left Dr. King School. This teacher against our better judgment became our daughter's teacher in the fourth grade. After that encounter, she never taught in a classroom again. The point is she was never able to damage the psyche of another black student in a classroom, as her actions were exposed.

This was the year the new principal and the vice principal lost control of the school and our last year at Dr. King School. The attitudes of these snobbish, uncaring African American teachers worsened, and the new administrators seemed to have no control over white or black teachers. Most of the teaching staff looked down on their capabilities and did not respect their authority.

The former principal and vice-principal hadn't allowed such behavior. If it surfaced, it was quickly quelled and dealt with. The parent did not know what corrective measures were taken to address the teacher's behavior. But the parent did know that her intervention would be swift, quiet, and discreet. The parent could also count on the problem or issue being handled fairly. Everyone in the school, like it or not, knew she was the head person in charge, no matter whether you were white or black!

Even though a lot of teachers loved us and our advocacy for our children, a lot of teachers at Dr. King (later throughout the district) didn't like the Billues. Everyone knew not to let the backlash show on our children. This was the point when that actually occurred. My husband is a big and tall man with a very deep voice. He is very passionate and loving, but if you mess with his wife and/or children, you will see a very different person. In the second grade, my husband accompanied my son to the school to inquire about the bruises on his arm, and he encountered one of these snobbish women.

The encounter in the office that day led to intervention by the former principal and an apology from the office staff. My husband had arrived to discuss the bruises on our son and to schedule a meeting with the teacher and others that day. However, the encounter with this snobbish African American staff person caused my husband to leave the school (with our son in tow). He had to take off the remainder of the day from work, and it also caused me to leave work early to address the matter.

The apology was not going to be good enough because now we had two issues. When teachers lose respect for the students they teach and the people they work for (the parents who are also taxpayers), it may be time to realign priorities, ask for professional development, or prepare to lose your ability to teach. I am not saying they must be fired immediately, but they must be taken out of the classroom and/or mentored by a master teacher. It the teacher is not receptive to the idea or the possibility, then they should lose their job, and that's a real possibility when dealing with the Billue family.

This encounter was not about the bruising issue. Now we wondered why this African American woman was providing a buffer for this teacher's behavior. My husband was there to speak with the social worker, not the principal. This snobbish African American woman thought he was unemployed and uneducated, but she was wrong. More importantly, it should not have mattered because no matter what, he deserved respect. She told him, pointing her finger and speaking through her nose, "We are too busy to help you. Write it down, and I'll have someone call you." When my husband indicated he had an appointment, she turned around again, pointing her finger and stating, "Didn't you hear what I said?"

My husband's replied, "Yes, but first who are you?"

The woman now seemed incensed that he had asked any question and replied, "Why?"

Now upset, my husband responded, "Because you control nothing here, do you?" Now remember, our son was with my husband, and this woman was about to attempt to block his path to leave, since he was standing in the middle of the entrance leading out of the main office. Suddenly my son told his father to call me, and that's when the behavior ceased, according to my husband's account. My son tugged on his father's hand, stating, "Daddy! Call Mommy! She will stop yelling if you call Mommy!" The look of bewilderment came across her face, and she now asked my husband, "Are you Mr. Billue?"

It was too late; the look on my husband's face must have indicated. All she could do was move back behind the counter and remain silent as he proceeded to leave the school. The principal was with another parent in her office, but she had heard portions of the encounter. We both thought her attempt to interfere with the social worker's involvement was peculiar. We had been warned about her behavior toward black males, but this encounter and because the social worker was an older black man verified the superior and elitist attitude. This very dark-skinned African American woman made negative comments about black colleagues, parents, and now to my husband during the encounter. The comments didn't sit well with my husband, the social worker, or the principal, and the teacher was removed from front office duties. A meeting was scheduled concerning the bruises, which will be discussed later.

This is when I realized that there were lots of African American female teachers in this school district who do not have any regard for responsibly educating African American children.

My husband reminded me of the statements of Dr. Carter G. Woodson prior to the meeting. The comments were from the book *The Miseducation of the Negro*.

Dr. Woodson asserts, "The educated Negros have a contemptuous attitude toward their own people because they are taught to admire the Greek, Latin, etc., and despise the African during their education." Sadly, we found this to be true. Hearing the words "a large majority of Negro educators are all but worthless in the development of their people" was disheartening, but we also found it to be true. Our experiences within this school district and the experiences of others proved that many African

American teachers do not allow their children to attend public schools (*Miseducation of the Negro* 2005).

This was an eye-opening experience; moreover, I couldn't just continue to ignore that it was a real problem. Dr. Woodson realized this attitude existed in the black community, and now we were face-to-face with it. This black woman had been warned that I was dangerous, but she had never met my husband. When he presented himself at the school that day, she made assumptions based on partial knowledge and his work clothes and the tone of his voice. This woman was not prepared for this meeting, but now it was unavoidable. My husband is a very respectful man, but if you attempt to publicly belittle his children or him, you will be in for an unexpected surprise.

At the beginning of the meeting, the teacher once again attempted to apologize, but it was too late. My husband's words and comments rang out like Malcom X, making "the Ballot or the Bullet" speech, but he used the powerful "cut you off at the knees" words of Dr. Carter G. Woodson. His words were so powerful the people in the room (all African American) began to tear up. The point that she made assumptions based on partial knowledge and her attempt to demean him in front of his male child was the reason for his anger. He outlined what her actions as a black woman meant in promoting self-hate.

I didn't say a word when they looked at me to stop his comments so they could provide a voice of reasoning. When he asserted his belief that "this black woman had a hatred of black men" and that her personal issues should not be played out in school, the teacher and the principal were floored, absolutely speechless. This was his first personal encounter with this staff person, and it was highly negative due to her snobbish attitude and her assumptions based on false knowledge.

This was not my husband's assertion, but she needed to know that her snobbish, elitist attitude was consistent with the "educated Negro" as described by Dr. Carter G. Woodson. She needed to know the epitome of the educator or the educated Negro who believes in the "inferiority of the uneducated Negro." However, by now, everyone had understood exactly who my husband was and that he was not that stereotypical Negro!

Dr. Woodson asserts, "The inferiority of the Negro was drilled into her in every class this African American female took at the institute of higher education she attended and now she was able to miseducate the uneducated Negro she despises (that messes it up for her advancement) and she feels no connection to the Negro life only the white life" (2005).

Silence fell over the room, but no one dared to challenge the comment. The point was made clear, and the attitude and behavior were checked. We received another apology, a very humbling apology, but it was too late. From that point forward, this teacher avoided us like the plague. Our feelings didn't change after the meeting because the behavior had to be checked.

Realizing that my husband was forewarned was disturbing because it indicated the behavior toward African American male teachers and students had been occurring for a while. I didn't know why the new administrators and parents feared these teachers' attitudes and behavior, but it was checked that day. It never reared its ugly head again, at least not with our family.

Not every African American educator has the snobbish attitude, but it does exist, and it can harm your child if not checked immediately. This was real. This black female teacher's hatred for the black male was being played out in the classroom with the black boys. This experience is so covert you may not realize it is occurring because the teacher is an African American, so it throws you off balance. It took me by surprise but not my husband; he called it the educated Negro syndrome.

What I once thought was impossible, I now knew was the truth—the whole ugly truth.

How is a student of color supposed to succeed when the snobbish black teacher or administrator despises him or her and the white female and male teacher historically fears him?

This was during the time frame when my niece was living with us; she was having issues with her classmates and her teacher. We were not aware this aspiring young teacher was a snobbish African American teacher, but we soon found out that indeed she was that type of "educated Negro"—one with an enslaved mind-set regarding their own race.

For some reason, this woman didn't like the fact my niece's rights were upheld, and she decided to inflict another type of teacher bias on her psyche. This was not due to her being intellectually gifted; it was something much worse. This teacher was hand-picked by the principal to motivate and nurture our niece's exceptional talents; however, this teacher had a different idea in mind.

A lot of teachers talked about our hand in her previous teacher's removal or leaving Elmwood, and most resented our tactics. It seemed no one had dealt with anyone like the Billues prior to 1996 in Syracuse. I took advantage of that power and asserted my privilege and knowledge every time we needed to equal or level the field. Sometimes, regardless of color, we have to bring those in authority (especially those with the HNIC mind-set) to their knees! Everyone in Syracuse knew my husband and I were not afraid of the long, hard fight, and no one welcomed the battle.

If you mess over or with my children or any child, you would definitely feel the whirlwind.

My niece was a good-sized child, but she was always well dressed as were all our children. Her size was never an issue until that school year. My niece alleged that the teacher made fun of her and allowed several girls in the classroom make fun of her size and her medical condition. My niece indicated the teacher had commented on her outfit, stating she didn't know "Talbots Kids made clothing that large." Then according to my niece, the teacher told her, "Don't go running to your aunt. I was playing." Was she being teased or bullied by the teacher? Was the comment coded for "Tell your aunt what I said"? I was not sure what was going on; why did she attempt to engage me, and why did her size matter? Now I had to look into the comments. Why did it matter that her clothing was from Talbots or even Talbots Kids or the sizes the stores made? Where was this coming from? Did the teacher really want a confrontation with me?

I became curious and decided that I needed to pay this teacher a visit, but my husband discouraged it due to the comments and my nature. My husband told me that he wanted to observe the classroom dynamics and did so the next day. For some reason, he knew there was much more going on, and he needed to switch up the players; instead of me, it would be him this time. This time he was going to investigate the situation during his lunch period. My niece is a very honest person, so he knew something more was going on.

Parents and readers, please note that while I reviewed law and policy, my husband studied master teachers such as Dr. Amos Wilson, Dr. Carter G. Wilson, Dr. Frances Cress Welsing, and many others who opened his consciousness in ways that allowed him to see things I didn't see. Everyone wants to see and think the best about a person, even denying what may be obvious. My husband will not stand idly by and let certain behavior, comments, bias, racism, prejudices, or stereotypes from anyone just pass. He has to call it out and expose them. He has a unique ability to call it what it is, no matter where he is, but he is especially perceptive when the fury is against his children.

During his visit the next day, he was bothered by the attitude of the teacher toward him while he was visiting the classroom. He mentioned the condescending tone she used to describe my niece and her assumptions about her home life (again assumptions based on partial knowledge), including a previous encounter she had with my sister.

Once my husband told the teacher she lived with us, the teacher replied, "Oh, that's why she dresses better now."

My husband turned around and said, "What did you say?"

To his surprise, this African American female teacher said, "Don't you live in the projects?" Of course, from there her feelings were hurt and now my husband was a "mean person." It was her assumptions based on partial knowledge, not his comments. Assumptions based on partial knowledge can be detrimental to the person making the assumption; this teacher found this out quickly.

Now pissed off, he replied, "Where we live is none of your business. Your business is teaching, and you need to pay more attention to teaching instead of things that are not your concern." As he left the room (now angry), he told the teacher, "Our niece is not responsible for buying her clothing or her living arrangements, but I will inform my wife of your concern." He described the look on teacher's face and her expression as fearful, as if her nemesis was being summoned, and she knew the outcome was not going to be positive.

The teacher quickly stated to my husband, "Getting your wife involved is not necessary. Let me explain," but it was too late.

As far as he was concerned, it was time to release the whirlwind of the lioness! This teacher didn't know me at all. She only knew of gossip regarding my sister and that my sister was known for chaos. I am sure she had heard through the grapevine about me, but it was based on assumption. The thing everyone knew was that I was known for taking action and understanding how to use policies and laws to protect the rights of our children!

Now visibly concerned, this teacher didn't realize she had clearly upset the one person that usually didn't lose his cool. Now he needed to leave before he said something else, and he didn't trust this teacher's intentions concerning our niece. Even more troubling than her statements was that my husband felt the need to call me (something rarely done) to handle a situation.

For my husband to demand that I go to the school and speak to "this woman" meant it was a serious situation. It indeed had escalated from concern about my niece, and now he felt that he had been dismissed and that both my niece and he were disrespected.

When he filled me in, I decided to take my lunch break at the school. I arrived at around 11:30 a.m. during the second lunch, so I decided to have lunch with my son and niece. Then during the third lunch, I could have lunch with my elder child, my daughter. This was something we did regularly each week, but today it was to monitor this situation. It was also to monitor things since our experiences at Dr. King School and at the Solace School left us in a defensive watchdog state.

As I walked into the lunchroom, my son immediately motioned me to his area. I told the teacher he was having lunch with me, and we moved to another area. I didn't see my niece, and then my son told me she was in the hallway crying. I left to find her, and once I did, I saw that she was indeed in tears as she came out of the bathroom. I noticed she had a disposable ice pack wrapped in a paper towel on her face, so I asked her what had happened. She told me a classmate had punched her in the face, and the ice pack was given to her by the nurse to prevent bruising.

Now I was puzzled as we didn't get a phone call that she was hit and needed to visit the nurse. As I turned to ask her teacher what had happened, she replied, "Ms. Thing here got smacked in the face by another student"! I thought out loud, "What did you just say? What did you just call my niece?" The teacher stepped back, but before I could think, I stepped forward, making the space between us small and uncomfortable.

It is important to note that I choose to be nonviolent instead of violent, but don't take it for weakness or take me for granted when it comes to my children. While I studied, researched, and reviewed law and policy, my husband studied master teachers such as Dr. Amos Wilson, Dr. Carter G. Wilson, Dr. Frances Cress Welsing, and many others who talked about this very behavior of black educators, but there comes a time when *you have to be ready and willing to name it and call it out!*

No one was ready for this, absolutely no one. My husband believes wholeheartedly in Dr. Woodson's comments, especially about the educated Negro despising his or her own people, and the concept being fresh propelled me to confront it head-on. The hallway began to shrink, and before I realized it, the teacher was backed into a corner.

The principal overheard my questions, and as she turned the corner and realized who it was; she was surprised and it showed on her face. She didn't interfere just yet because she was assisting another student, but she had spoken with my husband and she knew I was at the school.

None of us knew my niece had been assaulted by another student until that point. The principal didn't even know until then. After speaking to my husband, the principal had planned to call a meeting between the teacher and my husband, but now it had escalated and was much more serious.

Assumptions based on partial knowledge can be deadly for a relationship as this teacher had no idea who my husband was or his relationship with this African American principal.

This African American principal was his former elementary teacher—one that made an impact on who he is today. This principal held him in tremendous regard and gave him the highest respect, especially as he was an involved parent.

My questions to the teacher were relentless: "Why was my niece assaulted by another student in the classroom? Why was she sent to the nurse and the parent or the guardian was not notified? How was this allowed to happen? And who the hell is Ms. Thing?"

My niece was not a fighter; in fact, she would not fight back even to defend herself. Normally my daughter or my son would stand up for her or defend her, but this time neither was around. The teacher was surprised to see how upset I had become, especially regarding the Ms. Thing comment, and she tried to re-explain what had happened.

I cut her off at the first utter of sound! I put my hand up in a "stop or talk to the hand" position, warning her that "one more Ms. Thing could result in fisticuffs," and she instantly became silent. Then the ramifications of her actions got real for this teacher. I looked over at my niece and suddenly realized that as much as I wanted to set her straight I had to retreat.

I saw fear in this teacher's eyes and on the face of my niece. My niece feared for the safety of her teacher. Violence had a real impact on my niece, as it was one of the reasons that she lived with us. She was not an abused child, but violence was a part of her life's situation. She was physically hit by another student and she was punished while the other student was touted for the act, and this alone could affect her psyche.

My sister arrived at the school, and when she entered the lunch corridor, she heard my loud comments (my husband had also informed her of the incident) and began to rush to the area where we were. I looked up when I heard the principal telling her to calm down and that the situation was under control. The principal knew that if my sister heard the commotion and that her child was assaulted by another student and that no discipline was applied, there was going to be chaos. I knew it too!

My sisters are known as the "smack you first and ask questions later" in matters concerning family. Striking a teacher, fighting a large man, or even tussling with a police officer was a possibility, depending on her mindset. This sister was known as my bodyguard, as captioned by my husband in earlier years. If she thought I was being challenged, disrespected, or the focus of gossip, she was known to jump in your face without hesitation regardless of the potential for arrest. It was even worse when it came to her children or my children, and everyone seemed to know her reputation.

Just wait until she found out her child had been assaulted by another student and blamed for the behavior. Just wait until she heard her child was referred to as "Ms. Thing" and was told "her child got what she deserved it for getting smart with the other student." I almost felt sorry for this teacher, but it was reckoning time. The look on the principal's face said it all, and I could see this wasn't going to go well if I didn't calm my sister down. Never underestimate a child's level of perception, especially two gifted children. My son called out his aunt's name and ran into her arms, causing a shift in her demeanor. As she reached down to hug and kiss him, my niece called out "Mommy" and ran to her as well. They somehow directed her to the lunch line while I spoke with the principal. I didn't realize it until later on, but their excitement in seeing her turned the tide of the tension. They provided a much-needed buffer as she learned about the assault and the subsequent visit to the nurse.

We met with the principal at 1:30 p.m., and my husband was now present. Mrs. Williams informed the teacher that this meeting had been requested by Mr. Billue with regard to comments made during his earlier visit. In particular, it was about the comments made in the classroom and about her clothing and her physical attributes. The last thing we would discuss was the hitting incident that had not been reported to the parent or the principal.

Immediately, the teacher became defensive and adversarial, making a smart under-the-breath remark to the principal. However, this principal didn't allow whispers and innuendos; instead, she stated what the teacher had whispered. The principal asked the teacher, "So you are stating that since Mr. Billue's visit wasn't announced, you may not have been welcoming?"

The teacher turned toward my husband and was about to say something when I cut her off. I told her to quit while she was ahead any smart-assed thing she was about to say. "Keep it to yourself and just listen." I really felt the need to let this woman know this was not a joke!

I informed the teacher if she attempted to assert her snobbish and condescending attitude instead of accepting responsibility for her actions and respecting my husband's feelings in my presence, it was not my sister she would have to worry about.

I guess my expression and body language said it all; there was not another word uttered by anyone except my husband while we all sat there and listened. The teacher was not in the mediation between the two students the next morning, but it was during that meeting we learned about the teacher-led teasing and bullying. The other student's parent was offended that her child was encouraged to tease and hit another student. However, the student's version of the incident happened to match our niece's story, especially with regard to teasing by the teacher regarding her size and clothing. This did not excuse the assault, but it provided some clarity on the matter.

This child indicated she was encouraged to tease my niece by the teacher, but this time my niece stated, "I am telling my cousin (that is my daughter)," and she smacked her in the face. Somehow, that was a signal for the teacher to add the "call your aunt and your momma too" remark according to this student. Of course, the teacher denied telling either student anything of the sort, but even so, the allegation was out there. My husband had to break this vicious cycle by asserting his privilege and calling out the snobbish behavior, using the powerful words of the master teachers.

This snobbish attitude is still reflected by the same individuals in our school district today. Now the attitudes are reflected in their "suspending authority," and it shows in the suspension rate at their schools. These are African American teachers and administrators who seem to despise black children so much they suspend them at will. Some of the teachers mentioned are either now retired, the current dean of students, or vice principals, but most left their suspension mark and used it to make their despise for students of color known.

In 2013, two were school administrators; their schools are among the highest suspending schools in the district.

During the 2010–11 and 2011–12 school years, I accompanied our eight-year-old great-nephew and his mother to several meetings regarding his "disruptive behavior" at Frazer School. Each time I attended, there was a noticeable number of K-8 grade students who were being sent home at 9:30 a.m. The students were not suspended but sent home to cool off or calm down because the teacher had removed the student from the classroom.

I noticed immediately that the policy of teacher removal of a student was being implemented incorrectly, but at first, it fell on deaf ears. The principals attempted to justify the need for sending the student home by indicating disruptive behavior. Then I realized most of the students were not sent home by the teacher; it was the principal or his or her designee. It was the resurfacing of the snobbish black teacher or administrator.

Parents began to contact me regarding the matter, in particular about the attitude of school administration, i.e., principals, vice principals, and dean of students. These conversations often led to attending school meetings with the parent and the student, and I began to experience firsthand the condescending tone used by administrators, but I was especially disturbed by the condescending and insulting attitude of the African American administrators.

I remember this vice principal at a school located on Wall Street on the city's Westside. This African American female administrator displayed a very snobbish upper-class disposition while speaking to black parents (including parents I worked with). Several complained about this African American woman and asked me to attend the meetings. But I never had the pleasure of meeting this woman except for observing from a distance.

What I did witness was very noticeable: This administrator would show certain courtesy to the white parents that the black parents were not shown—courtesies such as acknowledgment, handshakes, and salutations—but when it came to African American parents, there was no interest. There were no good mornings, just snub-nosed looks from head to toe and rolling eyes. Our relationship became adversarial instantly even before I had attended a meeting with a parent.

In the second week of school, we had a transportation issue regarding our nephew's pickup time. We waited for over thirty minutes for the vice principal, but we didn't know she had no intention of meeting with us. When she entered the office, the secretary told her I was waiting to speak with her regarding transportation. The vice principal walked over to where I was seated, looked at me from head to toe, and stated, pointing her finger in the air and speaking through her nostrils, "I don't have time to deal with your transportation issue right now."

Now I had waited for over thirty minutes and I was standing right in front of this woman, and she didn't have time to "deal with my issue." I was standing there, looking at this woman, and I said, "What did you just say?"

The vice principal grabbed a post-it note from the desk of the secretary and a pen, pushed them onto the counter in front of me, and replied, "Write your issues or questions down on this piece of paper and go home. I will call you later when I have time to deal with it."

She turned and walked away, throwing her scarf across her shoulder, then I stated, "Excuse me, who do you think you are talking to?" My expression must have been powerful because my thoughts were *What the hell did this woman just say to me? I know she didn't just brush me off and flick her scarf? Calm down. She has no idea of who you are or does she?*

This was my first experience with this African American school administrator, and this was the 2010–11 school year, not the 1996–97 school year, but the attitude was the same, if not worse. Many parents had complained about this vice principal's attitude, but it had fallen on deaf ears until now as I had proof of the superior attitude. Little did she know I could also assert a superior attitude, especially when I know I have more power and the person is my equal, who is pretending to be my superior.

This African American snobbish female let stereotypes and my physical appearance fool her into thinking I was her subordinate. She had no idea of the power and privilege I possessed and commanded, but she was to learn quickly about me. This vice principal was about to find out about me in the worst way, the hard way as an adversary, instead of as an ally, and that was not good.

As she attempted to walk away, I raised my tone and said, "No, actually you are going to assist me and assist me now!" She turned around abruptly, and I firmly stated, "If you are the person in charge of transportation for the school, you will assist me now!" Before she could utter a word, to the contrary, I continued, "I am here now, and you will address my issues now. You will not treat me like you do others!" I told her very firmly, looking her in the eyes and without expression, "I am not an uneducated parent. You are not my superior. You will meet with me now because I am your equal and because I am here now!"

When the vice principal again attempted to reply, I silenced her, looking straight into her eyes and stating, "Why do you give black people such a hard time? I don't work for you! You work for me, and you must speak to me with dignity and respect if you want it in return!"

Silence fell over the office; everyone was looking down, but it was very quiet. I was not loud or disorderly but honest, respectful, and firm. I continued to publicly question her consistent, condescending tone and snobbish attitude, asking, "What have I done to deserve the treatment?" Then I told her what I had witnessed (in front of everyone in the office) the week prior while assisting a parent and what I had witnessed today while waiting to see her.

I indicated, "The parent you assisted prior to me (white and well dressed) was extended niceties, salutations, and handshakes. He was treated with dignity, respect, and courtesy, the very things you denied my child and me this morning. Why?" I added that I worked just like she did and that my time was just as valuable as her time. Now she was becoming aware that I was not the type of person that "you can dismiss like a subordinate" and it was "not going to be easy to mistreat us." I firmly stated, "I am here now and late for work, and you will not send me home like a child. You will deal with me as if I am your equal. Do you have a problem with that?" I was not loud, vulgar, or cursing.

Of course, I had that look in my eyes (everyone who knows me knows the look), but I was very relaxed, regal, and confident. I didn't fit the angry, ghetto black woman stereotype this vice principal assigned me to be. She anticipated hands flailing about, head shaking, hands clapping, speaking slang, and cursing. In fact, that is exactly what she expected; instead, she was educated the hard way.

This changed the whole dynamics of the encounter; the vice principal was visibly upset, but she did not dare retort. Instead, she crumpled up the post-it and asked me to follow her to her office. Our transportation issue was resolved within five minutes, no more, no less. Upon my departure, I told the vice principal that we still needed to have a larger conversation with the principal about our now strained relationship.

This was our very first interaction, our first occasion to meet, and it was not a positive interaction. When the only person who can resolve your child's issues treats you with this "I am better than you are. Kiss the ground I walk on" attitude, students and parents need to be prepared for a rocky road. I later learned my calm demeanor and manner of speaking put fear in the room, or at least that was the rumor in the school and that I was not the typical Negro.

Dr. Umar Johnson was able to shed some light on the issue for us in 2011. This was one of the reasons that led him to become a certified principal. He acknowledged, "There are some very effective and committed African American principals who fight for the proper education of students of color." However, he noticed something disturbing: "The amount of African–American principals who did not appear to have any commitment or regard for the education of African–American children."

This was not his theory, but Dr. Johnson had witnessed it throughout his experience as a school psychologist. I knew he was being blatantly honest, and as much as I wanted him to say "No, it's not true," I needed to be reminded that indeed there were many educated Negros, especially among black teachers and administrators, who despised their own race. These elitist African American teachers and administrators view those who have not achieved what they have to be a lower class of African Americans.

Dr. Johnson acknowledges, "Elitist blacks including many principals often feel superior to parents and children" and "that education is the venue to tell African American mothers and fathers how to become better parents." The difference is that these African American teachers and administrators and principals "are not receptive to parents telling them how to become better principals." I was not surprised when he also referred to Dr. Carter G. Woodson's statement: "The college-educated African American is seldom of any use to his race."

Now just because the road is rocky doesn't make it impassable; it makes it slower and longer to travel on, so don't back down!

Remember, at all times, no matter who you are dealing with "you are my equal. You are not more than me or less than me. You must always remember we are equal and you must respect me!" Don't be afraid to pull the carpet out from under the person or knock the wind out of them with words and facts. When you lose sight of who you are, it is easy to disregard those you think and feel are different. When you lose respect for others because you feel you are superior to that person, your vision and ability to treat the person equally is blurred. You must be willing to bring that blurred vision back into alignment by asserting your rights and privileges.

There can no longer be acceptance of an elitist demoralizing the parent or the child, engaging the parent into an argument so the teacher or the principal can dismiss them and the issue. The day of reckoning is on the SCSD and the educated Negro teacher or principal.

The days of the parent being unheard, banned from the school, or escorted out of school building by police are over. "Schools must be controlled by the community" (Johnson, pg. 35).

My husband calls these elitist teachers the COINTELPRO agents residing in our community who aid in the miseducation of our children and destroy the black family structure. They are professional African Americans who denounce other African Americans, who they consider are living a lesser life or who have not achieved what they have achieved. These African American professionals are doctors, lawyers, teachers, etc., and they despise:

1. Black people who are loud in public
2. Black people who draw unnecessary attention to themselves
3. Black people who listen to loud music, rap, or hip-hop music
4. Black people who use poor grammar or slang
5. Black people who wear dreadlocks, do-rags, or a natural hairdo, considering them as unkept hair.

My weapon was different from that of my husband's. I was using policies and my rights to assert a certain privilege that no one seemed prepared to deal with.

Who is teaching our child? Where did they receive their education? Who are these people?

Since so many assumptions were being made based on partial knowledge or from gossip, we needed to flex our rights and privileges, and this didn't make folks happy. These snobbish African American female teachers and administrators had a lot of personal and confidential information about our family so now we wanted to know who these people were as well.

This did not go over well with these snobbish African American female teachers. The mere fact that I had requested information about their qualifications, schooling, and certification and/or licensing and whether they were qualified to teach the grade assigned was like the FBI prying into their lives.

Our weapon, which you will hear more about in the next chapter, was the FOIL now covered under No Child Left Behind. Once the principal notified the teacher, we inquired about them or complained to the district and NYS. The elitist, snobbish attitude instantly ceased with regard to my husband, our niece, and our children each time it appeared during the period 1994–2011.

It was strange how the attitudes changed each time, even this time, because parents have a right to know. Now even the staff asserted a new attitude that "our students and learning came first." The tools in our toolbox became weapons in our arsenal. Why did we have to go to war to stop the BS? By this time, I didn't mind sending the message that the Billues are serious and that they don't play around when it comes to their children. Some admired our efforts and some did not, but everyone respected how we wielded our power, asserted our privilege, and exercised our rights.

To stop these African American snobbish teachers from sharing gossip and transferring biased personal opinions of us (the parent) and of our children, we used a hidden component of FERPA to stop these copy room sessions. Personal written notes and opinions of teachers that were not in the public realm could not be shared with school staff.

Family Educational Rights and Privacy Act Regulations
(FERPA) 34 CFR Part 99

FERPA states your child's biometric record cannot be shared. This means a record of one or more measurable biological or behavioral characteristics that can be used for automated recognition of an individual cannot be shared without your written consent. A teacher's personal notes about a student should not be made available or viewable to other school personnel, especially when the details of the notes are only of personal nature or biased or if the details are not publicly known by other school personnel.

Not even the district legal department knew how to answer this assertion. We never got a response, but that gossip toned down, especially once the teacher at Solace School found out who we are from the facts instead of believing the gossip. That stopped the gossip and the teachers from planting negative seeds. It stopped the transfer of private information and the projected stereotypes based on assumption from becoming a part of freely discussed topics among teachers—all under the allegation that it may negatively impact our child's learning environment.

The snobbish African American female teacher is a dangerous person to trust regarding educating our children. They loathe the very student they are responsible for educating and the very student who belongs to the same race as they do. Dr. Woodson stated that the consumer pays the tax, and therefore, as such every individual of the social order should be given unlimited opportunity to make the most of himself and not to be judged or treated substandard by the very person receiving the payment for their services, i.e., the snobbish African American teacher or administrator or, as my husband calls both male and female African American teachers, the "educated Negro or the miseducated Negro."

Coming to Syracuse from the Washington DC area, I was used to black teachers teaching black students—dedicated teachers committed to making more out of less in the most dangerous neighborhoods in the city. I was also familiar with the light-skinned versus dark- skinned fight among African American males and females. I was used to the booshie black folks who lived in upper Marlboro and other parts of the DC, MD, or VA area; some are my family members. I was used to uppity Long Island and Queens African Americans, but I was also used to the unity of the people in the Chocolate City and in NYC. This unity made me naive, and I was not prepared for this snobbish, zero-tolerance attitude among lots of African American female teachers or administrators in Syracuse. This sinister attitude is being used to push out students of color.

Prior to 2010, this topic was not discussed publicly; instead, it would be played out in the classroom and only dealt with when the parent and the teacher or the administrators had a communication breakdown. Parents felt something was going on but couldn't describe it.

Parents, educating your child has nothing to do with the following:

1. Where you live
2. Where you work
3. How much money you earn
4. How many children you have
5. What type of car you drive
6. How you and your children dress
7. Where you shop
8. If you receive public aid

Suspension of your child should not be based on the following:

1. Where you live
2. How much you family earns
3. Your child's disability
4. A family member's reputation or encounters with law enforcement

All the above *can be* reasons for a child to be sent out of the class, using the policy of teacher removal, especially if the removal is occurring routinely by an African American teacher.

All the above can play a role in suspension of students of color, especially among the few African American administrators or principals in Syracuse in my experiences. Understanding that this was actually occurring didn't ease the anxiety, but it did give me a good reality check.

These are just a few of the experiences that prepared me for the fight we are in today with our school district and suspension of students of color. *All the stories given here are for your reference.*
It could be you or your child who has experienced or is currently experiencing something similar. It could be something a friend or a family member's child has experienced or is experiencing.
It may be that you cannot put what is occurring into words, so you dismiss it and leave it alone.
These are some of the reasons we felt compelled to share our experiences and these stories. There were a lot of times we felt alone.

We often wondered, *Was this happening to other parents and students?* The unequivocal answer is yes! This is why we are committed to supporting and conducting trainings for parents to assist them in taking charge and control of the education their child is receiving.

Dr. Woodson acknowledges that the "Negro will never be able to show his originality as long as his efforts are directed from without by those that socially exclude him."

These uppity educated Negros are willing to help the master hold back the masses that they consider to be of lower class or caste African Americans for a paycheck and to be accepted by white society. It benefits their social standing (in their imagination) if they carry out the order to attack their own race. It is up to the parent to take a stand.

Chapter 19

The White Teacher's Implicit Bias Played Out in the Classroom

Simply stated, public education is a white female dominated profession that is use to treating black boys in a less than respectable manner.
—Dr. Umar Johnson

You can't teach a child you do not know, understand or respect.
—Dr. Jawanza Kunjufu (1986, pg. 12, 14)

Writing this chapter (Chapter 19) and the one before it required a lot of contemplation on my part—not because I am afraid of what anyone may think or say but because they are real experiences involving real people. These experiences were real, and they were painful in some instances. Our children, our niece, and the others who gave permission to use their experiences in this book are not fictitious; they have had real-life experiences, some with long-lasting effects. On the other hand, these chapters expose the bias of some teachers and administrators.

I know the statements will cause some to think that I am a racist and some to dislike my intentions even more. That's OK because the hidden agendas need to be exposed. The treatment of African American children is actually inherited from the fear of the black father and mother. At times, you and your child may doubt the obvious; you may even believe your child did something wrong, when they didn't, to excuse the bias. Again, it was Dr. Umar Johnson's insight, visits, e-mails, and phone calls that helped me to understand this problem in clear terms. My "thinking was not off track," and he was able to give me guidance on calling it what it is—implicit bias!

Before any person or person of color says this attitude doesn't exist, you should read the following:

1. Zoe Cornwall's *Human Rights in Syracuse: Two Memorable Decades:*
   A Selected History from 1963 to 1983

2. Dr. Carter G. Woodson's *The Miseducation of the Negro*
3. Jawanza Kunjufu's *Countering the Conspiracy to Destroy Black Boys Vol. 1–4*
4. Dr. Umar Johnson's *Pyscho-Academic Holocaust: The Special Education and ADHD Wars against Black Boys*

5. Dr. Ruby Payne's *Bridges Out of Poverty Strategies for Professional and Communities*

6. Dr. Frances Cress Welsing's *The Isis Papers: The Keys to the Colors*

Before person or person of color says this attitude doesn't promote the unfair suspension of a student, especially students with a disability, you should view the following DVD or watch it on YouTube: ***Special Education to Special Medication Learning Disabilities and ADHD* by Umar Johnson**

I used to be a proponent of "any teacher being able to effectively teach black students without bias" until I came to Syracuse. I am not saying that white teachers shouldn't or can't effectively teach black children. However, effective teaching methods will not work if their bias isn't checked at the door. I do believe that when a teacher understands diverse cultures or has been raised in a city center, they can truly understand the needs of their children.

I am not saying there are not good white male and female teachers and administrators in Syracuse because there are some excellent and dedicated teachers or administrators in our school district. Teachers and administrators who go the extra mile for a student use their own funds to make sure every child has an equal opportunity and nurtures that child as if they are valuable. However, the teachers and administrators mentioned in this chapter are leaps and bounds away from being that kind of educator. These white teachers are not compassionate, nurturing educators; in fact, they are the total opposite.

This chapter and the one before it address certain types of teacher's attitudes, stereotypes, and prejudices that have resulted in unfair treatment, routine referrals, and/or unnecessary disciplinary actions for very minor infractions. All the experiences are true and real examples of implicit bias being inflicted on African American students. Whether the bias is intentional or implicit, all parents must be aware it exists. Whether consciously or unconsciously motivated, the racially biased mind-set exists, and it is being played out in the classroom. There are people who do not want to talk about this issue, and I am sure they will call us something other than honest for writing these two chapters, and that is OK.

I feel people like Dr. Kunjufu and Dr. Johnson are bold and courageous enough to publicly state that this mind-set and stereotyping exist and give the parents the credibility to state that bias exists! Parents often feel like they are not believed when they request for assistance, especially when they express experiences in teacher bias, in particular with white female teachers. Dr. Johnson and Dr. Kunjufu's courageous actions made me include these chapters to point out that the implicit and hidden bias exists and that may be occurring in your child's classroom.

The suspension data coupled with the 2009–10 UCLA report and Syracuse's long implanted history of Jim Crow tactics made it evident that bias is a factor in referral and suspension. However, increasing the class size was also a factor due to teacher cuts. These cuts, especially in the support staff such as teaching assistants and paraprofessional staff, are just one indicator of how implicit bias can affect teaching and learning.

Bias and stereotyping result in unequal teaching and unequal discipline. White students get the attention, and African American students, especially the males, students with disabilities, and the intellectually gifted, are ignored or labeled as disruptive. The main consequences for expressing "frustration in learning" is "teacher removal of the student" or even suspension of the student.

The bias mind-set will often result in unfair treatment, but it is indoctrinated in the mind-set of the white female teacher, making removal a common practice. Even when the behavior is symptomatic of the disability or if the student is intellectually gifted, if they are assertive, they are sure to be warehoused in in-school suspension or pushed out using out-of-school suspension (OSS).

This chapter is also written to make the parents aware it is not in your mind; it does exist! You are not a crazy racist or a hateful person for speaking out about the matter. Parents, if you feel you are going through something similar and need assistance, e-mail us at twiggybillue@gmail.com or contact us at Hotep Resource Center and Coffee Café (Community Advocacy for Family Empowerment) at (315) 395-2644.

1994–2012

May–June 2013

On the night of the board meeting in that segregated room, white teachers and white parents were blaming African American parents for lack of discipline and African American parents were blaming white teachers for not teaching and for using suspensions to push students of color out of the classroom. Although the blame game was clearly being played out publicly, the students still suffered!

Anonymous Facebook and Twitter posts clogged social media in Syracuse with mainly white teachers and parents voicing the belief "if a black child is having behavioral problems at school, then discipline isn't being administered properly at home." I firmly disagreed with the statement.

Historically, white people have accused African American parents of "lack of discipline." They have described African American children as unruly, unteachable, and potential criminals. Disturbingly, I have found these stereotypes are asserted by a growing number of white teachers and administrators.

Historically, the fear some white people have of black men has been assigned to black boys.

African American children and parents have no control over the economic factors that plague the city and their neighborhood. The demolition of the 15th Ward indicated that African Americans in Syracuse have no power to control factors and variables that cause the socioeconomic decline within the community. If teachers do not understand the culture of the community historically and the factors that contribute to the negative climate, our children are doomed.

That night, white parents and teachers judged and stereotyped African American children and their parents. They blamed the parents for the students not learning—due to lack of upbringing and parenting skills.

I realized that night that I had not missed the mark in 1993–94 when my son was experiencing the wrath of bias at Dr. King Elementary School. It was kindergarten, and our son's teacher attempted to label him as a Jamaican criminal when he was five years old. Nor did I miss the mark when he was in the first grade when the teacher attempted to ignore him and not teach him or when he was demeaned for his appearance in an attempt to kill his self-esteem. I was not off base or crazy when he was transferred to Solace, and his teacher attempted to make him pay for our advocacy and tried to warehouse him in ISS.

Looking back, I realize there was an intense battle or war from 1991 to 2006. The battle intensified when the teacher attempted to kill the spirit of my gifted and talented niece at Elmwood in 1994–95 and when she was isolated in the IB program in 2004. Looking back, all the above fights and battles leveled the learning field for our children and threatened to expose the systemic push-out of our son and niece.

Those experiences provided me with strength and perseverance to defend my children and to use the knowledge of law and policy to initiate necessary changes in this school district for children of color and all children. This strength still propels me today. I didn't realize that I would rely on these experiences later during the 2008–13 school years. However, it has been those experiences that allow me to assist other parents in taking control and calling out bias in their child's education.

Yes, I am blacklisted. Yes, I am a hated parent and community advocate, and yes, I still bring the whirlwind! What else could we do? Remember, my husband relies on our master teachers such as Dr. Asa Hillard, Amos Wilson, Dr. Frances Cress Welsing, and Dr. Umar Johnson, and I rely on their teachings, as well as local, state and federal policies and laws.

I believe we are effective in creating change because we use the correct tools. Parents, you may be wondering what tools to use or what can a parent do even if the experience is similar.

Our weapons (proven strategy) are listed below:

1. Creating a paper trail—writing letters
2. Requesting information—on teachers and administrators—using our right to know (NCLB)
3. Filing student and parent grievances
4. Appealing decisions
5. Consulting outside assistance

There will still be those people who, no matter what you say, will think you are a racist until you prove the point. We don't mind proving the point. In fact, we are glad to show our evidence to anyone that states implicit bias doesn't exist in the classroom. In fact, just refer the nonbeliever to Harvard University's Project Implicit or encourage them to look at the Implicit Association Test (IAT) to explore bias with teachers in the classroom.

A report by Clark & Fillwalk published on the Teaching Tolerance Web site indicates that our "schools are populated by teachers who do not reflect the race, the language, or the communities of the students they teach" and that 80% of European American candidates express a strong predisposition to work in a majority setting. Another study referenced in the report indicates that "high quality teachers, both black and white, actively avoid schools with a large percentage of minority students," and this was the case in Syracuse.

Implicit bias is at play more than we would like to admit. Ignoring it is not possible because it's more overt than covert, and now it's played out at the expense of our children. You must understand that some parents and students live in very violent or impoverished neighborhoods and these children are carrying a heavy weight, a weight that other children in other neighborhoods don't ever have to carry.

Recently, I had heard about the concern of parents on the matter, so I conducted a workshop using Harvard's Project Implicit to prove the point and the association with the classroom. Teaching Tolerance, Dr. Umar Johnson, and Dr. Jawanza Kunjufu's insight give some much-needed clarity and background on the issues of white teachers and the bias inflicted on the black boys they educate or miseducate. I will let you make the choice.

I remember reading a passage indicating that "for white teachers their black male students may be the first black male they have ever had direct contact with," and for me, that was also profound (Kunjufu). Everything in that statement rang true for me because we have heard white teachers admit it when the behavior or attitude is called on the carpet. This is how the stereotyping and the historical fears were being played out—using implicit bias.

It was true for our learning-disabled son, our gifted niece, and hundreds of other students. It was an uphill battle that we fought for years. Although we fought a winning fight and eventually won the battle, why was it a fight at all?

My husband always recognized it for what it was: "old slave tactics by white men and women to eliminate black boys and men" in the twentieth century. The historical story of the predatory black men is a fictitious story, but it contains coded messaging, telling the white female teacher to beware. The coded message causes white people to quickly lock the car doors in certain neighborhoods and to clutch their purse closely on elevators and on certain streets, if black males are near.

When you fear someone or something, you put space or distance between that person and the thing. In the classroom, this plays out by sending the African American students out of the class or to the office, which often results in sending the students home for the day or a couple of days. Again here, as quoted at the beginning of the chapter, "how can you teach a child whom you do not know or understand" or, simply stated, a child you fear? (Kunjufu, 1986).

The collective fear of the black men has a rich and detailed history that has been encoded in their mind-set and in their DNA. The origin of the fear has been rooted in this nation's consciousness and unconsciousness from the time when Nat Turner led the revolt and the fear of miscegenation. Why is this fear being played out in the classroom by white females and a growing number of white male teachers?

I realized and witnessed in the school year 2013–14 that if you put twenty-eight rambunctious third-grade students (majority students of color) with a white female teacher, it will not take long before several of them are sent out of the classroom. The reasons for the removal are disruptive behavior, symptoms of a disability, and nonviolent, goofy behaviors.

Dr. Kunjufu asserts, "We cannot afford to have teacher placing negative value judgments on black culture." In turn, it devalues our children and affects their right to "fair and equal education." The "language of the child's environment should not bring about an attack on their self-esteem or condemnation," but quite often it does in our district. How can any white teacher (or black) "teach a child you do not understand or respect?" "For the African–American students, education is a matter of life or death" (1996, pg. 12, 14).

2010-2011 school years

During the second week of school, I was invited to a parent–teacher conference with my nephew's mother. Once we entered the classroom, I immediately noticed his desk. The seating arrangement for the other students was separate from where his desk was placed. His desk was in a corner, facing the wall. Later we found out this was called the disruption corner. Next, I noticed the condescending tone the teachers used with his mother. The icing on the cake was the suggestion that his alleged disruptive behavior could be a sign of a learning disability because his mother had dyslexia.

I was outraged; this was the child's first experience with school and his mother's dyslexia was a precursor to his demise. This child was five years old, and this was kindergarten. His alleged behavior issues or disruptive behaviors were described by the teachers as uncontrollable and his attitude made her feel uncomfortable. The teachers also indicated the "need to set up a plan to pick the child up when he can't settle down, just for the day," not a suspension but time to cool off.

I could not believe what I was hearing. Did this teacher just suggest that he be sent home instead of learning to acclimatize to a school setting? Why is the classroom size so large? What are the teaching supports in the classroom? Is co-teaching happening or is it the time-honored classroom management technique called teacher removal of a disruptive student the real foundation here? I was not convinced of the teacher's assessment, so I asked, "Why isn't he allowed any time to acclimatize to school, which is a new setting? Are you qualified to make the decision that he needs testing? Why are you suggesting a plan to push him out at five years old instead of Early Intervention services or a 504 plan?"

The bombarding of questions seemed to confuse the teachers, so they indicated that since his mother was diagnosed with dyslexia, it was possible the child had it as well. Again, I was not convinced, so I asked the teachers, "Which one of you is qualified to make that assessment?" Now I needed to know if the school psychologist or the social worker had been notified of the concerns. They had not.

These questions seemed to stun and anger this teacher, but she remained quiet and fumbled through some paperwork. Then she replied, "Can you give us a day or two to process this?"

"Absolutely not! No, we cannot," I responded. "We will schedule a meeting with the school social worker and the psychologist before we leave today."

We scheduled the meeting and were literally ignored until we inquired about the incident in writing. The school district responded by holding a series of meetings to address the issues. We arrived at the school and signed in at the office for each meeting, and then something became noticeable to my husband. As we waited to be called for our appointment or meetings, we noticed that during each visit at least eight students were being sent home at 9:45 a.m. We encountered parents, grandparents, guardians, or significant others who picked up a child. Even more disturbing was the fact that the child was being removed for disruptive behavior and being sent home for the day even when they had a disability.

We became angry at this point as we realized this was an overt attempt to warehouse this child in special education. This was an overt effort to kill his self-esteem and push out this five-year-old and his uneducated mother! Normally, the push-out is a covert secret dynamic that is initiated in middle school. However, since his mother mentioned she was dyslexic, he was being deemed feebleminded, unfit, or, in today's terms, unreachable and unteachable because of his so-called disruptive behavior.

I could not believe this; he was literally on the way to being pushed out of the educational system, in the guise of concern for him at five years old. When the teacher began to inquire too much about the family background, in particular his racial makeup, the warning light came on. Was this child actually paying the price of being a black boy and being raised by a multiracial mother with a documented severe learning disability?

Dr. Umar Johnson acknowledged that "learning while black" is tough, but often "black boys experience white education racism as early as kindergarten" (Johnson, 2011). That year alone (2013), I had heard many white teachers and administrators publicly make racist and insensitive comments about black parents and children than ever before. However, this time it was different; the comments were up close and personal. The comments from the teachers became disturbing when judgments and assumptions based on partial knowledge were made about our nephew's behavior based on his racial makeup.

To these white female teachers, his racial makeup was his presentence to criminal activity, mischief, and educational failure. To us, if we didn't act fast, these assumptions would become a lifelong label and sentence that we had to prevent. We knew the ramifications of children being pushed out of the educational system, and the alternatives were not productive alternatives.

I knew this would be a life sentence that would follow him the rest of his youth and adult life if we didn't act fast.

I often asked: Why is the focus always on this child? Was this child acting in a manner not consistent with a five-year-old's behavior? Why are the socioeconomic status, education, disability, and race of his mother and father prevalent factors when considering his educational and behavioral needs (especially since he lived with neither parent, and the child has resided with us for three years)? Why is his mother's diagnosis of dyslexia a consideration in his lack of ability to achieve? Why is his future being limited instead of thought about with great expectations and by virtue of programs designed to assist the school-aged child potentially in need of special supports?

I knew this was not just occurring with the child in my care, as I have heard and documented hundreds of similar stories in recent years. When Dr. Kunjufu and Dr. Umar Johnson spoke about this, it raised my awareness. I didn't want to believe that white teachers' implicit biases could be at work. I wanted to dismiss what had happened but it took me to a painful place in the past with my own children and family members. Now it was occurring with my great nephew and I could not dismiss it. Don't get me wrong. I believed it was occurring, but I had no real proof until now.

The next school year, we transferred him to a school closer to our home. From day one, we would arrive in school at 9:00 a.m.; by 9:15 a.m., we would again witness this common illegal practice. There were at least twenty students being sent back home for the day or a couple of days by mainly white teachers for disruptive behavior.

Now I know you are all thinking this person is a racist. I am not a racist. I do believe there are a lot of good white teachers. My experiences, however, cause me to believe the best white teachers take the time to learn and understand the culture of the students in their classrooms. Why would any teacher suggest that "raising a bi/multiracial child is harder when the mother is LD?" Implicit bias is at work when race is mentioned in the educational setting!

Our nephew wanted to learn and was excited, but somehow during the first two weeks of school, "his desire to learn was being stripped by unfair disciplinary treatment and premature determinations about his ability to learn" and his behavior (Johnson, 2011). This reminded me of the white teacher bias that was intentionally occurring with our sons. When parents cause unwanted change to occur, there is backlash—teacher backlash, administrator backlash, and even support staff backlash, which is OK as long as the backlash misses our children. When it does affect them, watch out for parent whirlwind—the Billues!

White teachers and administrators had heard the words "watch out for the Billues" and would talk about our assertive tactics. However, the conversation took a dangerous turn when comments were made in anger because of hidden implicit bias and were directed at our child. Assumptions based on partial knowledge are dangerous; however, they are the very root of implicit bias.

Our son was transferred to the innovative teaching school, the Solace School, in 1997. This new location was located on the city's east side and was the old Our Lady of Solace school building. His new teacher was touted for innovative learning applications; however, when she encountered our son, her fear of the black males made her feel uncomfortable. This discomfort played out in the classroom via implicit bias.

What role can race play in the failure of children in the educational system?

Dr. Johnson asserts, "Racial biases and assumptions play out in the classroom giving room for the teacher's lack of belief in the black students' ability to achieve," and this was our experience. It was the same for our son in 1997 at Solace as it was in 2011 for our nephew. The contempt that was displayed toward our son by his white teacher due to our advocacy efforts was real and played out in the classroom. Failure and frustration are the only winners when "contempt and negligent attitudes are responsible for educating our children." When a person's contemptuous mind-set takes over, especially that of a teacher, they begin to lack compassion and empathy for their African–American students. This is one way racial bias can enter the classroom, and we must not be naive about the issue (Johnson, 2011, pg. 71).

Due to our first two experiences with white female teachers, we requested for an African American teacher for our son. The school district dismissed the request by indicating the Solace School's innovative techniques would address our son's needs in the best manner. His new teacher was touted for her background in implementing culturally diverse classroom curriculum and also for being able to relate to her students' culture and bringing that unique understanding into the classroom. However, that was not this teacher. This teacher did not care about the culture of the students or their community and did not encourage participation in the classroom. In fact, she was more into being touted as something she was not—gossiping about black parents and students, rumormongering based on hearsay or partial knowledge, and overt stereotyping.

The most effective tools in our arsenal with regard to both biased white teachers and administrators and snobbish African American female teachers and administrators are the following:

1. Creating a paper trail regarding the issues—written documentation of the issues
2. Who it is sent to—the distribution list
3. Using your right to know—written requests for information on the teacher and/or the administrator and for anyone providing instructional support for your child
4. Taking advantage of the grievance or complaint processes.

Most teachers and principals are utterly surprised to receive a written documentation of incidents and requests for information about their teaching skills, certification, and/or licensing information. Some are more than willing to sit down without being defensive when you file a grievance or complaint, as you are afforded certain rights.

Parents, do you know who is teaching your child and that you have the right to know?!

Since so many assumptions were being made about our children and since the school had virtually all our information including social security numbers and birth records, we wanted to know who these people were as well, especially since our advocacy efforts were being used against my son, including biased comments and teacher removal. Remember, my son is intellectually gifted and has the ability to discern whether you are genuine or pretending, and his justice orientation was already developing.

My husband and my son were talking one evening when he indicated, "My teacher said I was going to be a bum." My husband called me into the room and asked our son to repeat his comment. It got a little deeper when we questioned him further, and he indicated, "She said tell your mother I am not afraid of her." Now I didn't know what to believe, but I knew my son did not make up the comments. The next morning, I contacted the principal and told her about our discussion and requested a meeting with the teacher after school. She called me back to indicate the meeting had been set and that my son was spending the day in another classroom for disruptive behavior.

Now could this be my imagination or did it happen after the principal indicated we had requested the meeting due to the comment? I inquired about the reason for the removal and was told he "made the teacher feel uncomfortable." The anger in my voice was noticeable when I replied, "What?" The principal was silent and indicated it was not ISS, but he was being moved until she investigated the incident. I strongly stated that I did not agree with the reason for the removal. I refused to have my son removed, and I was on my way to the school. This halted everything until we arrived at the school for the meeting. By the end of the day, the teacher had written our son up for fighting with another classmate and recommended he be sent to another classroom for the next two days. We arrived at the school for the meeting, and the tension was noticeable as we walked into the office.

The principal and our child were present, but the teacher was not. She indicated that our son received a referral and was going to be sent to ISS earlier during the school day; however, her investigation proved the allegation was unfounded. We indicated we wanted to know what our child did to make the teacher feel uncomfortable. The principal indicated she had not got to the bottom of the uncomfortable comment but that the teacher was coming to the meeting.

To make a long story short, the teacher indicated the bum comment was made jokingly and that she meant no harm. However, my son's comments in response made her feel uncomfortable, so she sent him to another teacher's classroom. My husband quickly spoke out and stated, "Your comment regarding our son being a bum was yesterday. What occurred today?" Silence again fell over the room, but my husband was not having the nonsense. He immediately mentioned the historical significance of a white female stating "a black male made her feel uncomfortable." He reminded the white female teacher and African American female principal that it was the stereotypical mind-set of the teacher that caused her to refer to his son as a bum. We are strong black parents, working parents, so to infer our child would "grow up to be a bum" was biased and we wanted to know the real reason why it was said.

We wanted real answers for the comments and the behaviors, not excuses for the teacher's behavior. The principal was an African American female principal, who was familiar with our family and our son. She was actually the vice principal at his previous school and one of the reasons that we agreed to the transfer. The principal was speechless until the teacher indicated that our son had a "strong will and personality," one that she had never experienced. The principal stopped her from commenting and told us she was going to change his classroom. Until the change occurred, he would report to her office for instruction. I knew it was her way of protecting our son, as well as giving the teacher a buffer from the whirlwind, but it was too late. I asked the principal how my child was receiving a punitive measure and the teacher was not. How could you change his placement without a determination hearing? Now the storm was brewing, and Solace was in the path of the whirlwind.

My arsenal was developed; now it was time to flex my muscle to show "you do not mess with my children!" Who is this woman whom the district touts as innovative and diverse, but in reality she is not? Was implicit bias preventing this teacher from being an effective teacher for all students or just for some students whose backgrounds reflected her background? Now our son's "strong will and personality" was being used to express contempt for our child from his teacher. Everyone knew our son's justice orientation and that he was a truthful child and very articulate, so his response to being called a bum and a negative comment about his mother would cause discourse and he would tell us immediately.

I wanted to know about the ability of this highly touted teacher and her ability to nurture and develop students for success since she was the teaching model. Everything she was described as—highly touted as effective and innovative—was a farce as we found her to be total opposite. Now it was time to assert my right to know who this biased white teacher was up close! Was this teacher even qualified or licensed to teach the grade assigned? Was she or had she ever been under review? When I produced the letter requesting information about this teacher and support staff, it seemed as if the building shook. My husband had another plan, and it was calling his old teacher, now the principal at Elmwood School. His request was for an immediate transfer and an African American teacher. This principal honored the request, and this was the start of the real education of our son to counter the miseducation that had occurred in previous years.

From 1993 to 2000, we used the FOIL to request the information. We sent a copy to the building principal, the director of pupil services, and the superintendent of school. We never received a written response, but once the letter was received, we knew the behavior and attitude would change or be suppressed.

We could count on a call from either the principal (if the request was not regarding them) or the superintendent's office, stating that NYS (superintendent's excuse) doesn't allow parents access to the information. The principal would always indicate it is a district's policy while the district would indicate it is a state policy. Of course, we requested the information from the NY State Education Department. It didn't matter if we got the information or not. Once the teacher or the principal found out we inquired about them or complained to NYS, the bias instantly ceased or was hidden.

It was strange, but it also proved the power of written requests and complaints. We didn't have the right to information regarding teachers. It was confidential, so my question to my state legislators and federal congressmen and senators was: "Why is the school allowed to collect and share so much confidential information about my child and family and we are not allowed to have information on staff?"

It was also amazing to see the changes in attitude, as well as suppression of anger in white female teachers when they found out the FOIL had reached the state level and the district was directed to respond. All parties involved knew the FOIL letters outlined the alleged biased attitudes and described incidents, and we suggested these incidents could be related to institutionalized racism or the possibility. "The teacher was not qualified to teach the grade and the subjects they taught." It pissed off the district administration and the teachers to find out we had the right to information. Right to know—As a parent, you have the right to request information regarding degrees and schooling and if there are any provisional status regarding the teaching certification or the license imposed by the state.

We would request for information on teaching assistants, tutors, or any person providing instruction support over the years, especially when white teachers, administrators, and district administration used implicit bias or racist tactics instead of teaching and nurturing our children.

Our most effective tools include the following:

1. Written documentation
2. FOIL letter
3. Appealing decisions
4. Filing grievances and filing complaints with the district and the state

We would get some information using the above prior to NCLB legislation, but mainly it put every teacher or administrator on alert. The FOIL request bothered the principals, upset lots of teachers, and caught the district off guard, but they could not prevent the request. The FOIL requests continued for over seven years until the implementation of No Child Left Behind.

Apparently, we were not the only parents who requested this information or felt the right to know information regarding teachers. According to the federal government, "Parents have a right to know"—most of what we had requested. Now we had a right to know the information, and no one was ready or willing to release it from 2005 to 2008. It was still a battle to obtain this information.

I used policies and laws to initiate confusion and fear (the same that was done to my children using implicit and hidden bias) and to communicate: "If you mess with my children, especially because of race or assumptions, you have a fight on your hands. I am not afraid of the system or to make noise and push back. Attempting to silence my efforts or dismiss us only makes the fury worsen."

For your benefit, our district's form to request teacher information is provided in this book's appendix section. In 2005, the federal "No Child Left Behind" legislation allowed parents to request information regarding the professional qualifications of your child's classroom teacher(s) and paraprofessional staff.

Under this law, parents may request information regarding the following:

1. Whether the teacher has met state qualification and licensing criteria for the grade levels and subject areas in which the teacher provides instruction
2. Whether the teacher is teaching under emergency or other provisional status through which state qualification or licensing criteria have been waived
3. The baccalaureate degree major of the teacher and any other graduate certification or degree held by the teacher and the field of discipline of the certification or degree
4. Whether the child is provided services by paraprofessionals and, if so, their qualifications.

Parents, remember when you use this policy or any of the other steps above, you may receive backlash, but stand your ground. You are the only person who can protect your child's rights and ensure your child receives a FAPE.

Even when you point out implicit bias is at work, it is not well received. It is actually taboo. If you are afraid to name it and your child is being affected, be prepared for a rocky road. If you are ready to fight the bias, start by documenting every incident that exposes the implicit bias, put it in writing, and send it to the building principal!

Make sure to put all inquiries in writing and send a copy to the superintendent's office. It makes the school staff very nervous, but if the staff is not biased and is teaching every child the same, the teacher has nothing to worry about.

This is only one option to use, which definitely straightens out any adverse behavior on the part of the teacher; the rest are yet to come.

Chapter 20

Implicit Bias and the Code of Conduct—Minor Infractions: A Tool to Push Out (Suspend) and Arrest Black and Disabled Students

During the 2006–08 school years, parents and students began to complain that the code of conduct did not follow the progressive discipline model outlined. Often minor offenses, including dress code violations, resulted in one- to two-day suspension.

At this time, we also noticed the authority the school resources officer commanded inside the schools. The SRO could recommend suspension or arrest for a disruptive incident such as "failing to respond to a direct request." A non-criminal matter could be made a criminal matter by the SRO without the principal's intervention. Additionally, we learned about the use of abusive tactics by the resource officers as an excuse to subdue (calm or restrain students) in most instances for non-criminal matters.

At first, the district's superintendent, the principals, and the police department denied any sort of incidents had taken place or were occurring. The denial ended when the district was face-to-face with proof that a SRO used abusive tactics on a female student. During the 2006–07 school year, we entered into a MOU with a local high school. The services provided included debriefing traumatic incidents, working with suspended students, returning to a regular setting from an alternative setting, and providing conflict resolution services.

This particular day, I didn't have students; instead, we were meeting with counselors from the student assistance center at the school. I remember the day very well. After leaving the school, I was off to pick up the birthday cake for my son's dinner party later that evening. Within five or ten minutes of leaving the school parking lot, my cell phone began to ring. I was driving without my earpiece, so I let the messages go to voicemail. The grocery store (Wegmans, Onondaga) was less than a mile away from the school, so I decided to wait until I arrived at my destination to listen to the messages. I arrived at the parking lot of the grocery store and noticed I had missed seven calls and received six text messages. Several message headings stated, "Emergency at the school."

Unknown to me, one of the students I worked with had called my office and spoken to a co-worker; she was upset and asking if I was available. The co-worker's granddaughter had also called her cell phone. When she picked up the phone, she first heard crying and then her grandchild asking, "Grandma, is Twiggy at the office?"

Note to the reader: I always answer my cell phone, just in case a student, teacher, or administrator needs assistance, so this was unusual to my students. The Director of Onondaga County Human Rights, an African American teacher and a community resident, had also called. The teacher taught in the AVID program and was close to many students. I had the opportunity to work closely with her and developed a friendship. I listened to her message; she was upset. You could hear it in her voice. There also seemed like someone was crying in the background, but then I heard, "If you are in the building, come to my classroom immediately." Now I became worried and sent a text, indicating I was not in the school.

The level of urgency came when my office called twice. It was my co-worker (Mrs. Williams) calling repeatedly from the office. When I answered, she immediately indicated that she had two students on hold, "who need you to come back to the school." In a firm voice, she and the executive director said, "Twiggy, we don't know what is going on, but you need to go back to the school!"

I responded OK, hung up the phone, immediately left the parking lot of the shopping center, and drove to the school. I was denied access to the school by police, and I got worried, so I began reading the text messages. Student after student had left messages, indicating that "a female student's nose was broken by the school officer" and the SWAT team had to lock down the school to conduct sweeps.

This day I remember well. A female student with a legal hall pass to the restroom was beaten by a white police officer as if she was an animal. District staff members or any staff member could request police intervention for any matter or issue, and nine times out of ten, the black student was sent out or arrested and the white student was not. Apparently, I was in the school when the incident happened, but I left just minutes before it became known school-wide. The principal granted me access to the school, and that was when I began to document what teachers and students had witnessed. It was not good, and now I was determined to expose it all!

The exposure of the incident to the public caused a series of meetings regarding unfair suspensions, the role of officer in the school, and revisions to the code of conduct. The director of the NYCLU and the Onondaga County Division of Human Rights assisted in documenting witness accounts. The series of meetings, discussions, debates, and subsequent revisions enabled me to have an intimate understanding of this entire document—the code of conduct.

Understanding the code of conduct is vital to your child's success. If your school district is considered a high-suspending district, you must become familiar with this document. In Syracuse, suspension rates are much higher than the national average, meaning that the code of conduct recommends suspension in all instances, minor and major.

In 2010, the Department of Justice led a leadership group in determining the proper language for revisions of the current code of conduct, related to the role and responsibility of the SRO. Later that year, several community organizations and the school district signed a mediation agreement and continued to meet every three months until the suspension data was released.

This is one of the reasons I keep a current copy of the SCSD's code of conduct. This has also resulted in providing in-services and workshops for local PTOs and for other school districts within Upstate NY on revisions to the code.

This was starting to seem unreal—the fire (fight) that was rising in me. This fire I had not experienced since the miseducation of my elder son and the effort to dumb down my niece.

I did not want to believe in or concede to the old practice of deeming black boys' behavior as disruptive; instead, the normal behavior of adolescent children, white or black, would be so overt as to criminalize non-criminal behavior. But the practice of labeling minority children as disruptive for exhibiting frustration and warehousing them in ISS or pushing out using OSS has been a common practice since 1994.

Now in 2013, I was able to document the common practice and use the disciplinary data analysis to verify that this was still occurring. I didn't anticipate that UCLA's report would show a fuller, more morbid picture of the occurrences, but I was prepared for whatever would come. Now implicit bias seemed more out in the open, and it was occurring at a far greater rate than when my children attended school.

I was in disbelief, but I had to believe it because we or my son lived it and my niece lived it! I had to believe it because of the history of Syracuse and our city's history of police in schools.

Zoe Cornwall wrote *Human Rights in Syracuse: Two Memorable Decades* (a selected history from 1963 to 1983). In this piece, she noted, "Despite the 1954 Supreme Court ruling against racially segregated schools, our city maintained a segregated school district for another eleven years and it took another thirteen years to integrate every single school building with the exception of three."

So even though I was in disbelief, I had to believe it because it jogged memories of recent complaints of student segregation within a local high school IB program!

Moreover, I had to believe it because of the history of Syracuse and our city's school district. Syracuse also has a significant reason for assigning police in the schools. In 1969–70, a new police unit was put into schools. This was implemented after the Henniger High School Riots, giving paramilitary power to enforce zero-tolerance policies. This is just one example from the past history that led to an escalation of stereotypes promoting implicit bias, so one can see today how it is entrenched throughout the code of conduct.

Parents, our number one weapon as a parent is to become knowledgeable and do research prior to communicating with emotions. It was Prof. Dan Losen who uncovered that Syracuse School District principals and teachers have severe implicit bias problems, which were propelling suspension of African American students and African American students with disabilities.

Implicit bias plays a huge role in the history of how blacks are perceived and treated in Syracuse, especially our children. It also plays a clear role in developing the school district's code of conduct. The demolishment of the 15th Ward and the gentrification of downtown Syracuse were historically clear; now it has developed into education genocide, which is reflective of why we are experiencing the issues with education that we are facing today.

A failing school with predominately African American students is not a new trend in Syracuse. There has historically been a lack of investment in black children's futures. In fact, Syracuse has a rich and robust history of our schools having a failing status—black schools. Low achievement scores were the basis for the Madison Area Project in the late sixties and is the same basis for closing Elmwood Elementary School even with the implementation of the Say Yes to Education Program, a very large enrichment program similar to the Madison Area Project.

The SCSD's code of conduct is a detriment to any efforts for raising achievement in low-achieving black schools. It is really a weapon used against black students to suspend and push students out the doors of the educational institution. "You can't teach them if they are not in school," and clearly with the published suspension rates, black students are not in school. Without investment in our students, complaints about motivating students to learn and lack of discipline are an excuse to suspend. That was Syracuse's mind-set in the sixties—to deprive black students in the Madison Irving Project of FAPE by using biased curriculum—as well as in 2013.

Cornwall asserts that a teacher had a hard time finding real motivators because most of the curriculum material was white oriented, and there was no black history (Cornwall, 1987). Today that teacher's remark is profound, as our school district still remains culturally insensitive to curriculum development. No black history (black contributions) courses are offered in our district.

In the Madison Area Project, this enrichment program did not help bring up academic scores. In fact, even the teachers considered it second-class education: "Even with increased funding from the Ford Foundation it was still considered by a teacher as 'inferior education' for black students. Teacher attitudes regarding students were those kids at Madison can't read, can't learn, aren't motivated, and are all criminals whatever . . ."

This is why certain themes resonate with some people— common themes when rules and policies are used as Jim Crow and black codes to suppress black students. It was these very words that caused me to look back at the history of Syracuse school in the 15th Ward and at our code of conduct.

> *"Teacher attitudes regarding students were*
> *those kids at Madison*
> *can't read, can't learn, aren't motivated, are all criminals*
> *whatever . . ."*

Cornwall's writings cover the years 1961–64. What is most astonishing more than forty years later is we still have the same issues in our city's educational system!

Implicit bias pushes the education machine in Syracuse.

The code of conduct reflects the principal's and the teacher's attitudes regarding African American students, especially males, and African American students with disabilities of any gender. It is written to reflect a violent criminal element associated with African Americans as viewed by white educators.

Minor offenses often called disruptive behavior have historically been the basis for having the Syracuse police in Syracuse schools. Cornwall acknowledged that the Henniger Riots was the prerequisite for Syracuse police to enter schools to police black children. The mind-set that African Americans are more violent than whites (although a myth) plays a large role historically in deeming African American students as unruly, unteachable, and disruptive.

When parents are at the code of conduct table for revisions or changes, they are often not prepared to deal with the bias that is reflected in the document. No training is provided; guidelines are convoluted and skewed to minimize parent and student participation, even when it is required by state and/or federal laws.

The following are the questions that *every parent should* know the answers to:

1. Are you a member of the code of conduct committee in your school district?
2. Do you know someone who is on the committee? Who chairs the code of conduct committee?
3. How many parents and students versus staff and school board members participate on the committee?
4. Does your code of conduct committee review and/or revise the document yearly?
5. How often does the code of conduct committee meet?

6. Is the code of conduct reviewed at the beginning of each school year by teachers, administrators, SRO, students, and parents? If not, you must push for these meetings to happen!

Parents, if you are not familiar with how the document is created and who sits at the development table, how will you be prepared to advocate for needed changes?

How will you know the difference between the roles of SRO in school versus the officer on the beat? How will you be able to determine if a student or your child is being fairly or unfairly penalized?

Realizing that the document is created from the mind-set of implicit or hidden racial biases will enable you to see how the myth of black criminality is heavily placed on African American students when disciplinary action is developed. In the 1960s, teachers used phrases like "the filtering out" and "unteachable students" to describe the push-out process of African American students. In 2013, it was less subtle and known widely as teacher removal of students. It was the main weapon used to filter out unteachable, unruly African American students.

The teachers' removal often leads to immediate suspension and then the push-out of African American students begins. In 2008, a PTO member at Elmwood posed a question regarding teacher apathy, and the overall sentiment from the teaching staff was "These students are not motivated to learn" and discipline was necessary to control unruly students. The sentiment became more intense and overt during the 2011–12 school year. Now it is said about all African American students in this school district. The mind-set projected by implicit bias over and over again eventually was reflected in suspensions and the very low ELA scores at Elmwood Elementary. This very same school year, the district closed the school.

"Sometimes you have to recall the past to fully understand the present."

(Rev.) Dr. Hal Garman, the former pastor of University United Methodist, gave me a copy of this book in 1995 as we worked on a project together. The historical significance of past events, especially in education and community development, impacted the decision made regarding the African American community in 2013. We are responsible for learning the history of the community we live in, especially as it relates to the education, economics, and political landscapes we are facing today.

When I read Cornwall's work, I was not all that familiar with the 15th Ward, the Henniger Riots, or the Jeremiah Mitchell story. I needed a beginning point for historical research regarding Syracuse during Germaine Lougen's time to the demolition of the 15th Ward to the present day.

We were familiar with the Jerry Rescue, but the more compelling story of the Underground Railroad King was suppressed in Syracuse history. Cornwall's book would become the guiding research for learning about the African American community in Syracuse. Little did I know at the time it would become a piece of reading material that would become a valuable resource for learning about Syracuse's history that is often hidden.

This hidden history was needed to interpret the full impact of the disciplinary data analysis and the report by Professor Losen of the UCLA Civil Rights Project. Historical research also connected the dots from the past history of our schools to the present paramilitary or zero-tolerance atmosphere, propelling our suspension rates. It also offered legitimacy and origin of the disparities found, which led to filing the complaint with the NYS attorney general and the US Department of Education's Office of Civil Rights.

Chapter 21

Code of Conduct Minor Infractions—Disciplinary Action for Prohibited Student Conduct

In the SCSD, all parents and students are introduced to a code of conduct. This seventy-two-page document is also available online, and also portions are included in the calendar or handbook. The document is intended to inform parents, students, teachers, and visitors about the rules of the school district or its district-wide policy on conduct, behavior, and consequences.

This document defines disruptive behavior for all students; however, this broad definition too often leads to suspensions for very minor infractions. Once you learn the difference between major and minor offenses, you will understand that violent incidents and weapon offenses require expulsion from school. Minor offenses are the offenses African American students are being suspended under, and the biggest category is suspension for dress code violations and suspension of disabled students for behaviors resulting from their disability.

Whether your child is a regular student, a student with a physical disability, or a student with a learning disability, you must become familiar with the code of conduct and how your school district defines disruptive behavior. The Syracuse City School District states:

Student's Conduct That Is Disruptive

Examples of disruptive conduct include the following:

- Failing to comply with the reasonable directions of teachers, school administrators, or other school personnel in charge of students
- Running in hallways
- Making unreasonable noise
- Bringing in unauthorized pets
- Using language or gestures that are profane, lewd, vulgar, or abusive
- Obstructing vehicular or pedestrian traffic
- Engaging in any willful act that disrupts the normal operation of the school community
- Trespassing. Students are not permitted in any school building, other than the one they regularly attend, without permission from the administrator in charge of the building
- Computer or electronic communications misuse, including any unauthorized use of computers, software, or Internet or Intranet accounts, accessing inappropriate Web sites or any other violation of the district's acceptable use policy
- Unauthorized use of objects (cellular phones, beepers, iPods, MP3 players, etc.) during regular school hours or school events
- Bringing in unauthorized objects (i.e. laser pointers, obscene materials, etc.)

If your child has ADHD, autism, ODD, or a specific learning disability, you must become familiar with the term *disruptive behavior*. As we found in our district's code of conduct, the language is set to suspend your African American student for symptoms of their medical condition and/or if the disruptive behavior was a manifestation of child's disability. This is illegal!

Once you become familiar with the school's policies for conduct and behavior, you will be better equipped to deal with an unanticipated suspension or determine if past suspensions were fair and followed due process. You will also become familiar with how your child is being pushed out of the classroom and services.

The ability to appeal decisions having adverse impacts on your child's education such as ISS and OSS is often a missed step for parents. Staying conscious of procedures and processes for appeal is a must. They are covered within the code of conduct, but the appeal process may be hidden within different portions of the document. Parents must understand that implicit bias, zero tolerance, and "Bridges Out of Poverty" practices guide the development of the document. These biases cause students of color to be warehoused by in-school suspension, to routinely receive referrals to the office, and to be pushed out of the classroom and out of school by teachers and administrators under the auspices of disruptive behavior.

Teske stresses the problem today is that "school officials throughout the United States have adopted zero-tolerance policies to address student discipline, resulting in an increase in out-of-school suspensions and expulsions." Policing the Syracuse schools has become a topic of discussion, especially the separation of school police and street officer mentalities. However, zero-tolerance policies have allowed police to intervene in non-criminal matters, and thus disruptive behavior becomes the number one reason to justify the need for policing students.

As mentioned in the previous chapter, "the implementation of school police sets a paramilitary atmosphere on school campuses and also increases the referral of students to the justice system." "While school personnel generally view zero tolerance policies as a constructive measure, it denies recent research on adolescent brain development that mischief is a foreseeable derivative of adolescence." So that would indicate that students (in most cases) are suspended for asserting behavior consistent with being a child or, simply stated, for acting like children. Teske's study asserts "zero-tolerance strategies have not achieved the goals of a safe and disciplined classroom; on the contrary, some suggest the strategies are harmful to students and may make schools and communities less safe" (Teske, 2011).

Knowing the difference between suspension and expulsion is very important. Parents and community members were informed by the district in 2008 that "the suspensions were based on disruptive and violent behavior." We challenged the statement once we learned the differences between persistently dangerous conduct and expulsion versus suspension for minor nonviolent behavior. If you don't know the differences, you can be easily fooled. Remember, students that commit violent and disruptive incidents are expelled from school and reported in the NYS VADIR.

"Mischief is a foreseeable derivative of adolescence," not a violent disruptive incident or act!

Major code of conduct infractions are reported in this document, but it also requires the school district to document and report disruptive incidents in NYS under the Safe School Against Violence Act.

Understanding the Significance of the VADIR

According to the glossary of terms used in reporting violent and disruptive incidents:

Other disruptive incidents are incidents involving disruption of the educational process and that rise to the level of a consequence listed in the *Summary of Violent and Disruptive Incidents Form* (columns j–o). Reportable incidents are limited to those resulting in disciplinary action or referral.

However, clarity becomes evident when you realize the difference between violent and disruptive incidents and disruptive conduct or behavior. Most reportable VADIR incidents constitute expulsion from school while infraction to the code of conduct does not. Therefore, the mind-set of teachers and principal, for suspending African American students, is not in alignment or consistent with the code of conduct.

Glossary of Terms Used in Reporting Violent and Disruptive Incidents

Disciplinary or Referral Action: For purposes of reporting, a disciplinary or referral action includes a referral to counseling or treatment programs, teacher removal, suspension from class or activities, out-of-school suspension, involuntary transfer to alternative education program or law enforcement or juvenile justice.

Parents, note this section also identifies how many students were removed by a teacher. Teacher removal is not a new concept, but now it is being used out of context. Instead of being removed for the class or the period, the student is being removed for the entire day, including other classes. The overuse and misuse of the policy allows teachers to improperly remove disruptive or violent pupils from the classroom.

Teacher Removal: For purposes of reporting, a teacher removal means the removal of a disruptive pupil from the teacher's classroom pursuant to the provisions of Education Law §3214(3-a). Routine referrals of a student to a principal or assistant principal for possible disciplinary action should not be counted as a teacher removal.

How does your school district make parents and students aware of their rights and responsibilities?

Who reviews the code of conduct with parents and students at the beginning of each school year?

The SCSD's code of conduct states, "The purpose of this handbook is to provide students, parents, and staff with information about the Syracuse City School District's Code of Conduct and dress code. It will also describe student rights and responsibilities, as well as District policies and procedures."

Often I find parents are not familiar with the policies contained in the code of conduct or the document itself.

Therefore, the next step is to understand the aspects of the document that pertain to your child, i.e., discipline, disability, IEP, appeal procedures, etc. Your next steps will depend on whether your child is a regular student or a student with a disability.

Parents, do you know how to participate in CSE discussions and reviews? Are you familiar with manifestation of a disability?

If not, in addition to the code of conduct, you will want to become familiar with the NYS Education Department's laws and procedural safeguards notice—your legal rights under federal and state laws to be involved in, and make sure that your child receives "free appropriate public education."

Attempting to maneuver the educational system can be difficult; however, if you have a child or children that have been unfairly suspended, especially if they have a disability, it can seem like an almost impossible feat. Just know you are not alone. Unfair and disproportionate suspension of African American students and African American students with disabilities is a common practice in public school districts across the United States.

Parents must be prepared to defend their children and understand the lifelong impact or Life Sentence suspension has on African American children.

Parents must also understand the diagnosis and misdiagnosis of the specific learning disability. Specific learning disability means a disorder in one or more of the basic psychological processes involved in understanding or in using language, spoken or written, that may manifest itself in the imperfect ability to listen, think, speak, read, write, spell, or do mathematical calculations.

The term includes hidden conditions such as perceptual disabilities, brain injury, minimal brain dysfunction, dyslexia, and developmental aphasia. The term does not include learning problems that are primarily the result of visual, hearing, or motor disabilities; of intellectual disability; of emotional disturbance; or of environmental, cultural, or economic disadvantage. (http://nichcy.org/disability/categories#ld).

If your child has been suspended either out of school or in school, your level of concern should be raised, and your next steps should include studying the code of conduct.

Additionally, have you ever been told your child has a specific learning disability and will not achieve more than a D? The excuse to accept lower expectations from a student based on gender, race, or economic status is implicit bias at work. Knowing how to recognize and name the issues is the start of the journey.

You owe it to your child and yourself to become knowledgeable of the policies and laws associated with a FAPE and how to effectively assert your rights.

You must also expect more.

Your code of conduct's expectation regarding behavior may favor suspending your child, especially if he or she has a disability. Stay vigilant on top of all the changes, wording, and medical terms that are used to describe behavior.

Chapter 22

Learning the Language of Special Education: How to Understand the IEP

I am not an expert in public education, special education, disability laws, but as a parent of a regular student and/or a student with a disability, unfortunately you must become well versed in them all.

What do the terms *research-based testing* and *researched-based education practices* mean?

Next, how do you understand terms and the new language associated with a document you do not fully understand?

The Individuals with Disabilities Education Act (IDEA) Part B addresses the IEPs for school-aged children with disabilities. IDEA states, "A child attending a public school child who receives special education and related services must have an Individualized Education Program (IEP)." It also specifies, "Each IEP must be a truly individualized document." That is, it must be designed for your child.

I have found over the years that I spend a lot of time assisting parents in understanding their child's IEP.

IDEA created the opportunity for parents to be an integral part of the IEP team and work together with teachers, school administrators, and services staff, i.e., occupational therapists and speech therapists to improve the opportunity for educational success for their child.

The language used in the IEP often is written with a lot of terms most parents are not familiar with, especially the number of acronyms used in special education:

Acronyms	Expansion
IDEA	Individuals with Disabilities Education Act 2004
IEP	Individualized Education Program
IEP Team	Individualized Education Program Team
IEE	Independent Educational Evaluation
CSE	Committee on Special Education
CPSE	Committee on Preschool Special Education
BIP	Behavioral Intervention Plan
PBIS	Positive Behavior Intervention Support
IAES	Interim Alternative Educational Setting
FBA	Functional Behavioral Assessments
SEPTA	Special Education Parent Teacher Association
LRE	Least Restrictive Environment
FAPE	Free Appropriate Public Education
LAA	Level of Academic Achievement
SESL	Special Education School Liaison
SUPAC	Syracuse University Parent Advocacy Center
AT	Assistive Technology
PT	Physical Therapy
OT	Occupational Therapy
MDM	Manifestation Determination Meeting
VESID	Office of Vocational and Educational Services for Individuals with Disabilities
PLOP	Present Level of Performance

The purpose of an IEP is to prepare your child for future education and employment. Understanding your child's IEP ensures that your child receives appropriate learning opportunities, accommodations, adaptations, specialized services, and supports that are needed to assist your child with academic achievement.

What Is the IEP?

IEP is the tool used to document how your child's special needs will be met within the educational environment.

When Is the IEP Developed and Reviewed?

An IEP must be initially developed and annually reviewed and, if appropriate, revised by the CSE.

Who Develops the IEP?

The IEP team or committee must comprise the following people in New York State:

Each CSE must include, but is not limited to the following:

1. The parents or persons in parental relationship with the student
2. At least one regular education teacher of the student
3. At least one special education teacher of the student
4. If appropriate, at least one special education provider of the student
5. A school psychologist
6. A representative of the school district who is qualified to provide or supervise special education and who is knowledgeable about the general education curriculum and the availability of resources of the school district and may also be the same individual recognized as the special education teacher, the provider, or the school psychologist
7. Chairperson—this representative is from the school district and is a person who can interpret the instructional link of the evaluation results. This person may also be the regular education teacher, special education teacher, provider, school psychologist, or school district representative having knowledge or special expertise regarding the student.
8. A school physician, if requested in writing by the parent or any member of the school district, at least seventy-two hours before the meeting
9. An additional parent member of a student with a disability residing in the school district or a neighboring school district
10. A parent member may be the parent of a declassified student or a graduate student as long as the declassification period or graduation has not exceeded five years
11. Other persons having knowledge or special expertise regarding the student, including related services personnel as appropriate, as the school district or the parent(s) shall designate. The determination of knowledge or special expertise will be made by the parents or school district whoever invited the expert to be a member of the committee on special education
12. If appropriate, the student

The IEP

1. Identifies your child's special needs and/or circumstances
2. Describes how the school will address those special needs and/or circumstances
3. Provides a blueprint of how your child's education will be provided and with supportive staff
4. Ensures your child receives the same general education curriculum and standards as regular students
5. Directs how the special education services and resources will be implemented to address the individual need of your child at that school they currently attend
6. Measures your child's progress toward the benchmarks, goals, objectives, and outcomes
7. Assists a school in determining if they are able to use their school resources to reach the desired outcomes
8. Is an important accountability tool for school staff, parents, and students to determine if the services and resources of the school meet the desired outcomes for the student

A New Requirement from the New York State Department of Education

All IEPs developed in New York State beginning with the 2011–12 school year will be required to be consistent with the NYS model IEP form.

The model form became a state form required to be used by all local and state educational agencies for all IEPs developed for use in the 2011–12 school year and, thereafter, pursuant to section 200.4(d) (2) of the Regulations of the Commissioner of Education.

The IEP used herein is the NYS Department of Education's model form for IEPs.

The Contents of an IEP

Here we will dissect each section of the IEP and review each box.

Identifying Information

This section of the IEP includes identifying information for the student—name, date of birth, and local school ID#, the projected date the

IEP will be implemented, the disability classification for the student (which must be selected from the options that appear in the drop-down menu), and the projected date of the annual review of the IEP.

Individualized Education Program (IEP)

STUDENT NAME: DATE OF BIRTH: LOCAL ID #:	DISABILITY CLASSIFICATION:
PROJECTED DATE IEP IS TO BE IMPLEMENTED:	PROJECTED DATE OF ANNUAL REVIEW:

Note: The IEP must designate the disability classification of the student from one of the disability categories defined in NYS State Regulations. Only one disability category may be listed in the IEP.

The disability classification is picked from a list of disabilities. Make sure your child's classification is correct. This drop-down menu provides a list of classifications that can be selected by

by the IEP team (see above picture). Although ODD, ADD, or ADHD is not on the drop-down list, they are covered under the Other Health Impairments classification.

Present Levels of Performance and Individual Needs

The next section is referred to as the PLOP. It is the body of the IEP. I often see the acronym PLAAFP meaning Present Level of Academic Achievement and Functional Performance; however, in our school district, the acronym used is PLOP, meaning present level of performance, but the IEP calls it present levels of performance and individual needs, as seen below.

PRESENT LEVELS OF PERFORMANCE AND INDIVIDUAL NEEDS
DOCUMENTATION OF STUDENT'S CURRENT PERFORMANCE AND ACADEMIC, DEVELOPMENTAL AND FUNCTIONAL NEEDS ·
Evaluation Results (including for school-age students, performance on State and district-wide assessments)

This section continues to detail your child's disability and how it impacts his or her ability to access and make progress in the general education curriculum.

The PLOP begins to detail your child's academic achievement, functional performance, and learning characteristics, so it must be written clearly and concisely and tailored to the individual needs of your child. This section is written in a narrative form that gives a description of your child's strengths, weaknesses, and needs based on the following *four areas of needs:*

1. Academic achievement, functional performance, and learning characteristics
2. Social development
3. Physical development
4. Management needs

Parents, this is also a place for your concerns. The language may seem difficult to process; however, I will share a guide that is helpful in making sure your concerns are addressed in the present level or PLOP section.

NICHY states the following facts:

1. Objective data from evaluation—identifies if basic reading skills are at grade level or below, also describes if writing and math skills are at grade level or below grade level.
2. Strengths—which skills are strong, vocabulary, reading . . .
3. Weaknesses—difficulty with or in which areas, vocabulary, written expression . . .
4. What helps learning—aids, manipulative, hands-on learning, assistive technology, and/or modifications?
5. What hinders learning—maybe your child has trouble putting onto paper what is read. Here the student's ability to express what is on his mind may be better in verbal format than written. It could be hindering your child's learning, so you would definitely want this included.

If you want your child to receive additional services you feel are needed such as speech or occupational therapy, you may need to advocate for them. The PLOP is where the parent can put additional concerns including medical or therapist recommendations or diagnosis. Remember, this is the section that describes and initiates services for your child. Make sure you communicate and put your requests and outside documentation in writing and demand they be a part of the IEP. Communicate your child's needs, especially anything that indicates that your child has a need in that area. For example, if your child has a speech impediment and you have medical documentation or a private assessment indicating such impairment, the CSE or IEP team must take it under consideration. Remember, your child's academic and special education placement is also guided in the present level of performance and student needs.

Academic Achievement, Functional Performance, and Learning Characteristics

ACADEMIC ACHIEVEMENT, FUNCTIONAL PERFORMANCE AND LEARNING CHARACTERISTICS
LEVELS OF KNOWLEDGE AND DEVELOPMENT IN SUBJECT AND SKILL AREAS INCLUDING ACTIVITIES OF DAILY LIVING, LEVEL OF INTELLECTUAL FUNCTIONING, ADAPTIVE BEHAVIOR, EXPECTED RATE OF PROGRESS IN ACQUIRING SKILLS AND INFORMATION, AND LEARNING STYLE:

STUDENT STRENGTHS, PREFERENCES, INTERESTS:

ACADEMIC, DEVELOPMENTAL AND FUNCTIONAL NEEDS OF THE STUDENT, INCLUDING CONSIDERATION OF STUDENT NEEDS THAT ARE OF CONCERN TO THE PARENT:

Academic Achievement, Functional Performance, and Learning Characteristics

1. Current levels of knowledge and development in subject and skill areas, including as appropriate
2. Daily living (e.g., personal care, preparing meals, household activities, and managing resources)
3. Level of intellectual functioning (e.g., general intelligence, attention, memory, problem-solving ability, and language functioning)
4. Adaptive behavior (e.g., the effectiveness with which the individual copes with the natural and social demands of his or her environment, how the student makes judgments and decisions)
5. Expected rate of progress in acquiring skills and information (e.g., the pace at which a student learns new information or skills, in consideration of factors such as those associated with the child's levels of cognitive skills, interests, age, and history of rate of progress)
6. Learning style (e.g., how the student learns best such as through visual or auditory modalities, hands-on approaches, cooperative learning, or repetition).

Completing this section relies on parental involvement and the student's involvement, especially when age appropriate involvement is required. These considerations must include the strengths of the student and the concerns of the parent(s) for enhancing the education of the child.

Social Development

Plain and simple, it means how your child makes friends; how they interact with other students, teachers, and school staff; and social development concerns the parents may have. Social skills also mean social rules or how well your child follows concrete social rules or reasonable requests.

Social Development

THE DEGREE (EXTENT) AND QUALITY OF THE STUDENT'S RELATIONSHIPS WITH PEERS AND ADULTS; FEELINGS ABOUT SELF; AND SOCIAL ADJUSTMENT TO SCHOOL AND COMMUNITY ENVIRONMENTS:

STUDENT STRENGTHS:

SOCIAL DEVELOPMENT NEEDS OF THE STUDENT, INCLUDING CONSIDERATION OF STUDENT NEEDS THAT ARE OF CONCERN TO THE PARENT:

Pay particular attention to the social development section as this refers to your child's social adjustment to school and community environments. Note that there is also a phrase called "feelings about self." Let's take a moment to look at this aspect of social development. As parents, do we understand or ask our children how he or she feels about themselves? Do you consider how well your child is able to express his or her ideas? Is your child aware that their emotional needs are a part of their social development?

It can speak volumes about your child, so while you can report on adjustments in community environments, make sure you are aware of what is going on in the school environment. I had an experience with my son and another parent, where this section of the IEP did not report or reflect that the child had any social development strengths, only weaknesses (see below):

1. Fails to follow classroom or school rules
2. Does not listen attentively
3. Calls out or blurts out constantly during instruction
4. Talks excessively even after being asked to stop talking
5. Does not use time constructively
6. Does not work cooperatively with others or in group settings.

Monitoring the classroom and school environment for your child is something the parent must stay on top of. As you see above, not only are the comments in this narrative negative, but also none are measurable goals. For instance, what does "not listening attentively" mean?

In my experiences, "not listening attentively" translates into the real underlying issue that the student was not paying attention. This is a measurable goal if framed correctly—something like "to increase attention" and use language to ensure it is an achievable goal. Pay attention to the wording here; too many negatives can become burdensome or overwhelming. Again, just to be clear, IEP Team or CSE Committee considers the social development strengths and weaknesses of your child as well as the parents' experiences and/or concerns. If you want to add or disagree with any statement regarding your child or feel the social development goals are not measurable or achievable, staying active in the CSE and IEP development and review processes is vital.

Parents, note that the Committee on Special Education (CSE) and the IEP team includes YOU, the parent!

Physical Development

This is the degree (extent) and quality of your child's motor skill development such as articulation, fluency, and oral motor skills. Sensory development is about your child's vision, hearing, and sense of smell, to name a few. Also, your child's health and physical skills or limitations, which pertain to the learning process, are included here. Each section requires that the IEP states your child's strengths and weaknesses.

PHYSICAL DEVELOPMENT

THE DEGREE (EXTENT) AND QUALITY OF THE STUDENT'S MOTOR AND SENSORY DEVELOPMENT, HEALTH, VITALITY AND PHYSICAL SKILLS OR LIMITATIONS WHICH PERTAIN TO THE LEARNING PROCESS:

STUDENT STRENGTHS:

PHYSICAL DEVELOPMENT NEEDS OF THE STUDENT, INCLUDING CONSIDERATION OF STUDENT NEEDS THAT ARE OF CONCERN TO THE PARENT:

Parent's involvement is strongly suggested; even if you cannot make it to the IEP meeting, put your thoughts into writing and submit them or appoint someone to submit them for you.

Your comments in this section are just as important as in any section.

MANAGEMENT NEEDS

THE NATURE (TYPE) AND DEGREE (EXTENT) TO WHICH ENVIRONMENTAL AND HUMAN OR MATERIAL RESOURCES ARE NEEDED TO ADDRESS NEEDS IDENTIFIED ABOVE:

> **EFFECT OF STUDENT NEEDS ON INVOLVEMENT AND PROGRESS IN THE GENERAL EDUCATION CURRICULUM OR, FOR A PRESCHOOL STUDENT, EFFECT OF STUDENT NEEDS ON PARTICIPATION IN APPROPRIATE ACTIVITIES**

This next section is regarding the use of assistive technology, supplementary aids, and services, including accommodations and/or testing modifications needed to gauge your child's progress on state- and district-wide standardized assessments. Does your child need a special device, extra time on test or not? In this section, it already provides an example for a special device, so use this as a means to determine if your child needs a special device or assistive technology based on the disability.

STUDENT NEEDS RELATING TO SPECIAL FACTORS
BASED ON THE IDENTIFICATION OF THE STUDENT'S NEEDS, THE COMMITTEE MUST CONSIDER WHETHER THE STUDENT NEEDS A PARTICULAR DEVICE OR SERVICE TO ADDRESS THE SPECIAL FACTORS AS INDICATED BELOW, AND IF SO, THE APPROPRIATE SECTION OF THE IEP MUST IDENTIFY THE PARTICULAR DEVICE OR SERVICE(S) NEEDED.

Does the student need strategies, including positive behavioral interventions, supports and other strategies to address behaviors that impede the student's learning or that of others? ☐ Yes ☐ No

Does the student need a behavioral intervention plan? ☐ No ☐ Yes:

For a student with limited English proficiency, does he/she need a special education service to address his/her language needs as they relate to the IEP?
☐ Yes ☐ No ☐ Not Applicable

For a student who is blind or visually impaired, does he/she need instruction in Braille and the use of Braille? ☐ Yes ☐ No ☐ Not Applicable

Does the student need a particular device or service to address his/her communication needs? ☐ Yes ☐ No

In the case of a student who is deaf or hard of hearing, does the student need a particular device or service in consideration of the student's language and communication needs, opportunities for direct communications with peers and professional personnel in the student's language and communication mode, academic level, and full range of needs, including opportunities for direct instruction in the student's language and communication mode?
☐ Yes ☐ No ☐ Not Applicable

Does the student need an assistive technology device and/or service? ☐ Yes ☐ No

If yes, does the Committee recommend that the device(s) be used in the student's home? ☐ Yes ☐ No

If you feel that assistive technology or service should be used at home, this is the section to advocate for the assistance. If the student receives or uses an assistive technology device at school, you may be able to make a valid case to continue the usage at home, especially for homework and enrichment purposes.

Measurable Postsecondary Goals: Long-term Goals for Living, Working, and Learning as an Adult

According to the National Secondary Transition Technical Assistance Center, a postsecondary goal is to be "generally understood to refer to those goals that a child hopes to achieve after leaving high school" rather than "the process of pursuing or moving toward a desired outcome" (http://www.nsttac.org/tm_materials/post_secondary_goals.aspx)

Measurable Postsecondary Goals

BEGINNING NOT LATER THAN THE FIRST IEP TO BE IN EFFECT WHEN THE STUDENT IS AGE 15 (AND AT A YOUNGER AGE IF DETERMINED APPROPRIATE)
MEASURABLE POSTSECONDARY GOALS LONG-TERM GOALS FOR LIVING, WORKING AND LEARNING AS AN ADULT
EDUCATION/TRAINING:
EMPLOYMENT:
INDEPENDENT LIVING SKILLS (WHEN APPROPRIATE):
TRANSITION NEEDS In consideration of present levels of performance, transition service needs of the student that focus on the student's courses of study, taking into account the student's strengths, preferences and interests as they relate to transition from school to post-school activities:

The NYS Department of Education's Web site states that your child's IEP must include "measurable postsecondary goals." Postsecondary education is study beyond the level of secondary education, which is often referred to as any schooling beyond high school education.

These goals must be based on your child's choices and interests as they relate to transition into independent living, working, continued education, or training. This is your child's transition from high school to postsecondary activities, in the following areas as defined on the IEP:

1. Employment
2. Postsecondary education, technical or vocational training, or continuing and adult education
3. Independent living skills

(http://www.p12.nysed.gov/specialed/publications/iepguidance/
postsecondary.htm)

The New York State Department of Education's Web site is a valuable
resource for understanding and developing the IEP. It lists some "quality
indicators" of measurable postsecondary goals and need statements that:

1. Echoes the hopes, dreams, and aspirations of your child
2. Reflects your child's strengths and interests related to after-high-
   school activities
3. Includes your child's own words
4. Is reviewed and updated at least annually once your child turns
   fifteen years old
5. Progressively becomes more detailed and specific as your child
   approaches the end of high school
6. Is developed with direct student involvement from the age of fifteen
   until graduation
7. Identifies linkages to and recommendations for transition services
   such as services from VESID or community agencies and other
   community activities
8. Is based upon age-appropriate transition relating to training,
   education, work, and self-reliant living skills

The above section of the IEP indicates your child's transition into the
adult world, so making sure this section is based on your child's interest
and choices is a must.

So think about the following things with your child in mind:

1. Is your child able to advocate for him/herself and/or his or her
   needs?
2. How is your child with time management?
3. Is your child able to travel on his or her own? Will transportation
   be required?
4. Can your child complete an application for employment without
   assistance?
5. Is your child able to work with or without minimal supervision?
6. Is he or she able to attend and/or participate in community events,
   activities without assistance?

Being able to answer these questions will be key to your child
transitioning to the future. Be on top of it!

This is also a section where the student's comments should be heard. It states at the top of the section, "BEGINNING NOT LATER THAN THE FIRST IEP TO BE IN EFFECT WHEN THE STUDENT IS AGE 15 (AND AT A YOUNGER AGE IF DETERMINED APPROPRIATE)."

This is when I encourage parents to make sure the student attends every CSE and IEP meeting and review with the parent. I always hear the parent or the student stating, "This is not what I, he, or she wants to do," so it's really important to make sure your child's input goes here.

Every student is different; while some know now what they want to do after high school, others change their minds quite frequently. Check with your child often, and in the IEP meetings, remember this section is about your child's future, and making it a reality means listening to your child.

Measurable Annual Goals

This is the section where your child's progress toward meeting the annual goals will be measured and reported to you. NYS Department of Education indicates that the "IEP must list measurable annual goals, consistent with the student's needs and abilities; to be followed during the period in which the IEP will be in effect."

MEASURABLE ANNUAL GOALS

THE FOLLOWING GOALS ARE RECOMMENDED TO ENABLE THE STUDENT TO BE INVOLVED IN AND PROGRESS IN THE GENERAL EDUCATION CURRICULUM, ADDRESS OTHER EDUCATIONAL NEEDS THAT RESULT FROM THE STUDENT'S DISABILITY, AND PREPARE THE STUDENT TO MEET HIS/HER POSTSECONDARY GOALS.

Remember, these are the goals your child hopes to achieve during the secondary education period, they are designed to prepare the child to meet the postsecondary goals. This section must be reviewed at least once a school year, once your child turns fifteen years old. It is designed to become progressively more detailed and specific as your child approaches the end of high school.

In NYS, the makeup or membership of the CSE committee or subcommittee states, "If appropriate, the student is a member of the team." This is the time I have found that it is imperative for your child's involvement. If your child requires linkage to transition services such as VESID, it will begin at this point.

Annual goals mean just that: goals for your child's achievement for that particular school year, not multiple years, but what he or she will focus on each school year.

Annual Goals What the student will be expected to achieve by the end of the year in which the IEP is in effect	Criteria Measure to determine if goal has been achieved	Method How progress will be measured	Schedule When progress will be measured

The PLOP or "present level of performance" narrative will be a determining factor of what is written here, especially as it describes how your child's "disability affects involvement and progress in the general education curriculum and your child's participation in appropriate activities." It is important that you participate in this section, making sure there is a link between the present levels and the annual goals, long term and short term. Parents, in short, look at the present level sections and highlight strengths and weaknesses, making sure the long-term and short-term goals are based on building upon strengths and focusing on turning weaknesses into strengths.

I have attended a great number of IEP team meetings at the request of the parents and noticed that parents do not review the contents of the IEP in great detail. Some are so trusting that they just look over certain information and pay attention only to portions of the IEP.

We even noticed on this particular document due to a change in school personnel that my husband's brother was listed as a parent, but who made that assumption? See below:

Name: Addis M. Billue   ID# 749333   Home Phone:(315)475-0349
Birth date: 04/12/1988   Age: 16 Yrs. 08 Mos. Sex: Male
Address: PO Box 193
   SYRACUSE, NY 13207 Onondaga Cty.   Current School: CORCORAN HIGH SCHOOL
                   Current Student/Teacher Ratio: 5:1
                   Dominant Language of Pupil: English
Parent/Guardian: Karl Billue   Dominant Language at Home: English

Questioning the accuracy of the information is just as important as anything else contained in the IEP. Stay on top of things and make sure the school district makes the changes you request. Once the changes are made, parents must make sure the district reissues the revised IEP, it is very important.

Look carefully over the IEP to ensure the annual goals are linked to the "present level of performance" narrative. For example, in the case of one of my children, at the end of the eleventh grade, the annual goals did not reflect any of the things mentioned in the present level section. This is a major flaw with the IEP, so we had to protest it during the meeting and demand the appropriate changes.

You must read the IEP and re-read it. Then you may want to take it apart and compare the sections, especially when it first arrives and periodically thereafter. If you have not reviewed the IEP and your CSE committee review is already set, go over the IEP with a fine-tooth comb and enlist assistance as needed. You may even want to reschedule the meeting, which is within your rights.

We found mistakes in 2005 on our son's IEP, and this document set the goals for the twelfth grade. Our diligence was due to previous experiences, and we could not just trust that the district's information was accurate or reflected his transition interest. We were not surprised to see that the IEP goals did not reflect or link to the present levels, but we were surprised at the push-back we encountered when we asked for the changes.

However, now armed with the knowledge of policies and laws and our own views and based on documentation not included in this IEP, we knew the recommendations for long-term and short-term annual goals needed to be changed. We also suspected that the request for changes would contradict some teachers' and paraprofessional staff's recommendations, but it needed to be changed based on state and federal regulations.

The New York State Education Department "Offers This Guidance"

"Goals should not be a restatement of the general education curriculum (i.e., the same curriculum as for students without disabilities), or a list of everything the student is expected to learn in every curricular content area during the course of the school year or other areas not affected by the student's disability." In developing the IEP goals, the committee needs to select goals to answer the question: "What skills does the student require to master the content of the curriculum?" rather than "What curriculum content does the student need to master?"

Notice that the present level for the student states the student is having difficulty with math, English, and social studies. The identified learning disabilities are written expression and math, and it notes the student benefits from the use of assistive technology.

Present Levels of Performance: *Needs extra us Hst Reg*

1. **Academic/Educational Achievement and Learning Characteristics:** Address current levels of knowledge and development in subject and skill areas, including activities of daily living, level of intellectual functioning, adaptive behavior, expected rate of progress in acquiring skills and information and learning style. All three areas: Present Levels, Abilities and Needs must be addressed.

-Present Levels:
-Abilities:
-Needs:

- 11th grade student struggling w Math English SS
- Needs to use Resource time more efficiently + use a planner
- Has good verbal skills, has difficulty getting ideas written in organized form
- Benefit from graphic organizer, assisted technology.

None of the above are reflected in the IEP goals.

Remember, I indicated that you, the parent, must ask your child repeatedly about their future aspirations. Often what the teacher has written in the goals section may not entirely reflect your child's future aspirations. Additional assistance and tutoring was required to ensure our children achieved the general education curriculum. We had to put it together. If there is no assistance or services recommended in the measurable goals, how will our children be successful in passing those subjects they experience difficulty in?

Knowing your child's future intentions is key. Also, make sure the IEP includes your own (parent) and the student's own search efforts for post high school education and/or training services.

The excerpt below states there was no postsecondary education or training search by the guidance counselor, program manager, parent, or student. That was not the case or the reality. In fact, it was really confusing that the IEP indicated no search, but in the "Future Considerations" area, a mark indicates "Post High School Education 4-Year College."

Post High School Education/Training Search

___ No ___ Yes Date_____ Completed by:_____ Anticipated Contact_____

___ Guidance Counselor ___ Program Manager ___ Parent ___ Student

---

Future Considerations

High School Education	Post High School Education	Employment	Housing
	___ 2 Year College	___ Part Time	___ Parents/Guardians
Course of Study	___ 4 Year College	___ Full Time	___ College Dorm
___ Regents Diploma	___ Technical	___ Competitive	___ Supported Apartment
___ SCSD	___ Adult Education Program	___ Supported	___ Supervised Apartment
___ IEP Diploma	___ Armed Services	___ Job Coach	___ Apartment
___ GED	___ Other	___ Enclave	___ Group Home
			___ Community Residence
			___ Foster Placement
Adult Programs	___ Sheltered Workshop ___ Day Program	___ Day Habilitation	___ Not Applicable

Contact Agencies
___ VESID ___ CBVH ___ CNYDSO ___ Advocacy ___ Supported Employment Agency ___ Case Service Agency ___ SSI ___ Other

---

So you must pay close attention to the particulars of the IEP. Remember, if school personnel change, i.e., guidance counselors, special education staff, resource staff, PT or OT staff, this is the only description of your child they will have. Make sure it is accurate!

We were already aware of VESID services, and we had contacted the agency, scheduled, and attended an appointment prior to this year's IEP review. Once the date of the review was indicated, we invited the VESID representative to the meeting, and they agreed and attended. Initially, we approached VESID to inquire about their post high school services. The reason for the invite was that the interviewer was surprised to learn that our child was not referred by the school and because our child and the VESID high school representative had never been introduced at the school.

He was not on the VESID list for high schools, and this was a concern for them and us. VESID did not have any paperwork from the school, indicating our child had an IEP and was interested in receiving services or that he wanted to attend college and could benefit from their services. We had learned about VESID during a college visit earlier that school year, and once the end of the year grew closer, we filled out an application for VESID, which led to the interview.

We learned they provided educational support after high school, including assistive technology, and that VESID's representative at our child's school could attend our next quarterly or annual IEP review. We indicated this to the guidance counselor and the resource teacher but did not get a clear answer on what had happened.

On the IEP, VESID was still not marked in the "contact agencies" area. At this stage of his review, our child had had already been accepted at a two-year and a four-year SUNY college. This was our second child in position to graduate, and we knew that the college application process, especially the written essay deadline, was approaching prior to entering the twelfth grade.

Our child had indicated since the tenth grade at each CSE meeting that he wanted to attend college and major in music, and during the eleventh grade, we indicated we wanted VESID services; however, sometimes you must repeat and repeat your expectations until they are included in the IEP.

As you will see below in the goals, VESID was not pursued by the guidance counselor, so we (our child and us, the parents) were glad we had initiated the contact with this agency.

Once we were able to advocate, the changes above his annual goals now needed to reflect measures to assist with the difficulty encountered in math, English, and social studies because no goal or measure reflected this issue.

Below are a few excerpts from the updated Annual Goals and High School Transition section. Now you can clearly see that the PLOP recommendations are not linked to the annual goals, so a parent must know how to read and interpret the document.

Annual Goals *Addis will meet w his guid-ance counselor to:*

Instructional Objectives

1. *Determine courses for next year*

2. *Determine credits needed toward graduation*

3.

Name: *A. Billie* **ID#:** *749333*

Annual Goals *Addis will continue the College process.*

Instructional Objectives

1. *Addis will complete Collegboard elig. for test mods for SAT*

2. *Addis will attend a college fair*

3. *Addis will take SAT in 10/05*

4) *Addis will complete College applications*

5) *Addis will complete VESID application & meet w counselor*

Annual Goals

Next, take a look at the short-term goals section, although it is noted as an alternate section for students in the instructions. We noticed that both long-term and short-term sections of our son's IEP had been written, so we reviewed and commented on both sections.

ALTERNATE SECTION FOR STUDENTS WHOSE IEPS WILL INCLUDE
SHORT-TERM INSTRUCTIONAL OBJECTIVES AND/OR BENCHMARKS
(REQUIRED FOR PRESCHOOL STUDENTS AND FOR SCHOOL-
AGE STUDENTS WHO MEET ELIGIBILITY CRITERIA TO TAKE
THE NEW YORK STATE ALTERNATE ASSESSMENT)

MEASURABLE ANNUAL GOALS			
THE FOLLOWING GOALS ARE RECOMMENDED TO ENABLE THE STUDENT TO BE INVOLVED IN AND PROGRESS IN THE GENERAL EDUCATION CURRICULUM OR, FOR A PRESCHOOL CHILD, IN APPROPRIATE ACTIVITIES, ADDRESS OTHER EDUCATIONAL NEEDS THAT RESULT FROM THE STUDENT'S DISABILITY, AND, FOR A SCHOOL-AGE STUDENT, PREPARE THE STUDENT TO MEET HIS/HER POSTSECONDARY GOALS.			
ANNUAL GOAL WHAT THE STUDENT WILL BE EXPECTED TO ACHIEVE BY THE END OF THE YEAR IN WHICH THE IEP IS IN EFFECT	CRITERIA MEASURE TO DETERMINE IF GOAL HAS BEEN ACHIEVED	METHOD HOW PROGRESS WILL BE MEASURED	SCHEDULE WHEN PROGRESS WILL BE MEASURED
SHORT-TERM INSTRUCTIONAL OBJECTIVES AND/OR BENCHMARKS (INTERMEDIATE STEPS BETWEEN THE STUDENT'S PRESENT LEVEL OF PERFORMANCE AND THE MEASURABLE ANNUAL GOAL):			

What does this mean? This meant we had to exercise our due diligence read and compare both sections of the IEP with the recommendations asserted to ensure that it matched the present levels. Pay close attention to the short-term instructional objectives and benchmarks as this outlines how your child will reach the annual goals.

Measurable Annual Goals and Short Term Instructional Objectives/Benchmarks

Annual Goal: *The student will successfully complete course requirements in content area classes.*

Short-Term Instructional Objectives or Benchmarks	Evaluation Criteria	Evaluation Procedures	Evaluation Schedule	Code
1) The student will successfully complete course work and ✗ pass tests required for graduation.	Course requirements 65% or better	Teacher evaluation, Tests, final exams and reports and/or RCT exams	Quarterly + End of year exam ↓	
✗				

Annual Goal: *The student will develop work habits necessary for academic success.*

The lack of benchmark achievement would not have been noticed. We had both the long- and short-term goals included in the final IEP for the twelfth grade because *"short-term instructional objectives and/or benchmarks are the intermediate steps between the student's present level of performance and the measurable annual goals."* There was no mention of present-level "struggles with math, English, and social studies," so monitoring benchmarks can ensure your child's success, especially if your child struggles with English or written expression and twelfth-grade English is their next feat. Instead, this section for our child is focused on work habits, completing course work, and passing tests, so making sure it is based on present levels is a must.

Short-Term Instructional Objectives or Benchmarks	Evaluation Criteria	Evaluation Procedures	Evaluation Schedule	Code
1) The student will bring necessary materials to all classes	Complete 100% of time	Teacher evaluation	Mid End	
2) The student will approach the resource teacher for reinforcement, ✗ academic support + test mods.		+ Correspondence with Content teachers	of each Quarter	
3) The student will use his	↓	↓		

Codes: M = Mastered P = Progressing Toward Competence PM = Progressing Towards Minimum Competence N = Needs More Time NI = Not Introduced Yet

Notice there are no codes marked, indicating the present level of performance toward competence. This was another issue that needed to be addressed. See the codes above.

These are the only two short-term goals mentioned. There are no linkages to strengths and weaknesses in the present-level area, and no measures are being implemented to address areas of difficulty. This is the main reason why you must review the IEP thoroughly to ensure it really addresses your child's disability as required by law. (See the IDEA and your state rules on students with disabilities and IEPs.)

Taking the time to make sure linkages are correct here is very important to your child's future success; monitor it like an IEP watchdog.

The next section addresses reporting progress to parents.

REPORTING PROGRESS TO PARENTS

Identify when periodic reports on the student's progress toward meeting the annual goals will be provided to the student's parents:

The steps or the combination of methods used was to inform the parents of the decisions of the local school district. However, I recommend that progress is reported quarterly, or at the same time, school report cards are issued to ensure you are fully updated on progress and at the annual review.

There is also a section that states the "IEP must indicate the recommended program and services, including related services that will be provided for your child during that particular school year."

Addressing Special Considerations

- Describe provisions for Braille and Braille Instruction for students who are blind or visually impaired (if determined appropriate by the CSE).

NA

- Explain the communication and language needs for students who are deaf or hearing impaired (with peers and professional personnel in the child's language and communication mode).

NA

- For students needing behavioral interventions, describe the behavioral interventions, strategies and supports to address the positive behavior. See Functional Behavioral Assessment and Behavior Plan.

NA

Below is the NYS-required format used to identify recommended programs and services:

SPECIAL EDUCATION PROGRAM/SERVICES	SERVICE DELIVERY RECOMMENDATIONS*	FREQUENCY HOW OFTEN PROVIDED	DURATION LENGTH OF SESSION	LOCATION WHERE SERVICE WILL BE PROVIDED	PROJECTED BEGINNING/ SERVICE DATE(S)
RECOMMENDED SPECIAL EDUCATION PROGRAMS AND SERVICES					
SPECIAL EDUCATION PROGRAM:					
RELATED SERVICES:					

Below is a sample of what may be in this section; however, the above asks for more details than the excerpt from our child's IEP below:

Program:	Begin	End	Hours	Minutes	Days/Week	Location
Resource	01/2005	06/2005	0	40	5	Resource room
Resource	09/2005	06/2006	0	40	5	Resource room

NY State Department of Education states that options for choosing "special education programs and services" are as follows:

For preschool students, the drop-down options include the following:

1. Special education itinerant teacher services
2. Special class in an integrated setting
3. Special class

For school-age students, the drop-down options include the following:

1. Consultant teacher services
2. Integrated co-teaching services
3. Resource room program
4. Special class
5. Travel training
6. Adapted physical education

This is where service options such as speech therapy, audiology, interpreting, psychological services, PT, OT, counseling, school health or school nurse, and school social work intervention services are listed.

Supplemental Aids, Assistive Technology, or Supports for School Personnel on Behalf of the Student

Supplementary Aids and Services/Program Modifications/Accommodations:				
Assistive Technology Devices and/or Services:				
Supports for School Personnel on Behalf of the Student:				

* Identify, if applicable, class size (maximum student-to-staff ratio), language if other than English, group or individual services, direct and/or indirect consultant teacher services or other service delivery recommendations.

It also contains a section listing the recommendation or need for assistive technology, supplemental aids or services, program modification, and additional supports. So make sure this section of your child's IEP doesn't look like the one below for our son.

Supplemental Aids/Services/Program Modifications

Supplemental Aids & Services	Begin	End	Amt. of Time per Day	Days per Week	Location
Agenda Book	1-11-05	6-30-06	daily	5	Classroom/Home
Graphic Organizer	1-11-05	6-30-06	as needed		
Progress Reports	1-11-05	6-30-06	as needed		
Assisted Tech	1-11-05	6-30-06	as needed		

Describe the program modifications or supports for school personnel that will be provided on behalf of the student to address the annual goals and participation in general education curriculum and activities:

Reinforcement and modification of school work in resource

Reporting Progress to Parents

State manner and frequency in which progress will be reported. _Quarterly_

12-Month Service and/or Program

New York State Department of Education states that the IEP form must identify if the student receives special education services in July and

August. As per NYSED, "If it does, the IEP must identify the provider of services; and for preschool students, state the reason(s) the student requires special education programs during this timeframe."

12-MONTH SERVICE AND/OR PROGRAM – Student is eligible to receive special education services and/or program during July/August: ☐ No ☐ Yes					
If yes: ☐ Student will receive the same special education program/services as recommended above. OR ☐ Student will receive the following special education program/services:					
SPECIAL EDUCATION PROGRAM/SERVICES	SERVICE DELIVERY RECOMMENDATIONS	FREQUENCY	DURATION	LOCATION	PROJECTED BEGINNING/ SERVICE DATE(S)

Name of school/agency provider of services during July and August:
For a preschool student, reason(s) the child requires services during July and August:

If the program or services recommended for July and August are not the same as recommended for the ten-month school year, the July and August recommendations must be documented in the following section of the IEP.

Testing accommodations and modifications are listed in the area below. Be sure it includes all modifications and specifies the details of the modification. This area indicates the individual testing accommodations needed by your child.

TESTING ACCOMMODATIONS (TO BE COMPLETED FOR PRESCHOOL CHILDREN ONLY IF THERE IS AN ASSESSMENT PROGRAM FOR NONDISABLED PRESCHOOL CHILDREN): INDIVIDUAL TESTING ACCOMMODATIONS, SPECIFIC TO THE STUDENT'S DISABILITY AND NEEDS, TO BE USED CONSISTENTLY BY THE STUDENT IN THE RECOMMENDED EDUCATIONAL PROGRAM AND IN THE ADMINISTRATION OF DISTRICT-WIDE ASSESSMENTS OF STUDENT ACHIEVEMENT AND, IN ACCORDANCE WITH DEPARTMENT POLICY, STATE ASSESSMENTS OF STUDENT ACHIEVEMENT		
TESTING ACCOMMODATION	CONDITIONS*	IMPLEMENTATION RECOMMENDATIONS**
☐ NONE		

*Conditions – Test Characteristics: Describe the type, length, purpose of the test upon which the use of testing accommodations is conditioned, if applicable.
**Implementation Recommendations: Identify the amount of extended time, type of setting, etc., specific to the testing accommodations, if applicable.

It will identify if your child needs extended time, if the test is administered over several days, revised test directions, or the use of aids or assistive technology devices. It will also identify if your child can move to a location other than the classroom for testing. Assistive equipment can be a word processor, calculator, use of a scribe, or the ability to use a spell-check device or voice to text device, etc.

The testing modifications from our child's IEP do not describe the modification in detail.

Testing Modifications:
Administer tests over several sessions
Administer tests to a small group in separate location.
Read directions to student.
Amanuensis(scribe)
Spell check device
Access to word processor
Calculator-scientific
Kurzwiel text to speech

Assessments:

X Your child will participate in all New York State and district wide assessments.
___ Your child will participate in New York State Alternate Assessment.

Knowing how the modifications will be achieved must be indicated; what spell-check device will be used or the format or media that Kurzweil will be administered must be clearly stated.

Coordinated Set of Transition Activities

This is why it was very important to have VESID listed at the beginning and throughout the entire IEP. The transition services and activities here show the linkages and coordination of services and activities that encourage transition from school into post-school activities prior to your child graduating or leaving the secondary school setting.

BEGINNING NOT LATER THAN THE FIRST IEP TO BE IN EFFECT WHEN THE STUDENT IS AGE 15 (AND AT A YOUNGER AGE, IF DETERMINED APPROPRIATE).		
COORDINATED SET OF TRANSITION ACTIVITIES		
NEEDED ACTIVITIES TO FACILITATE THE STUDENT'S MOVEMENT FROM SCHOOL TO POST-SCHOOL ACTIVITIES	SERVICE/ACTIVITY	SCHOOL DISTRICT/ AGENCY RESPONSIBLE
Instruction		
Related Services		
Community Experiences		
Development of Employment and Other Post-school Adult Living Objectives		
Acquisition of Daily Living Skills (if applicable)		
Functional Vocational Assessment (if applicable)		

This section was incomplete for our child. It is required to be addressed every year once your child reaches fifteen, so you must monitor the IEP for proper transition assistance, especially linkages to local agencies, and it must include independent living skills. This will enable your child to gain his or her own independence, requiring minimal parental assistance. This process is when my child began to advocate for himself effectively.

Future Considerations

High School Education	Post High School Education	Employment	Housing
	___ 2 Year College	___ Part Time	___ Parents/Guardians
Course of Study	✓ 4 Year College	___ Full Time	___ College Dorm
✓ Regents Diploma	___ Technical	___ Competitive	___ Supported Apartment
___ SCSD	___ Adult Education Program	___ Supported	___ Supervised Apartment
___ IEP Diploma	___ Armed Services	___ Job Coach	___ Apartment
___ GED	___ Other	___ Enclave	___ Group Home
			___ Community Residence
			___ Foster Placement

Adult Programs ___ Sheltered Workshop ___ Day Program ___ Day Habilitation ___ Not Applicable

Contact Agencies
___ VESID ___ CBVH ___ CNYDSO ___ Advocacy ___ Supported Employment Agency ___ Case Service Agency ___ SSI ___ Other

---

District-wide assessments

The format has changed, but the information that goes into this section remains the same.

New Format:

PARTICIPATION IN STATE AND DISTRICT-WIDE ASSESSMENTS
(TO BE COMPLETED FOR PRESCHOOL STUDENTS ONLY IF THERE IS AN ASSESSMENT PROGRAM FOR NONDISABLED PRESCHOOL STUDENTS)

☐ The student will participate in the same State and district-wide assessments of student achievement that are administered to general education students.

☐ The student will participate in an alternate assessment on a particular State or district-wide assessment of student achievement.
Identify the alternate assessment:
Statement of why the student cannot participate in the regular assessment and why the particular alternate assessment selected is appropriate for the student:

Old Format:

Assessments:

X   Your child will participate in all New York State and district wide assessments.

___   Your child will participate in New York State Alternate Assessment.

Participation with Students without Disabilities

The following section of the IEP is used to document the extent to which your child's disability prevents his or her participation with regular students or students without disabilities.

This section indicates that our child can participate in all regular classroom and school activities and will participate in all general education classes with the exception of his resource class.

Participation in General Education

The IDEA presumes that all students with disabilities will be educated in general education classes.

Explain the extent, if any, to which the student will not participate in regular education programs and extracurricular and other nonacademic activities including physical education or adapted physical education and occupational education (if appropriate).

all, except resource

☑ Your child will participate in all New York State and district wide assessments.

This next excerpt is from the psychological report, so making sure these recommendations are linked to the PLOP, annual goals, and transition from high school is very important to ensure your child's success in postsecondary life.

It is important to consider Addis's transition after high school. He is entitled to and should get accommodations once he leaves high school at the post-secondary level. The following accommodations should be considered:

Access to text
Extended time on tests
Note taker
Test taking accommodations
Adaptive computer access
Assistance with proofreading and editing
Tutoring
Self-advocacy training

The indications from the above psychological report are all the proof needed to reinforce and ensure these transition accommodations are put in place prior to graduation.

Special Transportation

SPECIAL TRANSPORTATION
TRANSPORTATION RECOMMENDATION TO ADDRESS NEEDS OF THE STUDENT RELATING TO HIS/HER DISABILITY
☐ None.
☐ Student needs special transportation accommodations/services as follows:
☐ Student needs transportation to and from special classes or programs at another site.

The IEP must specify any special transportation, including any specialized transportation equipment (e.g., special or adapted buses, lifts, and ramps), required to assist the student. This includes school-related programs and settings other than the school where the student receives education or special education services.

If your child needs adult supervision on the bus, wheelchair assistance, or feeding assistance, this is the area for recommendation.

And finally, the last section of the IEP is on placement and recommendation.

PLACEMENT RECOMMENDATION

NYS Department of Education states, "IEP must indicate the recommended placement of the student." Your child's placement is the educational setting in which the student's IEP will be administered and implemented. This includes the setting where the student will receive special education services such as identifying the school district, BOCES, or other services that work with disabled students.

NYS Department of Education provides guidance on IEP development at http://www.emsc.nysed.gov/specialed/publications/iepguidance.htm

EVALUATION TOOLS USED FOR ASSESSING STUDENT PERFORMANCE ON STATE- AND DISTRICT-WIDE ASSESSMENTS

The list below was too extensive and long to list the acronym and the actual name of the test, so I included all the tests and reports our local district uses for this.

COMMITTEE ON SPECIAL EDUCATION DIAGNOSTIC AND EVALUATIVE INSTRUMENTS

The tests and reports checked below were used by the Committee on Special Education to recommend a special education program and/or related services for your child. Evaluation results and reports are available for inspection and interpretation through your child's school C.S.E.

ACHIEVEMENT
__Wechsler Individual Achievement Test (WIAT)
__Curriculum Based Measurement (CBM)
__Key Math Diagnostic Arithmetic Test
__Wide Range Achievement Test
__Woodcock Reading Mastery Test
__Woodcock Johnson Test of Achievement-R
__Diagnostic Achievement Battery (-2)
__Test of Early Reading Achievement(-2)
__Test of Reading Comprehension
__Kaufman Test of Educational Achievement
__Informal Reading Inventory
__Slosson Oral Reading Test (SORT-R)
__Test of Written Language (-2)
__Test of Early Mathematical Ability (-2)

INTELLECTURAL ASSESSMENT
__French Pictorial Test of Intelligence
__Kaufman Assessment Battery for Children (K-ABC)
__Woodcock Johnson Test of Cognitive Ability
__Leiter International Performance Scale
__McCarthy Scales of Children's Abilities
__Slosson Intelligence Test (SIT-R)
__Stanford Binet Intelligence Scale - IV
__Wechsler Adult Intelligence Scale - Revised (WAIS-R)
__Wechsler Intelligence Scale for Children - III-R
__Wechsler Preschool & Primary Scale of Intelligence (WPPSI-R)

PSYCHOLOGICAL PROCESS EVALUATION
__Detroit Test of Learning Abilities
__Visual-Aural Digit Span Test (VADS)
__Developmental Test of Visual Motor Integration (VMI)
__Motor Free Visual Perception Test
__Bender Visual Motor Gestalt Test
__Auditory Discrimination Test
__Lindamood Auditory Conceptualization Test
__Test of Auditory Perceptual Skills

MEDICAL
__Audiological Examination
__Neurological Screening
__Psychiatric Evaluation
__Physical Examination

OTHER
_____
_____
_____

SPEECH/LANGUAGE
__Boehm Test of Basic Concepts-R
__Bracken Basic Concepts Scale
__Clinical Eval. of Language Fundamentals (CELF-R)
__Expressive One-Word Picture Vocabulary Test
__Goldman-Fristoe Test of Articulation
__Peabody Picture Vocabulary Test-R
__Test of Adolescent Language-R
__Test of Auditory Comprehension of Language-R
__Test of Language Development P/I
__The Word Test
__Test of Problem Solving
__Language Processing Test
__Other

SOCIAL-EMOTIONAL DEVELOPMENT
ADAPTIVE/PROJECTIVE
__AAMD Adaptive Behavior Scale-School Edition
__Vineland Adaptive Behavior Scale -
__Classroom Edition __Survey Edition
__Woodcock-Johnson Scale of Independent Behavior
__Behavior Rating Profile (-2)
__Child Behavior Checklist
__Parent Form __Teacher Form
__Achenbach (TRF)
__Achenbach (CBCL)
__Youth Self-Report
__Children's Apperception Test (CAT)
__Hand Test
__Make A Picture Story Test (MAPS)
__Draw A Person
__Kinetic Family Drawing (KFD)
__House-Tree-Person (HTP)
__Behavior Assessment System for Children (BASC)
__Parent __Teacher __Student
__Rorschach Technique
__School Apperception Test (SAM)
__Thematic Apperception Test (TAT)
__Roberts Apperception Test for Children

INFORMAL CLINICAL MEASURES
__Adaptive Physical Education Checklist
✓Classrom Teacher Reports
__Individual Education Program (IEP)
✓Classroom Observation
__Psychological Interview
__Review of Student's Records

This chapter was created to give parents a better understanding of how the IEP is created, their role in the creation, and a sense of empowerment once it is fully understood. I felt it was necessary to use my own child's IEP as a means to give you a sense of past and present IEPs, nothing more, nothing less.

Remember, if it is not written down, it did not happen and will not happen. So, Parents, use this guide if you are having trouble understanding your child's IEP. Review the entire IEP from the first page to the last page, using the guide provided here or from your state. Write down your comments and your basis for including reports from independent physicians, psychologists, and psychiatrists or from other specialized providers and recheck it again prior to the quarterly or annual update or review period. Attend every meeting of the CSE and subcommittee if possible or have someone, even another parent, represent you (with your written statement). You, the parents, are your child's only line of protection during the IEP process; make it work for you and your child.

Mistakes happen as you see above. The IEP can contain incorrect contact information including the wrong address and the wrong parent, so be diligent and check all the information for accuracy. Make sure the school has your correct mailing and/or physical address, as well as the correct phone number.

Also, notice whether there are any behavioral interventions, which is very important, if your child has been suspended.

Parents, remember, according to Lipsitt, positive behavior supports "should be positive, not punitive, it should be implemented as a teaching instrument for a child struggling with attention, focus, impulsivity, distractibility, organization, problem-solving, and social skills." Positive behavior supports and interventions are widely used to prevent suspension.

Appendixes

Appendix #1

Patient's Bill of Rights

(Taken from St. Joseph's Hospital's Web Site)
As a patient in the hospital in New York state, you have the right, consistent with law, to:

1. Understand and use these rights. If for any reason you do not understand or you need help, the hospital MUST provide assistance, including an interpreter.
2. Receive treatment without discrimination as to race, color, religion, sex, national origin, disability, sexual orientation, source of payment, or age.
3. Receive considerate and respectful care in a clean and safe environment free of unnecessary restraints.
4. Receive emergency care if you need it.
5. Be informed of the name and position of the doctor who will be in charge of your care in the hospital.
6. Know the names, positions and functions of any hospital staff involved in your care and refuse their treatment, examination or observation.
7. A no smoking room.
8. Receive complete information about your diagnosis, treatment and prognosis.
9. Receive all the information that you need to give informed consent for any proposed procedure or treatment. This information shall include the possible risks and benefits of the procedure or treatment.

10. Receive all the information you need to give informed consent for an order not to resuscitate. You also have the right to designate an individual to give this consent for you if you are too ill to do so. If you would like additional information, please ask for a copy of the pamphlet "Deciding About Health Care—A Guide for Patients and Families."

11. Refuse treatment and be told what effect this may have on your health.

12. Refuse to take part in research. In deciding whether or not to participate, you have the right to a full explanation.

13. Privacy while in the hospital and confidentiality of all information and records regarding your care.

14. Participate in all decisions about your treatment and discharge from the hospital. The hospital must provide you with a written discharge plan and written description of how you can appeal your discharge.

15. Review your medical record without charge. Obtain a copy of your medical record for which the hospital can charge a reasonable fee. You cannot be denied a copy solely because you cannot afford to pay.

16. Receive an itemized bill and explanation of all charges.

17. Complain without fear of reprisals about the care and services you are receiving and to have the hospital respond to you and if you request it, a written response. If you are not satisfied with the hospital's response, you can complain to the New York State Health Department. The hospital must provide you with the State Health Department telephone number.

18. Authorize those family members and other adults who will be given priority to visit consistent with your ability to receive visitors.

19. Make known your wishes in regard to anatomical gifts. You may document your wishes in your health care proxy or on a donor card, available from the hospital.

Appendix #2

Questions and Answers Parents Should Know about Manifestation Determination Meetings and Children with Disabilities

(Taken from the Web Site of the National Dissemination Center for Children with Disabilities **http://nichcy.org/ schoolage/placement/disc-details/manifestation**)

1. Under what circumstance should a manifestation determination meeting be conducted?

    Whenever a decision is made to change the placement of a child with a disability because he or she has violated a code of student conduct.

2. What's the timeframe for conducting a manifestation determination?

    The manifestation determination must occur within ten school days of any decision to change the placement of a child with a disability because of a violation of a code of student conduct.

    There are two scenarios under which the manifestation determination would be "yes." These are when the conduct or behavior:
    Was a manifestation of the child's disability, or
    The direct result of the LEA's failure to implement the child's IEP.

If either condition is met, the student's conduct must be determined to be a manifestation of his or her disability [§300.530(e) (2)-(3) and (f)]. In other words, the manifestation determination is "yes."

But it matters which of the two conditions was the basis for the determination of "yes."

"Yes," for failure to implement the IEP. If the group determines that the child's misconduct was the direct result of the LEA's failure to implement the child's IEP, the "LEA must take immediate steps to remedy those deficiencies." As the Department explains, if such a determination is made:

[T]he LEA has an affirmative obligation to take immediate steps to ensure that all services set forth in the child's IEP are provided, consistent with the child's needs as identified in the IEP (71 Fed. Reg. 46721).

What about placement?

Unless the behavior involved one of the special circumstances—weapons, drugs, or serious bodily injury—the child would be returned to the placement from which he or she was removed as part of the disciplinary action. However, the parent and LEA can agree to a change of placement as part of the modification of the behavioral intervention plan [§300.530(f) (2)].

"Yes," for conduct directly related to disability. If the group finds that the child's misconduct had a direct and substantial relationship to his or her disability, then the group must also reach a manifestation determination of "yes." Such a determination carries with it two immediate considerations:

Functional behavioral assessment (FBA)—has the child had one?
Does one need to be conducted?
Behavioral intervention plan (BIP)—Does the child have one?
If so, does it need to be reviewed and revised?
Or if the child does not have one, does one need to be written? [§300.530(f)]

Thus, if a child's misconduct has been found to have a direct and substantial relationship to his or her disability, the IEP team will need to immediately conduct a FBA of the child, unless one has already been conducted.

According to the Senate HELP committee:

An FBA focuses on identifying the function or purpose behind a child's behavior. Typically, the process involves looking closely at a wide range of child-specific factors (e.g., social, affective, environmental). Knowing why a child misbehaves is directly helpful to the IEP Team in developing a BIP that will reduce or eliminate the misbehavior. [2]

In addition to conducting an FBA (if necessary), the IEP team must also write a BIP for the student, unless one already exists. If the latter is the case, then the IEP team will need to review the plan and modify it, as necessary, to address the behavior.

The IEP team must also address a child's misbehavior via the IEP process as well. As the Department explains:

When the behavior is related to the child's disability, proper development of the child's IEP should include development of strategies, including positive behavioral interventions, supports, and other strategies to address that behavior . . . When the behavior is determined to be a manifestation of a child's disability but has not previously been addressed in the child's IEP, the IEP Team must review and revise the child's IEP so that the child will receive services appropriate to his or her needs. Implementation of the behavioral strategies identified in a child's IEP, including strategies designed to correct behavior by imposing disciplinary consequences, is appropriate . . . even if the behavior is a manifestation of the child's disability (71 Fed. Reg. 46720–21).

Appendix #3

Sample Letter (1)—Appealing a School Suspension

Insert Date []

Principal's Name:
School:
Address:

Re: Pupil Name

On _____, 201() my child _____ was suspended (In-School/Out of School) for _____days for the alleged charges of _____. On_____, 201_ I spoke to_____ at _____school about the matter and was told _____ (insert date told student could return).

I explained that I did not agree with the suspension, the allegations charged, or the lack of a formal investigation into the matter.

I also am not satisfied with the decision to suspend my child for _____ days as she is missing valuable instructional time. This letter serves to request an appeal of my child's suspension and a request for a formal meeting to discuss these matters.

Thank you,

CC
Superintendent of Schools

Appendix #4

Sample Letter (2)—Appealing SCSD Student Suspension and Requesting Meeting with Principal to Discuss Appeal

Date Sent: _____

Principal _____
_____ School
_____
Syracuse, NY _____

Dear (Mr./Ms./Mrs.) _____

On _____ (day of week), _____ (month)
_____, 20__, my child _____, a ____
grade student in your school received OSS or ISS for _____ days
for _____.

On _____ (day of week), _____ (month) _____,
20__, I spoke with _____,
the _____ (principal/vice principal) about the matter,
but my concerns about the incident and/or the manner in which my
child was suspended were not resolved to my satisfaction. This letter

serves as a formal appeal of the ___ day OSS/ ISS suspension of my child _____.

I am also concerned that:

_____ the suspension is not an example of progressive discipline
_____ the suspension was harsher than this situation warranted.
_____ there was not a formal or sufficient investigation into the facts
_____ the allegations against my child are untrue
_____ the allegations against my child misrepresent the facts
_____ I have not received a written notification of the suspension within the time period required under NY State law
_____ my child has a disability yet there was no manifestation hearing held to discuss whether the situation arose because of my child's disability or in direct relation to that disability.

The decision to suspend my child for _____ days will interrupt her learning environment as (she/he) is missing valuable instructional time. I ask that you contact me at _____ (phone) _____ (and, or, and/or) _____ _____ (e-mail address) in order to schedule a meeting to discuss this at a time when we are both available. I also request that you allow _____ (child's name) to return to school immediately pending this meeting to discuss my appeal of this disciplinary action.

Thank you,

_____ (Signature of Parent)
_____ (Printed Name of Parent)

Cc:
Superintendent
NYCLU

Appendix #5

Letter to the US Department
of Education Office of Civil
Rights (NY Office)

(Also sent via e-mail)

The National Action Network Syracuse Chapter
700 South Avenue, Syracuse NY (315) 832-0026
President, Mr. Walter Dixie

May 11, 2013

New York Office
Office for Civil Rights
U.S. Department of Education
32 Old Slip, 26th Floor
New York, NY 10005-2500

• Information about the person(s) or class of persons injured by the alleged discriminatory act(s):
African American and Latino students, Kindegarten-12 graders throughout the Syracuse City School District.

•The name and location of the institution that committed the alleged discriminatory act(s): and
Syracuse City School District
Central Offices located at, 725 Harrison Street, Syracuse, NY 13210
Mailing Address 1025 Erie Boulevard West Syracuse, NY 13204 (315) 435-4499

• A description of the alleged discriminatory act: **We believe that the Syracuse City School District has been and continues to follow unfair and discriminatory practices when issuing suspension (out of school and in-school) for African American and Latino students. We believe that the report issued by the Syracuse City School District (attached) shows the District used unlawful discrimination in the use of exclusionary school discipline. We also believe that African American and Latino students are suspended at twice the rate of their white counterparts, for the same or similar infractions. As we looked at the District's report we noticed that suspension by race with gender revealed the possibility of unlawful discrimination. This District's report also suggests that students with disabilities (African American and Latino) are also suspended at higher rates than their white counterparts.**

Example - Percentage of Students Suspended Out of School-K-8 Schools 2010-11 & 2011-12 (see attachment)
• Blodgett Elementary School 37.6% during the 2010-2011 school year.
• Bellevue @Shea, which reports a 71.4% suspension rate
• Frazer's K-8 suspension rate was 21.1% in the 2010-2011 school year but rose, to 28.1% last year
• Clary Middle School 30.3% in 2010-2011 to 41.1% in 2011-2012
• Danforth Middle School 52.3% in 2010-2011 and 50.4% 2011-2012.
• Westside Learning Academy 69.0 % last year.
• Lincoln Middle School 36.3% in 2010-2011 to 51.5% in 2011-.

We send this correspondence requesting this office to use its investigatory powers to look into this matter.
Respectfully,

Syracuse Chapter National Action Network
Walter Dixie, President

Appendix #6

Letter or E-mail to Dr. Umar Johnson

Page 1 of 2

Sunday, October 31, 2010

Greetings Dr. Umar R. Abdullah-Johnson,

My Name is Sister Twiggy Billue and I live in Syracuse NY.

A few months ago my King and I heard a presentation you gave on learning disabilities in African American children. At that time, your words resonated with our memories of fighting for our children and the resonate today with my great-nephew's current experience in Kindergarten.

It was painful hearing your message and being taken back to a place (1994-1995) when we had to lobby for speech therapy and occupational services for a child with a visible speech impediment. Learn the law in order to effectively fight for learning disability testing and seek the assistance of Syracuse University's Law Clinic and painful to know I would have to do it again! This time we are fight the pushout of our great nephew.

This was again a painful time, a period of 6-7 years of engaging in a war to keep the much needed services and the designations once our sons began to excel. You reminded us of the struggle we encountered attempting to keep them both in regular settings and how we had to fight to change to mindset and pre conception that they would not achieve or excel being told "not expect grades higher than a D and that both would receive IEP Diplomas", which was unacceptable . All in an attempt to take advantages of the services and resources our sons needed rather than give services they tend to label them as disruptive-as in the case of my five year old great nephew.

September 2010 we received a call from our great nephew's mother asking for assistance with her son. It was the second day school and the child was removed from the class and now was sitting at the teacher's desk. Removed from class and will be suspended the next time I thought how could this be? I met her at the school later that day and she told me he was being but on behavior modification and was scheduled for testing. I was surprised as he is only 5 years old and according to his mother he has never been in a daycare, pre-k, or structured environment until now including his home environment this was the second week of school.

By the time we inquired about the testing, it was already completed and a date was set to deliver the results (2nd full week of school). It was after this his mother confided that she has Dyslexia and that all her life she was in a small setting and was not expected to do anything. As she struggled to tell me her story, I realized that her pain was also due to being bi-racial and abuse she received from a white mother that was convinced she was stupid.

We agreed to attend the meeting with her and decided take a proactive role with our great nephew. The following Monday (first full week of school) we met his mother and him at the school at 8am and stayed each day to observe. I noticed immediately that he could not focus in a large or small group, he could not recognize letter or numbers, nor could he complete the ABC song with confidence or recognize his own name.

I also notice that he had difficulty coloring, following instructions and needed constant reminders in class as well as during his time at our home. The testing determined that he need "intensive assistance with in a small group and needed assistance with social skills".

Pages 2 of 2

Since that time we have noticed that he indeed appears to be developmentally delayed and has difficulty discriminating size, shape, color, time and number recognition, letter recognition and copying accurately from a model. We are hoping that he will acclimate to the structure and rules soon however we are very concerned that even with constant reminders and reinforcements he has difficulty remembering basic rules and it is causing him to be labeled disruptive.

Currently we receive daily calls regarding his behavior and lack of social skills because :

Of his impulsive behavior and lack of thought prior to his actions

He becomes overly excitable during group play

He has poor social judgment

Of inappropriate, unselective, and often excessive display of touching, pushing, shoving

Displaying behavior inappropriate for the situation

Of his failure to see consequences for his actions

He is overly distractible and he has difficulty concentrating

He has difficulty making decisions

His mother has a learning disability and his father's side of the family has children with them as well. My nephews mother's disability is Dyslexia and since dropping out of high school at 15 she has not receive any services an in turn is not able to teach her son. I am worried because we are aware that learning disabilities tend to run in families and so we are worried that a learning disabilities may be inherited.
more slowly.

I understand that children develop and mature at a slower rate than others in the same age group and in turn they may not be able to do the expected school work however it seems he behavior at his age is leading to a permanent label.

To make a long story short, we need your assistance in testing our nephew and assisting us with developing an action plan to address his needs. Free free to call either of us at the numbers below.

Sincerely in need of your assistance!

Ras Simenon Anu and

Sister Twiggy Billue

Appendix #7

EARLY SUMMARY OF VIOLENT AND DISRUPTIVE INCIDENTS

July 1, 2012 through June 30, 2013

| Due Date: July 8, 2013 |
| vadir@mail.nysed.gov |

School Name: _____

BEDS Code (12 digits): _____

This form must only be used by schools that have been directly notified to submit an early summary of the violent and disruptive incidents that took place in their schools, July 1, 2012 through June 30, 2013. It only contains Sections 1 and 9 of the VADIR form that will need to be filed via BEDS IMF application in September of 2013. Please complete Sections 1 and 9, and make sure the information is certified. The completed form should then be sent via e-mail to vadir@mail.nysed.gov, no later than July 8, 2013.

Each incident must be reported in only one category. If the incident involves more than one category, report it in the category with the lowest category number. For example, if an incident involves a robbery (category 3) and an assault with physical injury (category 7), report the incident in category 3. Category definitions are summarized in this document and detailed in the *Glossary of Terms*. Incidents in categories 1 through 8, 14, 15, 17, 18, and 19 must be reported regardless of whether or not the offender was disciplined or referred to law enforcement. Incidents in categories 9-13, 16, and 20 must be reported if a weapon was involved or if the consequences result in a disciplinary or referral action listed in columns (j) through (o). When the offender is not known, such as in a bomb threat or false alarm, the incident still must be reported. For more information, refer to the documents at http://www.p12.nysed.gov/irs/school_safety/vadir_collection.html. Schools reporting no incidents must report zero (0) in categories 1-20 column (y). The superintendent's certification must be completed.

1. **Violent and Disruptive Incidents:** Report duplicated counts of offenders and victims. That is to say, offenders and victims must be counted each time they were involved in an incident.

Incident Category	Number of Incidents (a)	Number of Offenders (Duplicated count. Offenders must be counted more than once if they commit more than one offense.)			Number of Victims (Duplicated count. Victims must be counted more than once if they are victims of more than one offense.)			Number of Incidents		How many enrolled student offenders were assigned or referred to: (Report all consequences)						
		Students (b)	Staff (c)	Other (d)	Students (e)	Staff (f)	Other (g)	Involving Alcohol or Drugs (h)	On School Transportation (i)	Counseling or Treatment Programs (j)	Teacher Removal Section 3214 (k)	Suspension From Class or Activities (l)	Out-of-School Suspension (m)	Transfer to Alternative Ed Program (n)	Less Enforcement or Juvenile Justice (o)
Incidents Involving Physical Injury or the Threat of Injury															
1. Homicide: conduct resulting in the death of another person.															
With weapon(s)															
Without weapon(s)															
2.1 Forcible Sex Offenses: involving forcible compulsion.															
With weapon(s)															
Without weapon(s)															
2.2 Other Sex Offenses: involving inappropriate sexual contact (no forcible compulsion.)															
With weapon(s)															
Without weapon(s)															
3. Robbery: forcible stealing of property from a person by using or threatening the immediate use of physical force.															
With weapon(s)															
Without weapon(s)															
4. Assault with Serious Physical Injury: intentionally or recklessly causing physical injury that creates substantial risk of death or serious disfigurement, impairment of health, or loss or impairment of the function of any bodily organ.															
With weapon(s)															
Without weapon(s)															

314

5. Arson: deliberately starting a fire with intent to damage or destroy property.

			NA		NA		NA											

6. Kidnapping: to abduct a person or restrain a person with intent to prevent his or her liberation.

With weapon(s)																		
Without weapon(s)																		

7. Assault with Physical Injury: intentional or reckless act causing impairment of physical condition or substantial pain.

With weapon(s)																		
Without weapon(s)																		

8. Reckless Endangerment: subjecting individuals to danger by recklessly engaging in conduct that creates a grave risk of death or serious injury but no actual physical injury.

With weapon(s)																		
Without weapon(s)																		

Other Incidents: Report incidents that 1) involve weapons or 2) disrupt the educational process. (See instructions.)

9. Minor Altercations: involving physical contact and no physical injury.

With weapon(s)																		
Without weapon(s)																		

10. Intimidation, Harassment, Menacing, or Bullying: no physical contact - intentionally placing another person in fear of imminent physical injury. Incidents that do not result in a consequence (j-s) should be reported in Item 2 page 1.

With weapon(s)																		
Without weapon(s)																		

11. Burglary: entering or remaining unlawfully on school property with intent to commit a crime.

With weapon(s)																		
Without weapon(s)																		

12. Criminal Mischief: intentional or reckless damaging of school property or the property of another person, including but not limited to, vandalism and the defacing of property with graffiti.

With weapon(s)																		
Without weapon(s)																		

13. Larceny and other Theft Offenses: unlawful taking and carrying away of personal property with intent to deprive the rightful owner of property. Permanently or unlawfully withholding property from another.

With weapon(s)																		
Without weapon(s)																		

14. Bomb Threat: a telephoned, written, or electronic message that a bomb, explosive, or chemical or biological weapon has been or will be placed on school property.

			NA		NA		NA											

15. False Alarm: falsely activating a fire alarm or other disaster alarm.

			NA		NA		NA											

16. Riot: four or more persons simultaneously engaging in tumultuous and violent conduct and thereby intentionally or recklessly causing or creating a grave risk of physical injury or substantial property damage or causing public alarm.

With weapon(s)					NA		NA		NA									
Without weapon(s)					NA		NA		NA										

Incidents Involving the Possession of Weapons, Drugs, or Alcohol (not reported in Categories 1-16).

17. Weapon Possession Only: Report incidents where weapons were found through screening at the building entrance separately from other weapons possession incidents.

Weapon(s) confiscated through screening					NA		NA		NA									
Weapon(s) found under other circumstances					NA		NA		NA										

18. Use, Possession or Sale of Drugs

			NA		NA		NA											

19. Use, Possession, or Sale of Alcohol

			NA		NA		NA		NA									

20. Other Disruptive Incidents: incidents involving disruption to the educational process serious enough to lead to consequence listed in (j-s). These incidents are in violation of the district code of conduct.

9. Superintendent Certification

I certify that the data reported here are complete and accurate to the best of my knowledge.

Superintendent Name: _____

E-mail Address: _____   Date: _____

Phone: _____   Fax: _____
Area Code   Number   Area Code   Number

Unsafe School Certification:

Is the following statement true?	Yes	No
"This school is in compliance with the unsafe school choice provisions of the No Child Left Behind Act." (See instructions for a description of unsafe school choice provisions.)		

Appendix #8

More Terms Every Student and Parent Should be Familiar With

According to the glossary of terms used in reporting violent and disruptive incidents:

Other Disruptive Incidents are incidents involving disruption of the educational process and that rise to the level of a consequence listed in the *Summary of Violent and Disruptive Incidents Form* (columns j–o). Reportable incidents are limited to those resulting in disciplinary action or referral.

Disciplinary or Referral Action: For purposes of reporting, a disciplinary or referral action includes a referral to: Counseling or Treatment Programs, Teacher Removal, Suspension from Class or Activities, Out-of-School Suspension, Involuntary Transfer to Alternative Education Program or Law Enforcement/Juvenile Justice.

Teacher Removal: For purposes of reporting, a "teacher removal" means the removal of a disruptive pupil from the teacher's classroom pursuant to the provisions of Education Law §3214(3-a). Routine referrals of a student to a principal or assistant principal for possible disciplinary action should not be counted as a teacher removal.

Taken from the NYS VADIR Glossary of Terms Web site, New York State Education Department: http://www.p12.nysed.gov/sss/ssae/schoolsafety/vadir/glossary08aaug.html

Appendix #9

State's Department of Education

Alabama   **http://www.alsde.edu/home/Default.aspx**

Alaska

801 West 10th Street, Suite 200/PO Box 110500 Juneau, AK 99811-0500
Telephone: (907) 465-2800
TTY/TTD: (907) 465-2815 Fax: (907) 465-4156 **http://www.eed.state.ak.us/**

Arizona

1535 West Jefferson Street, Phoenix, Arizona 85007 (602)-542-5393 or
1-800-352-4558 Hours of operation: Monday through Friday, 8:00
a.m. to 5:00 p.m. **http://www.azed.gov/**

Arkansas

Four Capitol Mall, Little Rock, AR 72201 Phone: 501-682-4475 Offices
open 8:00 a.m.–4:30 p.m., M-F **http://www.arkansased.org/**

California   **-Post-secondary Education Commission**

770 L Street, Suite 1160 Sacramento, CA 95814 Phone: (916) 445-1000
Fax: (916) 327-4417 Monday through Friday, 8:00 a.m.–5:00 p.m.

excluding state holidays and furlough days **http://www.cpec.ca.gov/ SecondPages/Contacts.asp**

State Board of Education

California State Board of Education 1430 N Street, Suite #5111 Sacramento, CA 95814 e-mail: sbe@cde.ca.gov Phone: (916)-319-0827 or send a facsimile to (916)-319-0175. **http://www.cde.ca.gov/be/**

Colorado

Colorado Dept. of Education 201 East Colfax Avenue Denver, CO 80203 Phone: (303)-866-6600 Fax: (303)-830-0793 http://www.cde.state. co.us/

Connecticut

165 Capitol Avenue, Hartford, CT 06106 / Phone: 860-713-6543 http:// www.sde.ct.gov/sde/site/default.asp

Delaware

Main Office: John G. Townsend Building 401 Federal Street (Federal & Loockerman Streets) Dover, Delaware 19901
State Location Code (SLC): D370B Phone: (302) 735-4000 Fax: (302) 739-4654 http://www.doe.state.de.us/
Auxiliary Office: John W. Collette Education Resource Center 35 Commerce Way Dover, Delaware 19904 State Location Code (SLC): N510

Florida

Office of the Commissioner: Turlington Building, Suite 1514 325 West Gaines Street Tallahassee, Florida 32399 Phone: (850)-245-0505 Fax: (850)-245-9667 OR Commissioner@fldoe.org Web site http:// www.fldoe.org/

Georgia

205 Jesse Hill Jr. Drive SE Atlanta, GA 30334 PH.(404) 656-2800 Toll Free: (800) 311-3627 (GA) Fax: (404) 651-8737 e-mail: askdoe@ gadoe.org http://www.gadoe.org/Pages/Home.aspx

Hawaii   http://www.hawaiipublicschools.org/Pages/home.aspx

1390 Miller St. Honolulu, HI 96813 Phone: 808-586-3230 Fax: 808-586-3234

Idaho   http://www.sde.idaho.gov/

650 West State Street, PO Box 83720 Boise, Idaho 83720-0027 Toll Free: (800) 432-4601
Local: (208) 332-6800 Fax: (208) 334-2228 Superintendent: trluna@ sde.idaho.gov

Illinois   http://www.isbe.state.il.us/

100 N. 1st Street Springfield, IL 62777 (866)-262-6663 (217)-782-4321
100 W. Randolph, Suite 14-300 Chicago, IL 60601 (312)-814-2220

Indiana

South Tower, Suite 600 115 W. Washington Street Indianapolis, IN 46204
Phone: (317) 232-6610 Fax: (317) 232-8004 e-mail: webmaster@doe. in.gov website http://www.doe.in.gov/

Iowa

Grimes State Office Bldg. 400 E 14th St Des Moines IA 50319-0146 Ph. (515)-281-5294 Fax: (515)-242-5988 http://educateiowa.gov/

Kansas

120 South East 10th Avenue Topeka, KS 66612-1182 Phone: (785) 296-3202 Fax: (785) 296-7933 TTY: (785) 296-6338 e-mail: ddebacker@ ksde.org or price@ksde.org Web site: http://www.ksde.org/

Kentucky

Capital Plaza Tower First Floor 500 Mero Street Frankfort, KY 40601
Phone: (502) 564-3141 Fax: (502) 564-5680
e-mail: webmaster@education.ky.gov Web site: http://www.education.
ky.gov

Louisiana

1201 North Third P.O. Box 94064 Baton Rouge, LA 70804-9064 Phone:
(225) 219-5172 Toll-Free: (877) 453-2721 Fax: (225) 342-0781 e-mail:
customerservice@la.gov Web site: http://www.louisianaschools.net

Maine

Burton M. Cross State Office Building 111 Sewall Street 23 State House
Station Augusta, ME 04333-0023 Phone: (207) 624-6600 Fax: (207)
624-6601 TTY: (207) 624-6800 e-mail: tammy.morrill@maine.gov
or susan.gendron@maine.gov Web site: http://www.maine.gov/portal/
education/

Maryland

200 West Baltimore Street Baltimore, MD 21201 Phone: (410) 767-0100
Fax: (410) 333-6033
e-mail: llowery@msde.state.md.us Web site: http://www.
marylandpublicschools.org/MSDE

Massachusetts—Department of Elementary and Secondary Education

75 Pleasant Street Malden, MA 02148-4906 Phone: (781) 338-3102 Fax:
(781) 338-3770 TTY: (800) 439-2370 e-mail: www@doe.mass.edu or
media@doe.mass.edu Web site: http://www.doe.mass.edu/

Michigan

P.O. Box 30008 608 West Allegan Street Lansing, MI 48909 Phone: (517)
373-3324 Fax: (517) 335-4565 e-mail: carefootk@michigan.gov Web
site: http://www.michigan.gov/mde/

Minnesota

1500 Highway 36 West Roseville, MN 55113-4266 Phone: (651) 582-8200 Fax: (651) 582-8724 TTY: (651) 582-8201 e-mail: mde. commissioner@state.mn.us Web site: http://education.state.mn.us/mde/index.html

Mississippi

Central School Building 359 North West Street P.O. Box 771 Jackson, MS 39205 Phone: (601) 359-3513 Fax: (601) 359-3242 e-mail: cblanton@mde.k12.ms.us Web site: http://www.mde.k12.ms.us/

Missouri

205 Jefferson Street P.O. Box 480 Jefferson City, MO 65102-0480 Phone: (573) 751-4212 Fax: (573) 751-8613 TTY: (800) 735-2966 e-mail: pubinfo@dese.mo.gov Web site: http://dese.mo.gov/

Montana

P.O. Box 202501 Helena, MT 59620-2501 Phone: (406) 444-2082 Toll-Free: (888) 231-9393 Toll-Free Restrictions: area code 406 only Fax: (406) 444-3924 e-mail: cbergeron@mt.gov Web site: http://www.opi.mt.gov/

Nebraska

301 Centennial Mall South P.O. Box 94987 Lincoln, NE 68509 Phone: (402) 471-2295 Fax: 402-471-4433 e-mail: denise.fisher@nebraska.gov Web site: http://www.education.ne.gov

Nevada

700 East Fifth Street Carson City, NV 89701 Phone: (775) 687-9217 Fax: (775) 687-9202 e-mail: darnold@doe.nv.gov Web site: http://www.doe.nv.gov/

New Hampshire

Hugh J. Gallen State Office Park 101 Pleasant Street Concord, NH 03301 Phone (603) 271-3494 Toll-Free (800) 339-9900 Fax: (603) 271-1953 TTY: Relay NH 711 Web site: http://www.ed.state.nh.us

New Jersey

P.O. Box 500 100 Riverview Plaza Trenton, NJ 08625-0500 Phone: (609) 292-4450 Toll-Free: 1-877-900-6960 Fax: (609) 777-4099 e-mail: vocinfo@doe.state.nj.us Web site: http://www.state.nj.us/education/

New Mexico

300 Don Gaspar Santa Fe, NM 87501-2786 Phone: (505) 827-5800 Fax: (505) 827-6520 Web site: http://www.ped.state.nm.us/

New York

Education Building Room 111 89 Washington Avenue Albany, NY 12234 Phone: (518) 474-3852 Fax: (518) 473-4909 Web site: http://www. nysed.gov/

North Carolina—Department of Public Instruction

301 North Wilmington Street Raleigh, NC 27601 Phone: (919) 807-3300 Fax: (919) 807-3445
e-mail: information@dpi.state.nc.us Web site: http://www. ncpublicschools.org/

North Dakota—Department of Public Instruction

Department 201-600 East Boulevard Avenue Bismarck, ND 58505-0440 Phone: (701) 328-2260 Fax: (701) 328-2461 Web site: http://www. dpi.state.nd.us

Ohio

25 South Front Street Columbus, OH 43215-4183 Phone: (614) 995-1545 Toll-Free: (877) 644-6338 Fax: (614) 728-9300 TTY: (888) 886-0181 Web site: http://www.ode.state.oh.us/

Oklahoma

2500 North Lincoln Boulevard Oklahoma City, OK 73105-4599 Phone: (405) 521-3301 Fax: (405) 521-6205 Web site: http://sde.state.ok.us/

Oregon

255 Capitol Street, NE Salem, OR 97310-0203 Phone: (503) 947-5600 Fax: (503) 378-5156 TTY: (503) 378-2892 e-mail: gene.evans@state.or.us Web site: http://www.ode.state.or.us/

Pennsylvania

333 Market Street Harrisburg, PA 17126-0333 Phone: (717) 787-5820 Fax: (717) 787-7222 TTY: (717) 783-8445 e-mail: 00admin@state.pa.us or 00sec@state.pa.us Web site: http://www.pde.state.pa.us/

Rhode Island—Rhode Island Department of Elementary and Secondary Education

255 Westminster Street Providence, RI 02903-3400 Phone: (401) 222-4600 Fax: (401) 222-6178 TTY: (800) 745-5555 e-mail: angela.teixeira@ride.ri.gov or irene.monteiro@ride.ri.gov Web site: http://www.ride.ri.gov/

South Carolina

1006 Rutledge Building 1429 Senate Street Columbia, SC 29201 Phone: (803) 734-8815 Fax: (803) 734-3389 e-mail: cclark@ed.sc.gov or jfoster@ed.sc.gov Web site: http://ed.sc.gov/

South Dakota

700 Governors Drive Pierre, SD 57501-2291 Phone: (605) 773-5669 Fax: (605) 773-6139 TTY: (605) 773-6302 e-mail: betty.leidholt@state. sd.us or mary.stadick@state.sd.us Web site: http://doe.sd.gov/

Tennessee

Andrew Johnson Tower, Sixth Floor 710 James Robertson Parkway Nashville, TN 37243-0375 Phone: 615-741-5158 Fax: (615) 532-4791 e-mail: Education.Comments@tn.gov Web site: http://www.state. tn.us/education/

Texas- Education Agency

William B. Travis Building 1701 North Congress Avenue Austin, TX 78701-1494 (512) 463-9734 Fax: (512) 463-9838 TTY: (512) 475-3540 e-mail: teainfo@tea.state.tx.us or commissioner@tea.state.tx.us Web site: http://www.tea.state.tx.us/

Utah

250 East 500 South P.O. Box 144200 Salt Lake City, UT 84114-4200 Phone: (801) 538-7500 Fax: (801) 538-7521 e-mail: mark.peterson@ schools.utah.gov Web site: http://www.schools.utah.gov/

Vermont

120 State Street Montpelier, VT 05620-2501 Phone: (802) 828-5101 Fax: (802) 828-3140 TTY: (802) 828-2755 Web site: http://www. education.vermont.gov/

Virginia

P.O. Box 2120 James Monroe Building 101 North 14th Street Richmond, VA 23218-2120 Phone: (804) 225-2420 Web site: http://www.doe. virginia.gov/

Washington—Office of Superintendent of Public Instruction (Washington)

Old Capitol Building 600 South Washington P.O. Box 47200 Olympia, WA 98504-7200 Phone: (360) 725-6000 Fax: (360) 753-6712 TTY: (360) 664-3631 Web site: http://www.k12.wa.us/

West Virginia

Building 6, Room 358 1900 Kanawha Boulevard East Charleston, WV 25305-0330 Phone: (304) 558-2681 Fax: (304) 558-0048 e-mail: dvermill@access.k12.wv.us Web site: http://wvde.state.wv.us/

Wisconsin: Department of Public Instruction

125 South Webster Street P.O. Box 7841 Madison, WI 53707-7841 Phone: (608) 266-3390 Toll-Free: (800) 441-4563 Fax: (608) 267-1052 TTY: (608) 267-2427 e-mail: dpistatesuperintendent@dpi.wi.gov Web site: http://dpi.wi.gov/

Wyoming

Hathaway Building Second Floor 2300 Capitol Avenue Cheyenne, WY 82002-0050 Phone: (307) 777-7690 Fax: (307) 777-6234 TTY: (307) 777-8546 e-mail: supt@educ.state.wy.us Web site: http://edu.wyoming.gov/

Guam

Federal Programs Division P.O. Box DE 312 Aspinall Avenue Hagatna, GU 96932 Phone: (671) 475-0470 Fax: (671) 477-4587 Web site: http://www.gdoe.net/fedprograms/

Puerto Rico- Department of Education

P.O. Box 190759 Calle Federico Costa #150, Hato Rey, PR 00919-0759 Phone: (787) 773-5800 Fax: (787) 282-6017 e-mail: perez_da@de.gobierno.pr or barredaca@de.gobierno.pr Web site: http://www.de.gobierno.pr/

Virgin Islands

1834 Kongens Gade Charlotte Amalie, VI 00802 Phone: (340) 774-2810 Fax: (340) 779-7153 e-mail: lterry@doe.vi Web site: http://www.doe.vi/

Bibliography

American Psychiatric Association. 2000. *Diagnostic and Statistical Manual of Mental Disorders.* 4th ed. Text Revision (DSM-IV-TR). American Psychiatric Association: Washington, DC. DSM-IV-TR Diagnostic and Statistical Manual of Mental Disorders 2000 Psychiatry Online Web site accessed July 2, 2013 Arlington, VA. http://dsm. psychiatryonline.org//book.aspx?bookid=22

Children with ODD. 2011. Facts for Families. Publication No. 72. The American Academy of Child and Adolescent Psychiatry (AACAP). Web site accessed on April 3, 2012. http://www.aacap.org/App Themes/AACAP/docs/ facts for families/72 children with oppositional defiant disorder. pdf

Clark, Patricia Dr. and Zygmunt-Fillwalk, Eva Dr. *Using the IAT With Teachers to Affect Change.* PDF accessed on July 5, 2013. Teaching Tolerance-Ball State University: Muncie, IN. http://www.tolerance.org/ sites/tolerance.org.tdsi/files/assets/general/IAT BallState.pdf

Dohrn, B., Justice R. Barkett, and S. Biehl. School Expulsion: A Life Sentence? ABA Section of Litigation 2012 Section Annual Conference April 18–20, 2012: Where are the Lawyers? An Investigation of Access to Justice for Children with No Counsel 2011. http://www. americanbar.org/content/dam/aba/administrative/litigation/materials/ sac 2012/47-1 school expulsion a life sentence.authcheckdam.pdf

Editorial Board. Infant Mortality: Onondaga County has Made Great Strides, But Racial Disparity Persists. *Syracuse.com*, September 25,

2011. Web site accessed on January 2013. http://blog.syracuse.com/opinion/2011/09/infant_mortality_onondaga_coun.html

Education Resource Organization Directory, State Education Agency (State Department of Education). Web site accessed on August 8, 2013 US Department of Education http://wdcrobcolp01.ed.gov/programs/erod/org_list.cfm?category_ID=SEA

Gathright, Molly, and L. H. Tyler. *Disruptive Behaviors in Children and Adolescents*. pdf Web site, Psychiatric Research Institute, University of Arkansas for Medical Sciences. Web site accessed on May 2, 2013. http://psychiatry.uams.edu/files/2009/07/disruptive.pdf

Gibson, C. P. 2008. *Overcoming the Stigma of the Learning Disability Label: A Story of Survival and Recovery*. Academic Communication Associates, Inc.: Oceanside, CA. Special Education News, Article LD-8-3. http://www.acadcom.com/acanews1/anmviewer.asp?a=53

Guide to Quality Individualized Education Program (IEP) Development and Implementation 2010 Revised NY State Education Dept. The University of the State of New York. http://www.emsc.nysed.gov/specialed/publications/iepguidance.htm

Hayes, Edward. *White Female Teachers and Black Male Students: Kunjufu and Me*. December 5, 2009. Chicago Public Education Examiner.com. Web site accessed on April 2012. http://www.examiner.com/article/white-female-teachers-and-black-male-students-kunjufu-and-me

IEP Direct, Webinar Series: Measurable Annual Goals and Other Sections Frequently Answered Questions Centris Group. Web site accessed on May 5, 2013. https://www.iepdirect.com/downloads/FAQ%20%20webinar%20%20Goals%20and%20other%20sections.dec2010.pdf

Infant Death Rate in Syracuse Is Still Rising. *New York Times*, October 10, 1991. Web site accessed on May 2013. http://www.nytimes.com/1991/10/10/nyregion/infant-death-rate-in-syracuse-is-still-rising.html

Instructions and Descriptions of the National Spreadsheets, Suspended and Off Track, April 2013 Civil Rights Project/*Proyecto Derechos Civiles* http://civilrightsproject.ucla.edu/resources/projects/

center-for-civil-rights-remedies/school-to-prison-folder/federal-reports/out-of-school-and-off-track-the-overuse-of-suspensions-in-american-middle-and-high-schools/Instructions-to-Secondary-Schools-Suspension.pdf

Johnson, Umar. 2013. *Psycho-Academic Holocaust: The Special Education and ADHD Wars against Black Boys*. 1st ed. Prince of Pan-Africanism Publishing: Philadelphia, PA

Kessel, M., and J. Hopper. Victims Speak Out About North Carolina Sterilization Program, Which Targeted Women, Young Girls and Blacks. *NBC's Rock Center*, November 7, 2011. Web site accessed on May 9, 2013.

Knowing Your Child's Rights. National Center for Learning Disabilities, Editorial Team 2010. Web site accessed on April 4, 2013. http://www.ncld.org/parents-child-disabilities/ld-rights/knowing-your-childs-rights

Kunjufu, Dr. Jawanza. 1986. *Countering the Conspiracy to Destroy Black Boys*. vol. 2, rev. ed. African–American Images: Chicago, IL

Kunjufu, Dr. Jawanza. 1995. *Countering the Conspiracy to Destroy Black Boys*. vol. 4, 1st ed. African–American Images: Chicago, IL

Lipsitt, Marcie. 2012. Why and How to Read Your Child's IEP. National Center for Learning Disabilities. Web site accessed on April 5, 2013. http://www.ncld.org/students-disabilities/iep-504-plan/why-how-read-your-childs-iep

Losen, D., and T. E. Martinez. April 8, 2013. *Out of School and Off Track: The Overuse of Suspensions in American Middle and High Schools Executive Summary*. Civil Rights Project of UCLA. Web site accessed on May 2013. http://civilrightsproject.ucla.edu/resources/projects/center-for-civil-rights-remedies/school-to-prison-folder/summary-reports/out-of-school-off-track-reports-by-district

National Secondary Transition Technical Assistance Center, Post-Secondary Goals. http://www.nsttac.org/tm materials/post secondary goals.aspx

National Dissemination Center for Children with Disabilities (NICHCY) IEP Annual Goals September 2010. Web site accessed on May 2013. http://nichcy.org/schoolage/iep/iepcontents/goals#brief

New York State Education Department IEP Directions, Special Education Forms. Web site accessed on 2013. http://www.p12.nysed.gov/specialed/formsnotices/IEP/directions.htm

NYS Dept. of Education. *Violent and Disruptive Incidents.* VADIR NYS Student Support Services. Web site accessed on May 2012–August 2013 http://www.p12.nysed.gov/sss/ssae/schoolsafety/vadir

Payne, R. K., P. E. DeVol, and T. D. Smith. 2001. *Bridges Out of Poverty: Strategies for Professionals and Communities.* Aha! Process Inc.: Highland, TX

Public Health Law (PHL) 2803 (1) (g) Patient's Rights, 10NYCRR, 405.7,405.7(a)(1),405.7(c) Website accessed on April 2, 2013. http://www.sjhsyr.org/bill-of-rights#.UcoCqjvVCSo

Rebhorn, L. April 2009. *Developing Your Child's IEP, Parent Guide.* 3rd ed. National Dissemination Center for Children with Disabilities. Web site accessed on July 2013. http://nichcy.org/publications/pa12

Rossi, S and S. Stringfield. *Education Reform and Students at Risk: Findings and Recommendations.* vol. 1. Office of Educational Research and Improvement, US Dept. of Education. Diane Publishing 1995 and 1997

Syracuse City School District. *Handbook of Student Responsibilities and Code of Conduct,* rev. July 2011. Web site accessed on April 28, 2013.

Syracuse City School District. *2012–2013 School Calendar and District Handbook.* Web site accessed on April 26, 2013.

Syracuse City School District. *Disciplinary Data Analysis for 2010–2011 and 2011–12.* Web site and PDF document accessed on May 1–5, 2013. http://www.syracusecityschools.com/tfiles/folder514/SCSD%20Student%20Disciplinary%20Data%20Analysis.pdf

Teacher Removal of Disruptive Student. Ballston Hills-Ballston Lake Central School District Policies. Web site accessed on June 2013. http://www.bhbl.org/Policies/P5310.2.pdf

Teske, S. C. 2011. A Study of Zero Tolerance Policies in Schools: A Multi-Integrated Systems Approach to Improve Outcomes for Adolescents. *Journal of Child and Adolescent Psychiatric Nursing.* Wiley Periodicals, Inc. http://www.ncjfcj.org/sites/default/files/Zero%20Tolerance%20 Policies%20in%20Schools%20(2).pdf

UCLA Civil Rights Project. Web site http://civilrightsproject.ucla.edu/ resources/projects/center-for-civil-rights-remedies/school-to-prison-folder/summary-reports/out-of-school-off-track-reports-by-district

US Department of Education Office of Civil Rights. Web site accessed May 2013 OCR Data Collection Unit. Shea/Bellevue Suspension. http:// ocrdata.ed.gov/Page?t=s&eid=238209&syk=5&pid=1

US Dept. Of Education. *History: 25 Years of Progress in Educating Children with Disabilities through IDEA.* Web site accessed on June 5, 2013. Office of Special Education and Rehabilitative Services http://www2. ed.gov/policy/speced/leg/idea/history.html

US Dept. Of Education. *FERPA Regulation—Family Educational Rights and Privacy Act Regulations (FERPA) 34 CFR Part 99.* Web site accessed on June 1, 2013 http://www2.ed.gov/policy/gen/guid/fpco/ pdf/ferparegs.pdf

US Office of Education. My Child's Special Needs. 2000. *A Guide to the Individualized Education Program.* Office of Special Education and Rehabilitative Services, US Department of Education. PDF Document, Web site accessed on June 2013. http://www2.ed.gov/parents/needs/ speced/iepguide/index.html

Volokh, A. and S. Lisa. *School Violence Prevention: Strategies to Keep Schools Safe (Unabridged).* Policy Study No. 234, January 1998, Part 1 http://reason.org/files/60b57eac352e529771bfa27d7d736d3f.pdf

Weissman, M., E. Wolf, K. Sowards, C. Abaté, P. Weinberg, and C. Marthia. April 2005. *School Yard or Prison Yard: Improving*

Outcomes for Marginalized Youth. Working Paper. http://www. communityalternatives.org/pdf/sfs.pdf

Wilson, Amos. 1988. *Blueprint for Black Power: A Moral, Political, and Economic Imperative*

Woodson, Carter G. 2005. *The Miseducation of the Negro*. Dover ed. Dover Publications, Inc.: Mineola, NY

About the Author

Twiggy Billue

When there is a problem, Twiggy Billue believes in taking action rather than waiting for someone else to do something. This direct approach has led to her community organizing and advocacy efforts in Syracuse. It is also the reason she has been honored by many civil rights and community action groups over the years and is why she was one of persons honored as a recipient of the 2002 Unsung Heroes and Heroines Award at Syracuse University.

Among Billue's many community projects is the creation of the Rockland Avenue Neighborhood Association. "We created it because we felt voiceless when it came to neighborhood problems," she says. Twiggy has also been the president of the Elmwood Elementary and Shea Middle School Parent–Teacher Organizations, coached youth little leagues and basketball at Our Lady of Lourdes Elementary School, and has been involved in the Youth Enrichment Opportunity Program.

In 1989, Billue began exploring the issue of infant mortality in the Syracuse community. She was invited by Congressman James Walsh to testify before a senate subcommittee on infant mortality. The SHA adopted a program she wrote to combat infant mortality. The program involved educating parents who lived in zip codes where the rates of infant mortality were the highest about parenting techniques. As a result of her efforts, Billue was offered a job at the Syracuse Community Health Center.

Twiggy has been married for twenty-six years and has raised three children with her husband, Ras Simien Anu. Twiggy has also been involved in efforts to find out why the African American community has a high rate of alcoholism, school inequality and suspension, infant mortality, and gun violence. Mrs. Billue was a past member and co-chair of the Syracuse Partnership to Reduce Gun Violence Community Management Team and received training in trauma response from the Boston Trauma team and Dr. Robert Macy.

Twiggy participated along with Trauma Team members to respond to the scene of violence or traumatic incidents in the community and to debrief and offer assistance to community members. Twiggy is currently a member of the Syracuse Chapter of the National Action Network and co-chair of the Education Committee. Twiggy currently serves as the director of Project Hotep and the Copy Shop.

Despite her heavy involvement in community organizations, Billue still believes in dealing with problems directly. If a parent calls her because they can't find their child, Billue will go right out and look for the child. "I believe in the one-on-one community-building approach."